CHRISTIAN FAITH &
HUMAN UNDERSTANDING

Robert Sokolowski

CHRISTIAN FAITH &
HUMAN UNDERSTANDING

Studies on the Eucharist, Trinity, and
the Human Person

The Catholic University of America Press
Washington, D.C.

LIBRARY OF CONGRESS CATALOGING-IN-PUBLICATION DATA

Sokolowski, Robert.

Christian faith and human understanding : studies on the Eucharist, Trinity,

and the human person / Robert Sokolowski.

p. cm.

Includes bibliographical references and index.

ISBN-13: 978-0-8132-1444-3 (pbk. : alk. paper)

ISBN-10: 0-8132-1444-0 (pbk. : alk. paper)

1. Faith and reason.   2. Catholic Church—Doctrines.

3. Lord's Supper—Catholic Church. 4. Trinity.

5. Man (Christian theology)   I. Title.

BT50.S63 2005

230′.2—dc22

2005016827

To Alyce Ann Bergkamp and Reed and Roxolana Armstrong
For their friendship and kindness

CONTENTS

ACKNOWLEDGMENTS

I am grateful to friends and colleagues for their help in these essays as they were written over many years, especially John Brough, David Burrell, C.S.C., Peter Casarella, Richard Cobb-Stevens, Jean De Groot, Jude P. Dougherty, John Drummond, James Hart, Richard Hassing, V. Bradley Lewis, John C. McCarthy, Guy Mansini, O.S.B., Francis Martin, Susan Needham, Kurt Pritzl, O.P., Owen Sadlier, O.S.F., Brian Shanley, O.P., John Smolko, and John Wippel. I am particularly indebted to Francis Slade and Kevin White for their philosophical inspiration and conversation, and wish to recall the memory of Thomas Prufer, my primary mentor in philosophy and theology.

PROVENANCE OF THE ESSAYS

"The Autonomy of Philosophy in *Fides et Ratio*" appeared in *Restoring Faith in Reason*, edited by Laurence Paul Hemming and Susan Parsons (London: SCM Press, and Notre Dame, University of Notre Dame Press, 2002), pp. 277–91. "Philosophy and the Christian Act of Faith" was originally published as "Philosophie et acte de foi chrétien," *Revue philosophique de Louvain* 92 (1994): 281–94. "Creation and Christian Understanding" appeared in *God and Creation: An Ecumenical Symposium*, edited by David B. Burrell and Bernard McGinn (Notre Dame: University of Notre Dame Press, 1990), pp. 179–92, after having been presented at the Ecumenical Symposium in Comparative Religious Thought at the Universities of Chicago and Notre Dame, April 26–28, 1987. "Christian Religious Discourse" was published in the *American Catholic Philosophical Quarterly* 65 (1991): 45–56, after having been given as an address at the meeting of the American Catholic Philosophical Association in Washington, D.C., in April 1991.

"Phenomenology and the Eucharist" was given as the Peter Richard Kenrick Lecture at Kenrick-Glennon Seminary, Seminary, St. Louis, Missouri, on March 21, 2002, and published in *Theology Digest* 49 (2002): 347–58. "Praying the Canon of the Mass" appeared in the *Homiletic and Pastoral Review* 95 (July 1995): 8–15. "The Eucharist and Transubstantiation" was given at a meeting of the Catholic Theological Society of America on June 6, 1997, and published in *Communio* 24 (Winter 1997): 867–80. "The Office of the Bishop and the Theology of Disclosure" was given on November 14, 2003, as an address at a conference held at the John Paul II Center in Washington, D.C., under the title *The Call to Holiness and Communion: Vatican II on the Church*. It is scheduled for publication in a volume of proceedings. "Revelation of the Holy Trinity: A Study in Personal Pronouns" was given

at a conference at St. Meinrad's Abbey on April 8, 2000, and published in
Ethics and Theological Disclosures: The Thought of Robert Sokolowski, edited by
Guy Mansini, O.S.B, and James Hart (Washington: The Catholic University
of America Press, 2003), pp. 162–77.

"Soul and the Transcendence of the Human Person" appeared in *What
Is Man, O Lord? The Human Person in a Biotech Age*, Proceedings of the Eighteenth Bishops' Workshop, edited by Edward A. Furton and Louise A. Mitch-
ell (Boston: The National Catholic Bioethics Center, 2003), 49–63. It had
been given as a lecture at the Eighteenth Workshop of the American Catholic Bishops in Dallas, Texas, in February 2001. "Language, the Human Person,
and Christian Faith" was given as the Aquinas Medal Lecture at the annual
meeting of the American Catholic Philosophical Association in Cincinnati,
Ohio, on November 2002, and it was published in the *Proceedings of the American Catholic Philosophical Association* 76 (2003): 27–38. "The Human Person
and Political Life" was given at a symposium in honor of Jude P. Dougherty
at The Catholic University of America in November 2000 and was published
in *The Thomist* 65 (2001): 505–27. "The Christian Difference in Personal Relationships" was presented on February 14, 2003, as one of the John Henry
Cardinal Newman Lectures, sponsored by the Institute for the Psychological Sciences. It is scheduled to be published in a volume entitled *On Wings of
Faith and Reason: The Christian Difference in Culture and the Sciences*, by The Institute for the Psychological Sciences Press. "What Is Natural Law? Human
Purposes and Natural Ends" appeared in *The Thomist* 68 (2004): 507–29.

"The Art and Science of Medicine" was published in *Catholic Perspectives on Medical Morals*, edited by Edmund D. Pellegrino, John P. Langan, and
John Collins Harvey, Philosophy and Medicine, volume 34 (Boston: Kluwer Academic Publishers, 1989), pp. 263–75, © 1989 by Kluwer Academic
Publishers; with kind permission of Springer Science and Business Media.
"The Fiduciary Relationship and the Nature of Professions" was given at a
conference on professional ethics during Georgetown University's Bicen-
tennial celebration in 1989 and published in *Ethics, Trust, and the Professions*,
edited by Edmund D. Pellegrino, Robert M. Veatch, and John P. Langan
(Washington: Georgetown University Press, 1991), pp. 23–43. "Religion and
Psychoanalysis: Some Phenomenological Contributions" was given as the
Thirteenth Edith Weigert Lecture of the Washington School of Psychiatry
on October 30, 1988, and published in Joseph H. Smith and Susan Handel-

man, editors, *Psychoanalysis and Religion: Psychiatry and the Humanities*, pp. 1–17 © 1990 Forum on Psychiatry and the Humanities of the Washington School of Psychiatry (Baltimore: The Johns Hopkins University Press, 1990); reprinted with permission of the Johns Hopkins University Press. "Church Tradition and the Catholic University" was presented at a meeting of the Fellowship of Catholic Scholars and published in their Bulletin as well as in the *Homiletic and Pastoral Review* 96 (February 1996): 22–31. "Philosophy in the Seminary Curriculum" was given as an address at a meeting of the American Catholic Philosophical Association in November 2001, and was published in the *Homiletic and Pastoral Review* 104 (May 2004): 14–22. I am grateful to the journals and publishers who gave permission for these essays to be reprinted in this volume.

CHRISTIAN FAITH &
HUMAN UNDERSTANDING

INTRODUCTION

We are distinguished as human beings by our ability to think. Our reason is the specific difference that makes us human and thus differentiates us from the other animals. Furthermore, distinctions in the quality of a person's reason make him stand out among his fellow human beings, for better or worse, precisely as a human being.

Human reason is not just the power to move from one proposition to another; it is not just the ability to argue, infer, and compute. More fundamentally, it is the capacity to let things come to light, to let the intelligibility of things show up for ourselves and for others. Instances of such intelligence serve as both the starting points and the points of rest or stability amid the movements of argument. Reason, therefore, encompasses both reasoning and intelligence. Also, in its practical forms, reason is the power by which we are able to perform human actions and to fabricate things.

Human thinking occurs most specifically in the medium of speech, but it can also be exercised in depiction, dance, and music; there can be as much intelligence in a portrait or a landscape as in an essay, each of which has its own kind of syntax. Thinking also occurs in the rationalized motions we call sport and in the patterned conduct we call games. Playing tennis and playing poker are exercises of reason, and they have their syntax too. Thinking occurs in the establishment of political societies and the performance of political actions, and it occurs further in acts of courage, justice, and friendship, in the fabrication of roads, bridges, and houses, and in the medical treatment of an illness. It occurs in a distinctive way in the pursuit of mathematical science and the technology derived from it. These are all exercises of reason, and words function at the heart of them all, even though they are not reducible to words.

Christian faith affects us at the core of what we are, at the center of what makes us human. It is true that our faith must be expressed in our actions, but since our actions are formed by our understanding, faith must affect our thinking before it can affect what we do. God's grace serves both to elevate and to heal us, and faith, specifically, both elevates and heals our reason. It makes it possible for us to know certain things that we would otherwise not have been able to know, and ultimately it promises us the beatific vision as the crown of faithfulness; this vision is a completion of understanding that we in our own efforts would be entirely unable to conceive, let alone attain. But faith also remedies the deficiencies of our fallen nature, so that in its light we can think more clearly even about things we can know on our own.

Faith is the response that God enables us to make to his revealed words and actions; it is also the response we are enabled to make to God as the one who speaks in revelation. We not only believe what is revealed but also believe *in* the one who reveals, and these two beliefs are interconnected, because the words that are declared tell us about the nature of the one who speaks them. We could not believe in God unless we believed the articles of faith contained in the creed; without them, we would not know whom to believe in. Faith is a personal relationship but it involves an understanding, not obedience alone.

And although faith is God's work in us, it becomes our own work as well, precisely as being given to us. It is not something that merely happens in us, nor is it something we are merely clothed with; it is something that we ourselves do. It is a transformation by grace of the nature we receive as created by God. God's agency in us makes it possible for us to act toward him as our Father; we are enabled to act in union with the Son, under the guidance of the Holy Spirit. We act as befits rational agents, with the understanding and autonomy made possible by grace.

Through faith we accept the man Jesus Christ as the eternal Word and Son of the living God, the God whom he called his Father, and whom he taught and enabled us to address in the same way. Through faith we accept the death of Christ on the cross as our Redemption, an action whose life-giving force was revealed and confirmed by his Resurrection from the dead. We see his sacrificial death as the most perfect created manifestation of the love or charity that exists between the Father and Son in the Holy

Trinity, a love expressed within the Trinity as the Holy Spirit, who has been given to us and who vivifies the Church, which embodies sacramentally the continued presence of Christ in the world. The work of the Spirit is not to bring about yet another divine achievement, but to continue, until the end of time, the work accomplished in and by Christ before the Father, for the life of the world.

These articles of faith are held on the authority of God, who has revealed them to us. They have not been attained by human reason, but they inform our reason. They give it a certain shape and actuality, a form expressed in liturgy, words, actions, music, painting, and manners of conduct. These articles of faith also give us a certain confidence in reason, because if our reason is able to receive truths such as these, which concern God himself, it follows that the same reason must be trustworthy and capable of truth in its natural discoveries, where it works on its own, as in practical deliberation, skills, science, and philosophy. Human beings have in fact attained truths apart from revelation, and this achievement bears witness to reason's capacity to manifest the way things are, but reason's confidence in itself is enhanced by faith, by its revealed ability to receive the Word of God.

It is valuable for both faith and reason for us to study how they differ from each other. The relationship between the two need not be adversarial. By contrasting one with the other, we can appreciate more fully what faith is and we can come to see why we could attain its truths only by faith and in no other way; but this same contrast will also help us appreciate more clearly what we know *not* by faith but by our own insight and argument. If we know that we believe certain things, we will be able, in contrast, to get greater clarity on what we believe that we know.

What shall we focus on when we try to explore the difference between Christian faith and reason? The most fruitful topic to address is not the difference between two subjective dispositions, between knowing something on the authority of someone else and knowing it through our own thinking. Nor is it the difference between the modes of reasoning that are appropriate in each of these domains. Rather, the most important topic is the nature of the God who is believed in Christian faith: we must focus primarily not on faith and reason but on who and what is believed. The "object" of faith will specify what faith is and how it must be distinguished from reason. The most important issue is to explore how radically the God of Christian faith

differs from other divinities, from other understandings of the divine. The
point can be made most clearly in regard to the pagan world, from which
biblical faith, in both the Jewish and the Christian covenants, differentiated
itself. The pagan gods, whether depicted by poets or conceptualized by philosophers, were part of the world. They were the best, strongest, and most
admirable powers, but they were parts of the world and could not exist apart
from the larger whole. As Alain Besançon has put it, "It was not God who
created the world. It was the world that gave birth to the gods.... Gods were
born, engendered one another, proliferated, and, generation after generation,
descended from Physis: Zeus, Poseidon, Heracles, but also Murder, Famine,
and other children of Eris, thirty thousand nymphs, the Gorgons, Auro-
ra, Helios. Physis and Moira—the impersonal and indifferent order—stand
above the gods. They give gods their being, their shape, their powers."[1]

In contrast with this understanding of the divine, Christian faith accepts
God as underived and unobligated, as sheer existence and not just one kind
of existent. For Christian faith, God could be apart from the whole that is
called the world, and he would exist in undiminished goodness and greatness had he not created it; God is not made more perfect by having brought
things into being. Only if his Creation is so free of need can it be done out
of pure generosity, and only then can the created world be the signature
of the God who is love (I John 4:8, 16). God creates for his glory and our
good, not out of necessity. The Christian God is different from the gods that
are part of the world, and also different from the god whose goodness must
overflow into entities other than himself. God creates by choice and not by
emanation. This distinctive understanding of God is at the intersection of
faith and reason, and it opens up the logical space for the mysteries of the
Incarnation, the Holy Trinity, the Church and the sacraments, and grace.
Such teachings would be against reason, not beyond it, if they were to be
related to a god who was part of the world; in such a context they would be
incoherences, not mysteries.

The Christian distinction between God and the world is the theme of
the first group of essays in this volume, which discuss the place of philosophy in Christian faith, as well as some of the kinds of reasoning that are

---

1. Alain Besançon, *The Forbidden Image: An Intellectual History of Iconoclasm*, trans. Jane Marie
Todd (Chicago: University of Chicago Press, 2000), p. 13.

proper to Christian belief. The second section of the book discusses the Eucharist (the primary expression of Christian life), the episcopal office (whose highest role is eucharistic celebration), and the mystery of the Holy Trinity. The third section of the volume explores the impact that Christian faith has on our understanding of the human person. The essays in this section deal with the concepts of soul and person, with political life, and with natural law. A theme pervading this section is the claim that things have their own natures and ends, that is, they have their own intelligibilities, which must be respected by human action, science, and philosophy, and which must not be undermined by religious belief. Faith does not dilute the natures of things or turn the ends of things into purposes. The fourth and final section considers how Christian faith can shape practical as well as theoretical reason. The essays examine medicine, the professions, and psychoanalysis, and they explore some institutional implications of faith and reason in academic life and in seminary programs. The essays were written for various occasions and there are bound to be some elements that recur among them, but I think that the reappearances are illuminating and not redundant, because of the differences in context.

The way we are as human beings is determined in no small degree by what we know, by what is "in our minds." Our reason and our humanity are qualified by what informs our intelligence. The presence of God to our minds modifies us more than the presence of created things, because God is understood as the truth that is the origin of all other truths, and the good that has brought into being all the other things we desire. God's presence to the mind is now achieved in faith, through a glass darkly, but it is no less intense for that, and it could not be given in any other way; ours is not the time for vision. This presence in faith prompts both hope and charity. Like the burning bush in Exodus it calls not for curiosity but for a response (Exodus 3:1–6). It is not merely cognitional but manifests a good, something that we can love, but this good can be somewhat disorienting if we are used to thinking along the ways of the world. Through faith we are made capable of making a distinction and appreciating, as Evelyn Waugh puts it, "the difference in kind between the goodness of the most innocent of humans and the blinding, ineffable goodness of God."[2] The first kind of goodness is visible to

2. Evelyn Waugh, *The End of the Battle* (Boston: Little, Brown and Company, 1961), p. 79.

any reasonable man. It can be seen by the eye of human decency, and though it makes a great demand on us we can comprehend it in our own natural categories, our ways of predicating or making public. The second, however, becomes more and more present only to the "man of prayer."[3] It dazzles the mind but does not destroy it. It blinds by a surfeit of intelligibility, not a deficit; it is glimpsed as being understandable but more than we can understand, and it can be desired or loved as such. We may not be able to comprehend it, but we can distinguish it and thus allow it to work its effect on us.

3. Ibid.

PART I

FAITH AND REASON

THE AUTONOMY OF PHILOSOPHY
IN *FIDES ET RATIO*

The title of the encyclical names the two things that are to be brought together, faith and reason.[1] This essay will attempt to clarify each of the terms and to discuss the kind of autonomy reason, and specifically philosophical reason, enjoys within Christian faith.

Reason as intelligent articulation

Reason in its widest scope can be considered to be the insertion of syntax or categoriality into human experience.[2] To move from simple experience into rational experience is to introduce—and to become explicitly aware of—distinctions between wholes and their parts. Instead of just perceiving an object, such as a tree, and reacting to it, we come to register articulated facts involving the object: we register *that* this object is a tree, *that* the tree is blossoming, and *that* we could climb out on one of its branches; we move from sensibility to intellection, from things to their intelligibility. Reason brings articulation and syntactic form into human consciousness and into the things we are aware of.

Reasoning is often considered to be the activity of moving from one statement or proposition to another, from premises to conclusions or from effects to causes, but it is also true that the original registering of a situa-

---

1. *Encyclical Letter Fides et Ratio of the Supreme Pontiff John Paul II to the Bishops of the Catholic Church, On the Relationship between Faith and Reason* (Boston: Pauline Books and Media, 1998).

2. This is how Husserl describes and defines reason in the sixth of his *Logical Investigations*.

tion is a rational act, an act of intelligence. Reason is exhibited not only in propositional logic but also in predicational logic, when an object of any sort is taken as a whole (as a subject) and a feature or a part is declared to belong to it: that is, when *S* is said to be *p*. Reason does not just draw inferences, but also manifests by articulating. Reason is at work when a whole is unfolded for us into its various parts. In fact, this manifesting role of reason is much more elementary than the inferential; we cannot move from one proposition to another until we have accumulated a store of convictions. The inferential work of reason simply introduces further syntactic forms into what we intend: we present not only individual but also concatenated states of affairs, and their linkage with one another is but a more complicated kind of syntax.

Our rational articulation normally takes place in language, in predication and its various elaborations, but there can be other kinds of articulation that disclose the truth of things: the composition of a picture, for example, is also a "syntactic" manifestation with its own kind of logic, its own way of being consistent and inconsistent, coherent and incoherent. Picturing is an act of reason, and so are compositions and performances in music, dance, cooking, and gardening, as well as architectural constructions. They too are forms of conviction and they are humanly structured wholes. Practical conduct and moral action are also made rational by their categorial forms.[3]

Linguistic and mathematical exercises of reason can take place on a rather small scale, in rather localized articulations and collections, but they can also occur on a grand and systematic scale. We not only achieve episodic bits of knowledge; we also build up the various sciences, which have been defined as "organized knowledge."[4] In the encyclical, the Holy Father recognizes the wide range of reason and includes a moving tribute to scientists, "expressing my admiration and . . . offering encouragement to these brave pioneers of scientific research" (§106).

---

3. See Robert Sokolowski, *Moral Action: A Phenomenological Study* (Bloomington: Indiana University Press, 1985), pp. 1–6, and "What is Moral Action?" in *Pictures, Quotations, and Distinctions: Fourteen Essays in Phenomenology* (Notre Dame: University of Notre Dame Press, 1992), pp. 261–76.

4. See Joseph Owens, C.Ss.R., *Cognition: An Epistemological Inquiry* (Houston: The Center for Thomistic Studies, 1992), pp. 291–309.

Philosophy as the comprehensive form of reason

The encyclical is primarily concerned with one particular form of rational thinking, namely, philosophy: in the Introduction, John Paul II says, "I wish to reflect upon this special activity of human reason" (§5), and he says that by "reaffirming the truth of faith" he and his brother bishops "can both restore to our contemporaries a genuine trust in their capacity to know and challenge philosophy to recover and develop its own full dignity" (§6). Faith is to confirm our confidence in our natural power to understand, and it is to remind philosophy of its noble role in human affairs.

How is philosophy different from other forms of thinking? All the others, even the organized forms of knowledge that we call the sciences, are partial. Each of them is limited to one particular domain of the world, and each realizes that there are other domains that have their own claims on truth. Each science, each localized expression of truth, marks off a part of the whole for its attention, and, moreover, it *knows* that it restricts itself in this way. It is conscious of its limitations. It knows that to some extent it is specialized. It has its own expertise and it can be proud of it, but it also knows that other disciplines have other kinds of expertise. This limitation is reassuring. It draws borders on what the specialist is responsible for. He is obliged to know what is important within his domain, but he can defer to others in regard to their professional competence.

Philosophy, however, is the "specialty" that knows no borders. It is the attempt to formulate the whole, the big picture. By definition it takes on the challenge of trying to say something, not about a part, but about the comprehensive whole. In principle, the philosopher cannot make any disclaimers; he cannot say, "Well, that's outside my field." If, for example, a given philosopher tries to specialize in the philosophy of language, he cannot say, to a questioner, "You are asking me about change and stability, and about images and memories; I don't know anything about such things. I can only talk about language." Such a reply would indicate that the speaker has become a linguist, not a philosopher, because if he presents himself as a *philosopher* of language he cannot in principle refuse to entertain questions from any quarter. He has to be able to show how language fits into the whole of things, and to do so he will have to take into account how it is related, in the case of these particular questions, to stability, change, and representation. The philosopher of language might acknowledge his limitations by saying, "I haven't thought about that yet; I have been occupied with other things," but these are his personal limitations, not restrictions on his "field." He cannot disavow the effort by saying that it is outside his responsibility. He is responsible for the whole, and on this level everything is related to everything else.

The philosopher will know that it is a tricky business to think and speak about the whole. He will also know that language begins to act strangely when you apply it to this encircling domain, just as the natural elements behave oddly when they approach absolute zero.[5] One of his tasks, therefore, is to show how words become transformed, in both their semantics and their syntax, when they are taken from their birthplace in partial domains and applied to the most comprehensive context. Furthermore, sometimes one of the partial sciences tries to become the science of the whole: physics might try to provide the theory of everything, or history, psychology, or evolutionary biology may claim to be the encompassing science, but if any such partial science tries to take over the whole show, if it tries to become philosophy, it too will fall prey to the same difficulties that face philosophy. It will have to answer questions from all quarters and it will be unable to make any exclusions. It will have to absorb everything into itself. Physics, for example, if it tries to become the science of the whole, will have to account for such things as quotation, picturing, memory, and political decisions.

It is not the case that only professional philosophers take a position toward the whole of things. Every thinking person has some opinions about the whole, and every person inevitably gets into subjects that are philosophical: whenever anyone uses words such as *truth, falsity, change,* or *time,* he enters into issues that can be properly treated only in the context of the whole. Also, whenever a person becomes involved in moral debate, he activates terms, such as *virtuous* and *vicious, responsible* and *innocent,* that engage the widest context, that of the whole, because they get into the issue of moral truth.[6] Socrates perplexed his interlocutors by showing that they cannot

5. To draw out the analogy, it would be interesting to ask what in philosophical language corresponds to Bose-Einstein condensation as matter approaches absolute zero, when it has almost no thermal energy.

6. The encyclical often restates the claim found in *Veritatis Splendor,* and in other teachings of John Paul II, that freedom and morality must be based on truth: "Once truth is denied to human beings, it is pure illusion to try to set them free. Truth and freedom either go together hand

avoid philosophical questions. Generally, the opinions people have about the whole are just taken over from what others say, or they are projected from one particular special field. Only the philosopher sets out explicitly to think about the whole as such, on terms that are appropriate to it.

There is a fundamental veracity that is part of every human being; the encyclical says, "One may define the human being . . . as the one who seeks the truth" (§28), and it quotes St. Augustine in saying that while there are people who try to deceive others, no one wants to be deceived himself (§25). This inclination to truth develops into the regional understandings of the way things are, but the philosopher lets this veracity expand without confinements, into its widest setting, that of the whole of things. The philosopher reads authors who are judged to have explored this field with some success, and he spends much time reflecting on how difficult it is to think without the restrictions that mark out a domain to be cultivated. The encyclical also observes that no particular philosophical achievement can ever conclude human thinking: "Every philosophical system . . . must still recognize the primacy of philosophical inquiry, from which it stems and which it ought loyally to serve" (§4).

Philosophy as the inquiry into the first and highest things

Philosophy moves into the most comprehensive context; it is also concerned with the first principles of that context. One cannot think about the whole of things without having some inkling of what is first and best and original in the whole. The whole is not a flat, undifferentiated collection of particular issues. It is ordered around a first and best, around something that governs the whole. A concern with the divine has always been part of the philosophical impulse. All classical philosophers have thought about the first and ultimate principle or principles of the world. They did not think only about particular issues, or even about the cosmos as a whole; they also thought about the first principle of the universe.

Thus, Parmenides and Heraclitus, Plato and Aristotle, the Stoics and Epicureans, all thought about the divine, the first, and the best. To think about the divine was part of their philosophy. However, both the philosophical

---

in hand or together they perish in misery" (§90). In the same section he writes that without truth human beings are led "either to a destructive will to power or to a solitude without hope."

and religious thinkers of antiquity took the whole of things, the cosmos, as the ultimate setting for their thought. They did not conceive of the possible nonexistence of the cosmos; its factual givenness was quite properly taken for granted, and the divine principles, the god or the gods, were thought of as the highest and best entities within that setting. And because pagan thinking accepted the world as the final, unquestioned context, the two approaches to the whole, religion and philosophy, offered competing versions of how the whole and the divine principles should be understood. The philosophers considered the poetic stories about the gods to be inadequate and unworthy, and thought that their own interpretation of the divine, and consequently of the whole, should purify the inherited religious tradition: Plato refines Homer as the educator of the Greeks, and Aristotle demythologizes the poets. Philosophy claimed to offer a more appropriate expression of ultimate truth, but it did not try to replace religion, it only claimed the right to monitor it; the attempt to replace religion by philosophy—the attempt that defines the modern Enlightenment—would in this view destroy philosophy, because philosophy has to remain the concern of relatively few people, not of everyone.

In such a pagan setting, it is hard to avoid what was later called an Averroistic understanding of the relationship between theology and philosophy, between faith and reason. Religious belief and human reason each attempt to think about the whole of things, and they have rival views of what is highest and best in it. Religious belief and reason are in competition because both view the cosmos as the final setting for reason, and consider the divine to be the best, highest, and governing principle in the cosmos.

We should also observe that the philosophical search for the first and the divine occurs not only in ancient philosophy but in contemporary thinking as well. In our intellectual culture, the role of the governing, "divine" principle is usually played by evolution, on both the cosmic and the biological scale. People may say that the evolution of living things is based on purely accidental mutations, but when they speak more generally about it they attribute to it a providence and a superior intelligence that strongly resembles the Mind *(Nous)* that the Presocratic philosopher Anaxagoras said was part of nature.[7]

It is easy to see that philosophy enjoys a great autonomy in the pagan

7. See Aristotle, *Metaphysics* I, 3, 984b15–18.

understanding of things. There, philosophy stands in judgment on poetic and religious truth, distinguishing the valid from the invalid and retaining only what it considers acceptable to human thinking. Aristotle gives a philosophical interpretation of the ancient legends and concludes, "Only thus far, then, is the opinion of our ancestors and of our earliest predecessors clear to us."[8] He accepts what he can reformulate philosophically and discards the rest as poetic fictions added in order to persuade the multitude.[9] And Plato, after criticizing Homer, says that "only so much of poetry as is hymns to gods or celebration of good men should be admitted to a city."[10] Philosophy, in this conception, is obviously the governing knowledge.

The autonomy of philosophical thinking in the encyclical

The encyclical *Fides et Ratio* also acknowledges the autonomy of philosophical evidence and truth. One of the places it does so is in the course of its recommendation of the work of St. Thomas Aquinas, which it praises not only for its intrinsic value but also for Thomas's willingness to learn from Jewish and Muslim thinkers. It also endorses and recommends Aquinas because he is such a good conduit of the classical tradition.[11] However, the encyclical insists that "the Church has no philosophy of her own nor does she canonize any one particular philosophy in preference to others." The reason for this reserve is very interesting: "Even when it engages theology, philosophy must remain faithful to its own principles and methods. Otherwise there would be no guarantee that it would remain oriented to truth and that it was moving toward truth by way of a process governed by reason" (§49).

In other words, the Church refrains from making any philosophy official *because she does not want to endanger the autonomy of philosophy.* Her restraint is based on a respect for philosophy and natural wisdom, and for the truth that they can attain. A philosophy based on authority would not rest on its own evidence, and hence it would not be philosophy. It is to protect philosophy that the encyclical allows it to function on its own: "A philosophy which did not proceed in the light of reason according to its own principles and methods would serve little purpose" (§49). The major reason for the Pope's

8. Ibid., XII, 8, 1074b13–14.

9. Ibid., XII, 8, 1074b3–8.

10. *Republic* X, 607a. *The Republic of Plato,* translated by Allan Bloom (New York: Basic Books, 1968).

11. Aquinas is mentioned often in the encyclical; see §§43–44, 57–59, 61, and 78.

reluctance to canonize a philosophy was this respect for the autonomy of the discipline, but there may be a historical and practical reason as well: having lived under an ideological regime in Poland and having seen how artificial, empty, and inauthentic an "official philosophy" inevitably becomes, he was all the more sensitive to the nature of philosophical evidence. A third reason why the Pope acknowledged the independence of human intelligence was the confidence in reason that his Christian faith gave him. Christian belief understands itself to be based on truth, and therefore it does not need to fear any other expressions of truth. In its view, the more understanding the better.

Does this acknowledgment of the autonomy of philosophy mean that reason can set itself up as the tribunal for faith, as it does in pagan thinking? Obviously not; in fact, there are passages in the encyclical that seem to make the opposite claim, to subordinate reason to faith, and to restrict the autonomy of philosophy.

Christian faith as deeper than reason

The most dramatic passage that declares the priority of faith is the following: "The preaching of Christ crucified and risen is the reef upon which the link between faith and reason can break up, but it is also the reef beyond which the two can set forth upon the boundless ocean of truth" (§23). The phrase, "the preaching of Christ crucified and risen," is somewhat ambiguous. First, it can mean the preaching that was accomplished by Christ in his Death and Resurrection; this decisive action of Christ, his Death and Resurrection, is the ultimate word that was uttered, the ultimate statement that was made, by the incarnate Word of God. It was a statement made through an action and not merely through words. Second, the phrase can mean the preaching carried on by the apostles and by the Church, who proclaim the Death and Resurrection of Christ through their words and actions. This second sense is probably the one intended by the encyclical, but the first sense is certainly a welcome overtone.

Still, if reason stands in need of the revelation that took place in the Death and Resurrection of Christ, how can it be autonomous?

The phrase "Christ crucified and risen" does not signify only the particular truth of the death of Christ and his rising from the dead; it also implies the Incarnation, and consequently the mystery of the Holy Trinity. That is, it signifies the understanding of God that is revealed through the Death and Resurrection of Christ. These events do not just reveal *Christ;* they also reveal *God.* The Death and Resurrection of Jesus are not simple facts that stand alone; they both manifest and presuppose a certain background, a certain understanding of God, which was revealed gradually through the words and events of the Old Covenant and brought to its final manifestation in the words and actions of Christ, as well as in the words and actions of the Church, enlivened by the Holy Spirit, in the aftermath of Christ. Biblical revelation did not take place against a neutral, universal sense of the divine that is common to all religious thinking, or common to all monotheisms. It did not merely confirm a generic understanding of the divine. It manifested a new sense of the divine, a new name for God.

In the Old Testament, God is revealed as radically different from the world. He is not just the best and highest entity within the world, as divinity is understood in paganism; rather, he is the one who created the world and is totally different from anything in it. He cannot even be represented by an image in the world. Israel was different from other nations because its God was different from theirs. It was not just that the Jews had the right divinity while the other nations had the wrong ones; rather, the very meaning of the divine was changed through the pedagogy and disclosure of the Old Covenant. The other "gods" were not gods at all, not in the sense of *God* that was now being revealed.

This revealed sense of the divine is then perfected in Christ, who shows, by his words and actions, and especially by his Death and Resurrection, that the God of the First Covenant is not only radically other to the world, but so other to it that he could become part of it without diminishing his divinity. The Father of Jesus Christ is the same God as Jahweh, but more deeply revealed and understood. Through the Old and New Covenants, God is understood to be so different from the world that he could exist, in undiminished goodness and greatness, even if the world had not existed; that is, God created the world out of sheer generosity and benevolence, not out of any need to perfect himself or to bring about any increase in the goodness and greatness of being itself. The charity of Creation is manifested by the even greater charity of the Incarnation, Death, and Resurrection of the Son of God.

This deepening of the sense of the divine makes possible a harmony between *this* kind of faith and human reason. In paganism, the religious or poetic grasp of the whole is necessarily at odds with philosophy, because both consider the cosmos as the ultimate context, and take the divine to be the greatest and best principle within the cosmos. Both religion and reason were able to reach this far by their own efforts. In biblical and Christian faith, which understands itself not as an achievement of reason simply but as the reception of the Word of God, the cosmos is no longer seen as the ultimate context, the encompassing whole. The cosmos is now understood as possibly not having been. The whole that served as the unshakable setting for human thinking is now seen as possibly not having come into being. God is now understood as not having had to create; he could have been all that there is, with no lessening of goodness and greatness. He is not just the best and highest entity in the whole of things. A new sense of the whole, a new sense of the divine, a new sense of the cosmos, as well as a new sense of the human person, are revealed to us in this kind of faith.[12]

In this new understanding of the whole and the divine, philosophy is not seen as an alternative or a rival to religious faith. Here, philosophy cannot see the religious formulation of the divine as inadequate or unworthy. It cannot demythologize the narrative that presents the action of God, as Plato and Aristotle could demythologize the stories of the poets. Philosophy could not say of biblical revelation what Aristotle, in a quotation, says about Simonides and other writers, "Poets tell many a lie."[13] In fact, St. Anselm's argument for God's existence in the *Proslogion* shows that reason can attain the insight that when God is understood as he is in Christian faith, he cannot be understood not to exist.[14]

This new understanding of God and the world was, historically, not reached by human rational inquiry.[15] However, once it is presented to us, through God's own Word, reason can rejoice within it and exercise itself to

12. See Robert Sokolowski, *The God of Faith and Reason: Foundations of Christian Theology* (Washington, D.C.: The Catholic University of America Press, 1995); also *Eucharistic Presence: A Study in the Theology of Disclosure* (Washington, D.C.: The Catholic University of America Press, 1993), chapter 5 and 10.

13. *Metaphysics* I, 2, 983a3.

14. For this interpretation of St. Anselm, see Sokolowski, *The God of Faith and Reason,* chapter 1.

15. The encyclical mentions the concept of "a free and personal God who is the Creator of the world" as one of the "truths which might never have been discovered by reason unaided, although they are not of themselves inaccessible to reason" (§76).

its fullest capacity: "What a challenge this is to our reason, and how great the gain for reason if it yields to this wisdom" (§23). Reason can be autonomous in the space opened by biblical revelation and Christian faith. Reason does not turn into credulity or mere acceptance of poetic legends, because the Word of God proposes an understanding and not just a statement, an insight and not just a legend or a tale.

In Christian faith, the world is no longer taken as the ultimate setting, with the divine as the best, highest, original, and governing principle in it. The world is to be understood as possibly not having existed, with God understood as undiminished in goodness and greatness even if he had not created. Creation becomes an act of unnecessitated generosity, confirmed and more deeply revealed by the even greater generosity of Redemption. This modification, this "gestalt shift" in the understanding of the whole, is not simply one among many of the teachings of Christian faith. It stands at the intersection of faith and reason, and serves as the pivot on which the meaningfulness of all the other mysteries depend. What Christians mean by salvation, for example, or grace, or the sacraments, or the role of the Blessed Virgin, cannot be properly understood if the new context is not introduced. The syntax and semantics of Christian belief presuppose this adjustment in reason's grasp of the whole. And finally, we must also remember, as the encyclical often reminds us, that this new understanding of God was not reached by an appearance that was glorious in the eyes of the world; it did not come to light through spectacular celestial phenomena or acts of earth-shaking terror. Rather, it was revealed through a shameful execution: "Man cannot grasp how death could be the source of life and love; yet to reveal the mystery of his saving plan God has chosen precisely that which reason considers 'foolishness' and a 'scandal'" (§23).

The human person and Christian faith

If reason can be defined as intelligent articulation, Christian faith can be defined as the acceptance of this new understanding of God and the whole of things, with the conviction that it was presented to us by God himself, in Christ and through his Church. Through faith, the final truth about God and the world is disclosed to us. Christian reasoning or Christian theology is then the articulation that can be carried out within the context opened by this new understanding.

Faith also presents us with the truth about ourselves, about the human person. In doing so, it responds to another aspect of philosophical inquiry. We have described philosophy as the form of thinking that examines the whole and the divine principles in the whole, but it is also the inquiry into what we ourselves are. We are not merely components of the whole; as persons, we are questions to ourselves that cannot be answered merely by discussing cosmic and natural principles. From its beginnings the search for wisdom was also an attempt to know ourselves, as the encyclical observes while quoting the admonition at the temple of Delphi (§1).

To shed light on the place of the human person in Christian faith, I would like to draw on a remark made by the Catholic philosopher from Munich, Robert Spaemann. He draws a contrast between Socrates and Christ. When we consider the way each of these men reacted to people who were hostile to them, we immediately notice "the difference between the harsh speech of Jesus against his adversaries and the friendly, ironic speech of Socrates."[16] Socrates is friendly and ironic, often playful, because he appeals to the evidence of the ideas, of the things he is conversing about. He tries to give reason its full exercise. His role is instrumental, in the service of the forms. His mission is to bring his interlocutors to the point at which reason and philosophy take over in them. He tries to help them overcome their ignorance, the confusion in their minds that keeps them from accepting the truths that they themselves would desire if only they were able to grasp them.

The opposition to Christ, however, is grounded not merely on confusion and ignorance, but on a steadfast resistance to the truth, on a love of darkness instead of light. Spaemann says that the New Testament introduces another dimension into human being, which it calls "the heart." He says that this concept is the foundation of the later concept of the person, and in fact its use in the New Testament "signifies something like the discovery of the person."[17] It is "the ground for the turning away from the good,"[18] and it is also, conversely, the ground for the turn toward the good and toward truth. Furthermore, according to Spaemann, this turning toward or turning against

16. Robert Spaemann, *Personen. Versuche über den Unterschied zwischen "etwas" and "jemand"* (Stuttgart: Klett-Cotta Verlag, 1996), p. 30: "der Unterschied zwischen der harten Sprache Jesu gegenüber seinen Gegnern und der freundlich-ironischen Sprache des Sokrates."

17. Ibid.: "Er bedeutet so etwas wie die Entdeckung der Person."

18. Ibid.: "Der Grund für die Abwendung vom Guten."

is not just a response to an argument or to an idea, but a response to some-one—God, and in the more immediate situation, Christ—who discloses the truth: ". . . The decision between good and evil, between light and darkness, is not a decision made before an idea, but before a person, who comes forth as the ineluctable *(unhintergehbare)* revelation of the truth."[19] Socrates knows that he himself may have been only a historical contingency; Christ, how-ever, is the only way to the truth that he himself brings to light—there is no possibility of taking another route or somehow "going around" him.

Spaemann also says that this introduction of "the heart" is not only a theological teaching, but also a philosophical one: "What is expressed here is an anthropological discovery, because it corresponds to something we ex-perience."[20] This concept of the heart is an ultimate "explanation" for the turn toward truth or darkness, and it is original in the New Testament: "The heart is the unfounded foundation in a sense for which there is no thinkable or conceptual equivalent in antiquity."[21]

I would like to observe that this "unfounded foundation" is not a Ni-etzschean will or a blind desire for pleasure or power, but the impulse for or against truth, the inclination that makes a person to be what he is. It is not just a power but the responsibility we have to let the truth of things disclose itself. The heart is not something that unfolds spontaneously; receptivity to the truth—or its correlate, the love of darkness—is not a merely natural pro-cess. Our relation to the truth cannot be automatic or necessary; it must be free, responsible, and most deeply our own doing. It would be misleading, however, to speak of it as a choice, because it is much more basic than that; it is not one choice among many, but the movement toward truth that un-derlies all our choices. It also underlies all our specific exercises of truthful-ness, all our particular disclosures, as well as all our true or false statements and scientific endeavors. It underlies both reason and will; it is not one act of the will among many. It establishes us as agents of truth. The way this im-pulse is exercised will determine what kind of person each of us becomes

---

19. Ibid.: "Die Entscheidung zwischen gut und böse, zwischen Licht und Finsternis [ist] nicht eine Entscheidung gegenüber einer Idee, sondern gegenüber einer Person . . . , die als unhinterge-hbare Offenbarung der Wahrheit gilt."

20. Ibid.: "Was hier zum Ausdruck kommt, ist eine anthropologische Entdeckung, weil es einer Erfahrung entspricht."

21. Ibid.: "Das Herz ist grundloser Grund in einem Sinn, für den es in der Antike kein ge-dankliches und begriffliches Äquivalent gibt."

before God. It can be either cultivated or blighted, and whichever occurs is our doing, which is why Christ so severely reprimanded those who refused the truth to which he bore witness.

The kind of manifestation that is at issue in Christian faith depends on the central and powerful authority of Christ. In the Old Covenant, God himself spoke to his people, but he did so through Moses and the prophets. In the New Covenant God spoke as a human being. The tone of Christ's words reflects this difference. He does not merely bear witness to the truth and point out the way, but asserts that he *is* the way, the truth, and the life, that no one comes to the Father except through him, and that whoever has seen him has seen the Father (John 14:6, 9). Christ is an unsurpassable and irreplaceable speaker. Socrates was the midwife who helped others discover the truth of things through their own powers, but Christ reveals the truth. When we were children, other people introduced us to the syntax of human intelligence, which we then took over and exercised on our own. Christ gives us the syntax and semantics we need to call God our Father, to understand the world as his creation and ourselves as his adopted sons. This understanding in faith, however, is not one that we can take over on our own; we can possess and exercise it only in union with "Christ crucified and risen," with whom we must remain affiliated in the Church, his body. Our willingness to accept the disclosure of God as our Creator and Father depends on our willingness to listen to Christ, to respond to the human presence that God has assumed in order to speak to us: "The Eternal enters time, the Whole lies hidden in the part, God takes on a human face" (§12).

The fact that we depend on other persons for the disclosure of things does not constrict the autonomy of reason. Every human being enters into reason—becomes elevated into syntax and language—only by being introduced to it by other human beings. Without the help of others we would never be able to introduce syntactic structure into our experience; we could never intelligently articulate our experiences and the things we know. The flowering of our reason requires the intervention of others; it does not occur by itself. It is not like the growth of our muscles and bones.

It is true that philosophy aims at a final responsibility for the truth and that it subjects our experience to a kind of relentless verification. It desires the most comprehensive truth of things, and it keeps rethinking, in the light of further truth, whatever we may know at any moment. However, in this very attempt at complete verification, we may come to realize that a certain kind of truth would be entirely unavailable to us had not someone else registered it for us and with us. The understanding that comes from Christian faith is like this. No philosopher did in fact grasp the radical transcendence of God that biblical revelation made known to us; still less could anyone have arrived at the mysteries of the Holy Trinity and Redemption. But when we reflect on these mysteries, and see how they extend beyond the context of the world, we can see with insight that they are beyond us. Our autonomy consists in recognizing our own limitations, in coming to know what we do not and what we could not know on our own.

And by knowing what we cannot grasp on our own—by knowing what we believe, and seeing that we can possess it only by believing it—we become much more aware of what we *do* know on our own. We become much more aware of and confident in our reason precisely in contrast with our faith. Faith justifies our reason. By going beyond reason we more vividly appreciate it for what it is.

Autonomy and limitation

Limitation need not be a deficiency, and the recognition of it need not be humiliating. In several places, the encyclical points out that limitation and dependence need not destroy human autonomy, but that they make possible certain perfections that are appropriate to human beings. It reminds us that in our natural exchanges with others we often "entrust ourselves to the knowledge acquired by other people" (§32). We believe what they tell us. Such confidence in others permits us to develop "the deeper capacity to entrust oneself to others." We are also told that "the capacity to entrust oneself and one's life to another person and the decision to do so are among the most significant and expressive human acts" (§33). Such remarks clearly reflect moral and religious intuitions made possible by the Holy Father's personalist philosophy and by his dealings with people in a lifetime of pastoral care. They are similar to thoughts expressed by Alasdair MacIntyre in his book *Dependent Rational Animals,* which discusses "the virtues of acknowledged dependence."[22]

---

22. Alasdair MacIntyre, *Dependent Rational Animals: Why Human Beings Need the Virtues* (Chicago: Open Court, 1999), p. 8.

Such confident dependence on others, furthermore, extends even into the philosophical life; the encyclical calls to mind "the teaching of the ancient philosophers, who proposed friendship as one of the most appropriate contexts for sound philosophical inquiry" (§33). It calls upon the Old Testament to warn us, in a phrase that might be considered an implicit critique of Machiavelli, that the path to human knowledge "is not for the proud who think that everything is the fruit of personal conquest" (§18). The discovery of truth involves reception as well as initiative. The Kantian desire for pure autonomy stems in part from too radical a disjunction between the spontaneity of reason and the passivity of sense, between the kingdom of ends and the kingdom of nature. Our moral excellence depends not only on the imperatives we legislate for ourselves, but also on what we give to and receive from others in friendship. Likewise, the dependence of philosophy on Christian faith, and ultimately its dependence on Christ as the Word of God, can also be seen not as a deficiency but as an opportunity that discloses a truth about things that could not have been attained in any other way.

In closing, I wish to return to Spaemann's remark about the difference between Socrates and Christ. The serious discourse of Christ is now part of the life of thinking, but there still remain situations in which Socratic irony is appropriate. Christian revelation elevates but does not replace human reason, and it leaves intact not only reason's power to discover the truth, but also its dialectical and playful manner of doing so.

2

PHILOSOPHY AND THE CHRISTIAN
ACT OF FAITH

How is Christian faith related to philosophy? What does Jerusalem have to do with Athens? Does our engagement in the one compromise our pursuit of the other? The first thing to be determined is the difference between the *act* of faith and the corresponding theological *virtue*.

Faith as a virtue and as an act

Through our Christian faith, we believe that certain things are true, and we believe them because of words spoken by someone. We believe certain truths and we believe in a certain speaker. Christian faith is a virtue, an abiding habit or disposition to believe the things in question and to believe in the person in question. Occasionally we move beyond the disposition and explicitly express our belief in the truths and the person, and when we do so we perform an act of faith. The act of faith is often performed in public, as we declare our belief before others by our speech or by our significant actions, but the act of faith can also be performed in solitude before the God in whom we believe. Indeed, even when we perform an act of faith in public before other men, what makes it an act of faith, an act of theological virtue, is the fact that we are also expressing it before and toward the God in whom we believe. The Christian act of faith always remains an assent and a submission to the word of God and to the God who has spoken the word; it is never merely a report to other men of convictions that we hold.

25

In the normal course of the Christian life, the act of faith is embedded in and flows from the virtue of faith. The act, which occurs from time to time, arises out of the permanent disposition. But we must distinguish from such occasional expressions the act of faith that originally establishes the theological virtue of faith, the act through which we move from unbelief to belief. The originating act of faith does not arise from the disposition but rather brings the disposition about. This first act is a conversion, an act in which we turn toward God and assert, to him, to ourselves, and perhaps to others, that we believe in him and in what he has said. This act is an affirmation; all the subsequent acts of faith are reaffirmations or confirmations, and the virtue of faith is a kind of latent continuation of the original act of faith.

In order to bring out the special features of this original act of faith, this conversion, let us compare it with actions that bring about virtues in the natural order. There are two differences between, on the one hand, natural virtues and the actions that establish them and, on the other hand, theological virtues and the acts that establish them.

First, in natural virtue it is the acts of the human agent himself that establish the virtue. The agent's own activities settle into the disposition. It is true that the agent often is helped by others: we absorb, so to speak, the courage or temperance of those who help us to become courageous or temperate; but still, it is our own conduct that gradually condenses into the virtuous dispositions of courage or temperance. In regard to the intellectual virtues, we may be guided at first by the mathematical or literary activities of our teachers, but ultimately it is our own intellectual activity, stemming from our own powers, that makes us able mathematicians or writers. In regard to Christian faith, however, we believe that the original act of faith (as well as the virtue of faith and any subsequent acts stemming from it) is the work of God's grace: we could not achieve the act of Christian faith by ourselves. It is true that we do act when we perform the act of faith, but our action is informed by grace, by God's action; our act is made to be what it is, it is defined, by God, not by our human powers. In the act of faith, we are enabled to act by what God does and our action is determined by what God does. God's work in us is different from the work of our human teachers, who only help us actualize the powers that are our own. The act of faith is God's work as much as ours; indeed, it is primarily God's work, since its form is achieved by God and shared by us.

Second, in natural action and natural virtue, it takes many human actions to establish a natural virtue, but the theological virtue of faith is established by a single act of faith. To become courageous, an agent must face dangers and deal with fear in many situations, sometimes with the guidance and help of others but more and more on his own, until the disposition to act courageously has been acquired, until, in the phrase of Yves Simon, the agent achieves a state of "existential readiness" to deal with the dangerous, the fearful, and the painful in an appropriate way.[1] But as soon as we make a full act of faith, even only once, the virtue of faith is there.

The transition from the one act to the habit of faith can be so sudden precisely because the virtue of faith is not simply acquired by human action; faith is infused in us and is the work of God before it is our work. We do not gradually shape ourselves into belief, as we gradually shape ourselves into courage or temperance or into mathematical or literary ability; we are elevated into faith by God's grace, and this change in us occurs not in partial stages but at the moment when God works in us.[2]

The two features of faith that we have described—its being primarily the work of God, and its being established by a single act of faith—are not made known to us through our perceptions or through our feelings. It is not because faith seems to come upon us suddenly, or that it seems to come upon us from without, or that it feels like something that we could never accomplish by ourselves, that we believe it is the work of God. Rather, it is our understanding of what we believe and our understanding of what it means to believe that makes us conclude that faith could not be our own work and that it must be the work of God. The features of faith that we have described are part of the understanding that is brought through faith itself.

---

1. "Existential readiness" is Simon's translation of the Latin *habitus* and the Greek *hexis*. See Yves R. Simon, *The Definition of Moral Virtue,* ed. Vukan Kuic (New York: Fordham University Press, 1986), pp. 71–79; also *Work, Society, and Culture,* ed. Vukan Kuic (New York: Fordham University Press, 1971), pp. 163–67.

2. Heresies dealing with grace and human action, such as Pelagianism and Semipelagianism, fail to distinguish clearly enough between moral and theological virtues, and the reason for this failure is a further failure to distinguish properly between the natural whole and the whole projected by Christian faith.

Christian faith and natural faith

What is it about Christian faith that makes it more than we can accomplish on our own? We can clarify this issue by contrasting Christian belief with the natural belief we have in other people and in what they say.

When we believe what another human being tells us, we believe both what he says and we believe in him. The same dual structure we have found in Christian faith is present in ordinary belief: belief in certain truths, and belief in a certain speaker. If Helen tells John that taking vitamin C will help him to ward off a cold, and if John accepts that claim, he both believes the fact and believes in the person who told him the fact. Let us assume that John does not know this truth from any other source; he has not studied medicine, he has not read about vitamins in the papers, he has not heard about vitamin C from any other people, and he has not found through his own experience that using the vitamin cuts down on the number of colds he has. He is entirely dependent on Helen for this information. And yet, even though he has not had such experience or confirmation concerning the content of what he believes when he believes Helen, he still has much in his own experience to rely on in regard to Helen herself: he knows that she exists, that she speaks to him, and that she has been trustworthy in the past. He has to believe in Helen and in her trustworthiness in this matter of vitamins, because he has no other access to the truths in question; but that she is there present to him, that she is speaking to him, and that she is reliable, are all things that he knows on his own authority and does not have to believe. Helen's credibility is nested within a context of knowledge and direct experience. The content of her speech, that which is believed, is also nested within a context of knowledge and direct experience.

In the act of faith, however, the content of the speech, the content of what is believed, comprehends even the existence, the speech, and the credibility of the speaker. The full understanding of who it is that speaks, the fact of his speech, as well as the understanding of the kind of speech that it is, are all part of what is believed. Our natural religious experience may give us a certain sense of the divine, but this sense is radically transformed by Christian revelation; in Christian faith we do not merely hear and obey the god that everyone who recognizes a divine principle acknowledges. The biblical and the Christian God is the speaker who is believed, and the being and nature of that God and the fact of his speaking to us are themselves part of what he reveals to us and what we believe.

When we believe another person in natural belief, there is a content to what we believe. John believes, on Helen's word, that vitamin C will help ward off colds, and he acts accordingly. We must be careful not to treat such belief psychologistically; we must be careful not to reduce the content of such belief to the status of "mere ideas." Belief is not concerned just with mental things or concepts or mere propositions; rather, in belief the world itself is made to show up to us in a certain way. If John believes what Helen has told him, then Helen has made the world appear to John in a certain way: the part of the world we call vitamin C and the part we call colds are presented as being related in a certain way; John takes them as so related. It is true that the parts of the world that appear to John may still be absent to him (he may never have tried to see whether vitamin C wards off colds), and yet he holds that the world, in regard to those parts of it, is as Helen presents it to be. Most of the beliefs we have are concerned with things that are absent to us: if they had become present in some way, we would know them through our direct experience and would not need to believe them. But the absence of what we believe does not destroy the fact that it is part of the world that we believe to be in a certain way. Our belief is not just a matter of assenting to a mental content, to a concept, or to a group of concepts arranged into a proposition. We are world-directed in our beliefs, and to believe something is to allow the world to become presented to us in a certain manner.[3]

Christian faith has the same intentional or presentational structure. In Christian faith we do not merely add our assent to concepts and propositions that exist in our minds. In Christian faith we take the world in a certain way; we accept that things are in a certain way, and we accept them not because we have indisputably found them to be so but because of the word that was spoken to us by God.

3. In stressing the world-directed character of belief, we are, of course, making use of Husserl's doctrine of intentionality. One of the great advantages of his doctrine is that it gives us resources to avoid making concepts and propositions the target of our knowledge; it allows us to see all thinking as being public and involved with the world. Many commentators on Husserl misunderstand this aspect of intentionality and read a Cartesian form of consciousness back into Husserl. One of the most common ways of doing this is to make the noema into a replacement for the modern idea or concept.

The content of Christian faith

What do we accept, how do we accept the world to be, in Christian faith? What is the content of what we believe? There are many articles of faith, articulations of how things are accepted as being: the creeds list many of them, and others, relating, say, to the Eucharist or the Church or the Blessed Virgin, were made explicit in the course of time. I would like to concentrate on one article or articulation. Although it is of particular importance in our day and age, it has always been at the center of Christian faith.

In Christian faith we believe that God is the Creator of the world; that is, we believe that God could be, in undiminished goodness and greatness, even if the world, even if everything that is not God, did not exist. Because God is so transcendent and so holy, the world does not add to the perfection and goodness of his being. Creating the world does not add to God's perfection and goodness. Because God exists in such independence, his Creation was done out of sheer generosity, not necessitated by any need or desire for completion. To believe this of God is also to believe, correlatively, that the world might not have been, that it exists through the divine choice to create. It is also to believe that we, the believers, would not have been but for the generous decision of God to create us. Through our faith we believe that we exist because God has chosen us to be. Thus, Christian faith opens a new perspective on the divine, the world, and ourselves, and gives us a new understanding of these three ultimate dimensions. The basic attitude we have in response to this new understanding is one of thanksgiving and adoration: thanksgiving for the gift of being, and adoration of the supreme holiness and glory of God. And as we have mentioned above, this belief is not merely an assent to propositions that formulate the world and ourselves and the divine in the manner we have described; it is an attitude that takes the whole of things to be in this way.

This understanding of God, the world, and ourselves, this content of Christian faith, is different from the understandings that have arisen in non-biblical religion, for which the divine is part of the whole, or for which the divine is everything, with the nondivine reduced to a mere apparition of the divine.[4] The God of Christian belief is not the same as the god or gods

---

4. On the special Christian understanding of the divine, see Robert Sokolowski, *The God of*

of Homer or of Buddhist teachings. And it is because the content of what is believed in Christianity is so distinctive that the Christian act of faith is a distinctive kind of achievement. The special features of Christian faith derive, not from a psychological inspection of what such faith is like, but from the content of the articles of faith.

The Christian act of faith is not the same as the religious response to the sacred. A religious response to the sacred could almost be called instinctual in human beings: it is the response men have to the best and the most powerful part of the whole. It arises in function of our awareness of the whole, an awareness that accompanies, at least implicitly, everything we do; every particular issue we face is appreciated as a part of the whole, and the whole, with the tonality that our cultural heritage gives it, hovers in the background of whatever we think and do.[5] Because we are rational, we always have a sense of the whole of things, of "the world," and we acknowledge that the whole contains beings and powers that are far beyond us, beings that are the source of ordering in the things we see, the origins of our own being, and even the judges of what we do. Natural religious traditions articulate this recognition of the best and the most powerful, and give a form to the piety that is appropriate to such recognition. (Even people who deny any presence of the divine in the world will still see certain principles and causes as ultimate and governing over the whole: evolution and the laws of nature are often credited with features that could be called divine in a Platonic or Aristotelian sense.)

The Christian act of faith does more than to articulate the natural sense of the divine and the piety that follows from it. Christian faith presupposes the natural religious sensibility, but transforms it radically. The Christian act of faith responds, not to the sacred, but to the word of the sacred. It believes that the divine has spoken to us and that it is therefore not simply the supreme power and placid origin of things, but something capable of the kind

---

Faith and Reason: Foundations of Christian Theology (Washington, D.C.: The Catholic University of America Press, 1995), pp. 12–20.

  5. On the human person and the sense of the whole, see Yves R. Simon, *A General Theory of Authority* (Notre Dame: University of Notre Dame Press, 1962), p. 67: "As a member of a species, distinguished within the species by the material components of his being, a human subject is more properly designated as an individual. Considered as a complete substance which owes to its rationality a unique way of being a whole and of facing the rest of the universe, he is more properly designated as a person."

of initiative that speaking involves: the divine has formulated a speech (it has not merely ordered the world), it has spoken that speech to us (it is not indifferent to our being), and it has acted toward us in accordance with that speech (it has not only created but also redeemed us and associated us into its own life). The act of faith is an act of hearing, understanding, assent, and obedience.

Furthermore, the Christian act of faith holds that the divine that has spoken to us, in the Scriptures and in the events of the Old and New Testaments, is not simply the same as the divinity that prompts natural piety. The speaker to whom the act of faith is a response is not simply the best and most powerful being or the source of being in the whole. The Christian divinity could be even if the world were not; its transcendence is of a different order than that of the best and most powerful being. Christian divinity is only analogous to natural divinity. The Christian God has created the world, everything that is not divine, and created it not out of any need or deprivation, but in sheer generosity. As Thomas Prufer once said, "God does not need to give, and does not gain from giving." Christians understand God in this way, not because of any sense of the divine they have received in their natural piety and through their religious perceptions, but because of what is contained in the word that God has spoken. Part of God's word is to tell those who accept it what the speaker of the word is like. Thus, it is not the case that the divine is somehow present to us naturally and then speaks to us in his word; his word makes him present to us and gives us a glimpse of what he is.

Christian faith thus involves a distinctive understanding of the divine, the whole, and ourselves. Because faith incorporates an understanding, it is not simply willful and it is not arbitrary; it involves and elevates reason. From the Christian perspective, however, unbelief, the explicit rejection of biblical faith, is not based on understanding. It may stem from an inadequate grasp of the biblical sense of God, as St. Anselm claims,[6] or it may be a choice not to believe, but in neither case is it motivated by a deeper understanding of the nature of the divine. According to Anselm's argument, the nonexistence of the God revealed in Christian faith is not intelligible.

---

6. St. Anselm, *Proslogion,* chapter 4.

Natural religion is not the same as faith

We have observed that when, in natural belief, we believe what another human being has told us, our belief is nested within much that is given to us through our own experience and knowledge: if John believes what Helen tells him about vitamins, his belief is situated within his own knowledge that Helen is there, that she speaks to him, and that she is reliable. Natural belief is supported by the authority of our own experience and knowledge. Christian faith, however, seems almost to be without any support and without any context: its content seems to encompass the existence of the speaker, his speech, and his credibility. Is there any sense in which there can be a support outside of faith for the belief that faith presents?

The sense of the divine that is present to us in nature, to our natural religiosity, serves as a kind of initial invitation to Christian faith. Such religiosity is more like experience and knowledge than like belief; we know from natural life what religion means and what the divine is. Through our own human experience, the divine is distinguished from the profane. This instinctual response to the sacred is not yet pure enough, however, to be an act of faith.[7] It is laden with the fears, attractions, and fascinations of natural religiosity. It remains, in the words of St. Paul, "enslaved to the elemental powers of the world" (Galatians 4:3). But still, it serves as a familiar basis for us; it serves as something like the natural presence of Helen to John in the exercise of natural belief. We *know*, just by being human and rational, something of the divine. This knowledge of "what all men call God, *quod omnes dicunt Deum,*" must be deeply transformed by Christian faith, which takes God to be not merely the best and most powerful being in the whole of things, but that which could be even if the whole were not, that which is the free origin of the whole and of ourselves.[8]

Thus, natural religiosity serves as a context within which the act of faith

---

7. On the act of faith as requiring a highly refined understanding of the divine, deeper than that available to pagan religion, see the remark of Alain Besançon, *Les origines intellectuelles du Léninisme* (Paris: Calmann-Lévy, 1977), p. 16, where he speaks of "un climat païen, où le divin n'est pas encore rassemblé ni séparé du monde par sa nature transcendante, et où l'appartenance religieuse ne se scelle pas, par conséquent, par un acte de foi."

8. St. Thomas Aquinas argues to the existence of God in *Summa Theologiae* I, q. 2, a. 3. He gives five proofs. After reasoning to the unmoved mover, he states, *et hoc omnes intelligunt Deum;* after reasoning to the uncaused cause, he says, *quam omnes Deum nominant;* after reasoning to the

can take place, but the act of faith purifies the sense of the divine given to
natural religion: it appreciates the world as created in sheer freedom, and it
understands the believer himself as chosen by the Creator and redeemed by
him. Christian faith adjusts the triad of the world, the divine, and the thinking subject; it moves this triad from the understanding given by natural religion to that given in revelation.

But there are other worldly speakers that play a more immediate role
for Christian faith than does natural religiosity. There are the speakers of
the Old Testament, Moses and the prophets; there is, preeminently, Christ
himself, not only in his words but in his actions; and there is the Church,
the continuation of the presence of Christ. For us now, the Church functions as the worldly presence in which the word of God is preserved and
proclaimed; the Church plays most immediately for Christian faith the kind
of role that a human speaker plays in natural belief. The Church expressing
God's word to us is analogous to Helen expressing a human claim to John:
we know through our own experience, knowledge, and authority that the
Church is there, that she is speaking to us, and that she is credible. And yet,
there is the difference that the full credibility of the Church never comes
from what we can discern through our own experience and knowledge. The
full truth of the Church is itself part of the content of what the Church proposes for belief. Once again, the worldly presence of the Church has to be
transformed by the faith that she proclaims. Through Christian faith we not
only believe in the radical transcendence of God, but we also believe that
this transcendence and the Redemption God has achieved are presented by
the Church. We do not *know* all this simply from our personal and historical
evidences. The natural credibility of the Church may bring us close to faith,
but by the very logic of Christian belief it cannot be enough to prove apo-
dictically the content of faith, which is at its core the acceptance of God as
Creator, the world as created, and ourselves as chosen and redeemed.[9]

---

being that is necessary in itself, he says, *quod omnes dicunt Deum;* after the fourth and fifth proof,
reasoning to the most perfect cause of all perfection and to the source of intelligent ordering in
natural things, he says, *et hoc dicimus Deum.*

9. It is true that Christ himself was a speaker and agent in the world. People "knew" him
through their own experience and reason. This bodily presence of Christ is now refracted to us
through the written words of Scripture, primarily the gospels, and so these writings can serve as
a "worldly" presence that we can experience. We can read them or hear them being read. They

Within the context provided by this new understanding of God, the world, and ourselves, we can go on to accept and understand the other articles of faith, such as those dealing with the Incarnation, Redemption, the Church, the Eucharist, and eternal salvation. All these other elements of the creed are important because they are parts of the way in which God has accomplished his Redemption and manifested his glory. But all of them have their true sense only when the new dimension of God as free Creator, the world as created, and ourselves as chosen and redeemed has been introduced. If this new dimension, this new slant on the whole, has not been brought into play, all the other doctrines will be given only a worldly meaning. They will be "demythologized" and turned into merely symbolic vehicles, not true doctrines. The teaching of Christian faith is not the addition of new items of information into the whole which we have by nature, but the introduction of an entirely new presentational or intentional dimension to the whole of things and to our noetic possession of them.

How faith is related to philosophy

Our discussion so far has been concerned with Christian faith. What is to be said about the other theme announced in the title of this essay, the theme of philosophy?

Philosophy and religion are always in some tension because both of them deal with the whole of things, with what the Greeks called *to pan*. The conflict Plato describes between philosophy and poetry is not a conflict between the practitioners of two literary forms, but between two attempts to formulate what is ultimate and comprehensive, two attempts to state the essentials about the divine, the world, and the soul. Philosophy is the attempt to articulate the whole and its parts by human reason, by what can be stated and confirmed on our own authority, while religion, in its poetic expression, is the attempt to articulate the whole according to ancestral sayings accepted on the authority of another. The struggle between philosophy and religion is carried out within the whole that is given to us by natural experience and knowledge.

---

can serve as a theological analogue to Helen's speaking to John. People can be brought to God's word by reading the gospels. But the Scriptures themselves, of course, are kept alive, as authoritative documents, in the Church.

What happens when the natural whole is transcended in biblical and Christian revelation? The Platonic struggle gives way to the theology and philosophy of the Fathers of the Church and to Scholasticism; reason is seen as capable of being fully exercised within faith, not as opposed to inherited religious beliefs about the sacred. Athens and Jerusalem do not need to be in conflict. A special indication of the integrity of reason in faith is given in the Christian understanding of the Incarnation, in which the divine Logos assumed a full human nature that was not diminished in any way through its union with the Word.[10] Human nature, as well as human reason, is healed, not replaced or overcome, by its union with the word of God.

The most systematic form in which philosophy has been achieved within Christian revelation has been the metaphysics of *esse* that was elaborated in the middle ages. The divine perfection and glory were expressed as belonging to *esse per se subsistens,* which was also seen as the cause of all limited forms of *esse.* I would suggest that philosophy can now perform another reflective and systematic role in regard to Christian faith. It can clarify the manifestation of what is believed. In doing this, it can draw on philosophical resources provided by phenomenology. It would be possible to call such a form of Christian thinking by the term "phenomenological theology," but this expression is unwieldy in English; I would instead propose terms like "the theology of disclosure" or "the theology of manifestation." In speaking about manifestation, such reflection would complement the reflection on being and substance that was proper to Scholasticism, and it would come to terms with the issue of appearances, which has been the dominant concern of modern philosophy.[11]

Such a philosophical reflection within Christian faith would dwell, for example, on the differentiation between natural religiosity and Christian belief, and also on the differentiation of the Christian sense of God from the natural sense of the divine. It would examine, as we have tried to sketch in this essay, the manner in which human self-understanding, as well as the understanding we have of the world, changes when natural thinking gives

10. On the relevance of the Christological councils to issues of faith and reason, see Sokolowski, *The God of Faith and Reason,* pp. 31–40.

11. On the relation of phenomenology to Christian theology, see Robert Sokolowski, *Eucharistic Presence: A Study in The Theology of Disclosure* (Washington: The Catholic University of America Press, 1994), chapter 13.

way to Christian belief. It would go on to show why a distinctive kind of analogy becomes necessary in Christian discourse, and how the "speaker" of Christian revelation and the "word" spoken in it are different from speakers and words in natural experience. It would discuss how the Christian God is more radically transcendent and hence more radically absent to the world than are pagan divinities, and how he can be more purely immanent in his creation precisely because of this transcendence. It would discuss the special character of sacraments as effective signs: since the sacraments differ from natural signs, they can be understood in their own proper definition only against the background of the Christian distinction between the world and God. This treatment of the sacraments would, of course, deal especially with the Eucharist, with its complex presentational forms, identities, and differentiations, which span not only the difference between God and the world but also the temporal differences of present, past, and future. These and many other issues of appearance are rich topics to be explored by a philosophical and theological reflection within Christian faith. They provide a new field in which reason can be exercised, one that not only leaves the achievements of natural intelligence intact, but also confirms and clarifies them.

It is true that such philosophical reflection must come after Christian faith; such philosophy does not move from natural experience to faith; it does not establish or prove the existence of the object of Christian faith and the dimension that such faith opens to us. But philosophy comes afterwards in regard to everything it studies; it always reflects on and does not establish or prove its object. Political philosophy, for example, assumes that political life is being led and examines what it means; it does not bring about or prove the existence of political life. Moral philosophy presumes that people have been virtuous and vicious, and strong and weak, and it reflects on what the moral life is; it does not originally bring about the moral life. Philosophy always reflects on what has come before it. It is true that philosophy can play a supportive and apologetical role when it clarifies the issues it reflects on; it helps us to realize that politics is not, say, economics, and that moral action is not merely an expression of self-interest. In the same way, philosophical reflection can help us appreciate the distinctiveness of Christian faith and make that faith and its object more clearly present to us; but the faith precedes the understanding that it permits.

3

CREATION AND CHRISTIAN
UNDERSTANDING

Creation can be understood in a narrow and in a wide sense. In the narrow sense, Creation is the divine activity in which the world—everything that is not divine—is made to exist. In this narrow sense, Creation refers only to the beginning of the relationship between the world and God. The continuation of this relationship would be called preservation.

But we can also discuss Creation in a wider and fuller sense. We can discuss it not in its character of being a beginning, but as establishing a distinction and a relationship, a distinction and relationship that remain after the beginning. We can discuss Creation as that which defines how we are to understand God, how we are to understand the world, and how we are to understand the relationship between the world and God. By discussing Creation in this way we also discuss God as Creator and the world as created.

Creation, in this fuller sense, is not merely one teaching among many in Christian belief. It is not one in a list of teachings along with, say, those concerning grace, the Eucharist, the Church, and the inspiration of Scripture. Creation is related to such other teachings in a way that is logically distinctive. We could say that the teaching about Creation enables these other teachings to be believed, in something like the way that the introduction of a mathematical interpretation of nature enables us to have Newtonian physics, quantum theory, relativity, and computer science. The teaching about Creation opens the logical and theological space for other Christian beliefs and mysteries.

Furthermore, Creation, as well as the creature and the Creator, have a special meaning in Christian belief. They are not understood in the same way as they are taken in many other religious traditions. It is not the case that, say, Creation and monotheism constitute a common ground, a common genus for Christianity and many other religions or philosophies, and that the specific difference that distinguishes the Christian religion from the others is to be found in the other Christian teachings, such as those concerning the Holy Trinity, the Incarnation, and the Church. Rather, the Christian understanding of God and Creation is itself given a special tone by these other beliefs. What appears as the more specific has an effect on what appears as the more generic. What appears in the foreground has repercussions on the background. It is not the case that the doctrine of Creation simply enables the other elements of Christianity to become believable but remains untouched by them, as a neutral background to them. Rather, the doctrine of Creation is affected by the beliefs that it enables, but it is affected in a way different from the way it affects them.

To pay attention, systematically, to relationships such as those I have just described is part of what I would like to call the theology of disclosure. It could also be called the theology of manifestation or a theology of epiphany, a theology of apparition. It is not just a psychology of religious experience; it does not examine simply the subjective consciousness we happen to have of religious realities. Rather, it examines how the religious reality presents itself, indeed, how it must present itself, how it must differentiate itself, in its own manner of being differentiated, from whatever is other to it. To reflect on the epiphany is to think about *how* something appears, but it is also to think about *what* discloses itself in the manifestation, and it is also to think about *ourselves* as the datives for this revelation, as those to whom it appears.

Traditionally, one of the tasks of theology has been to bring out the relationships, the nexus, among the various revealed truths. This task can be pursued in regard to not just the truths themselves, but the way the truths become presented. It is not just the truths that are interwoven; their ways of being disclosed are also interlaced, and we can better appreciate the truths themselves by reflecting theologically on how they come to light. In the course of this essay we will carry out such reflection in regard to Creation and its relationship to other Christian mysteries, but first we must determine what the specifically Christian sense of Creation is.

The Christian sense of Creation

Let us call "the world" everything that is not God. The world, obviously, does exist. We start with that. But in Christian belief the world is understood as possibly not having been. The world becomes understood as existing in such a way that it might not have existed. And, in the Christian understanding, if the world had not been, God would still be. Furthermore, God would not be diminished in any way, in his goodness and perfection, if the world were not. While the world is understood as possibly not having been, God is understood as not being perfected in any way, as not increasing in goodness, by virtue of the actual existence of the world. Both the world and God become understood in this special way.

At first sight these understandings might seem to drain the world of its goodness and perfection. It might seem that the being of the world is said not to add anything to God's perfection because the world is understood to have no value in itself. Clearly we would resent this implication. But the reason the world does not add perfection to God does not lie in any poverty of the world; the reason is that God's goodness, perfection, and independence are understood to be so intense that nothing could be added to them. God is so understood that it would be meaningless to say that Creation added to his goodness, that he created out of any sort of need. It is because of the greatness of God, not because of any worthlessness of the world, that Creation does not better the perfection of God.

To bring out the novelty of this understanding, let us compare it to the sense of the world and the divine that is reached by natural religion and by philosophical thinking, as such religion and philosophy are found, say, in the classical poets and philosophers of Greece and Rome, in many religious writings, and in many beliefs that are current now, and that will doubtlessly always be current, among scientists, intellectuals, and people who have religious convictions.

According to the natural and spontaneous understanding, the divine and the nondivine form parts of a larger whole. The divine may be recognized as the exemplary, the controlling, the encompassing, the best, and even in some sense the origin, but it is not normally conceived as that which could be, in undiminished goodness and excellence, even if everything else were not.

Natural religious thinking and experience, as well as philosophical thinking about the whole, do not attain to this extreme turn of the dial.

Natural and spontaneous thinking accepts the world as simply there. The initial understanding of the world as dense and ineluctable, as unquestioned in its existence, is not a deficient form of thinking. It is the appropriate beginning. It is sound and robust. At the recorded inception of Greek philosophy, in the poem of Parmenides, the goddess who addresses Parmenides is quite correct in prohibiting him from looking for an origin for what is in that which is not (Fragment 8). To accept things as simply and necessarily there is the way reason should start. We *ought* to be impressed by the density of the nature of things. Even the Christian understanding of the being of things needs this natural stability as its counterpart and ever-present foil. The Christian understanding would not be appreciated as revelation without it. But over against this pagan and spontaneous understanding, Christian belief distinguishes the divine and the world in such a way that God could be, in undiminished goodness and greatness, even if everything else were not.

The Christian understanding introduces a new horizon or context for the modes of possibility, actuality, and necessity. Each of these modes is understood in a new way. The being of things is now questioned in a new setting. Questions are raised that are different from those that, say, Aristotle would raise. If we were to think as Aristotle thought, we might ask how it is that the elements and powers of the world—of the world that is always there—become congealed into being this animal or that building, and how they acquire the centeredness and intelligibility of being one substance or one artifact. This is how Aristotle would inquire into the being and substance of things. But in a Christian understanding one can ask why the animal or the building exists at all. Things are profiled not against the world and its elementary forces, but against not being at all. Their possibility is rooted not only in the potentialities of what already is and always has been, but in the power of God to make them be. The necessity against which their contingency is contrasted is not the iron bonds of fate that border the world, but the still more extreme necessity of the self-subsistent God whose choice is the source of everything else that is, everything that is now understood as not having to have been. The introduction of this sense of Creation introduces a new slant on being, on what it is to exist, and on all the modalities

of being. It also introduces a new slant on ourselves. We to whom this understanding occurs come to understand ourselves in a way different from the
self-understanding of a pagan or a secular philosopher. A pagan would consider himself as coming to be from the actions of his parents and his people,
from the process of evolution, and from the physical and psychic necessities
of the world. He would be grateful to his parents and his people, with a filial
piety and loyalty, for they were responsible for his coming to be.

But even if a pagan accepted a divine principle in the world, he would
not have the kind of gratitude toward that divinity that a Christian would
have toward God. He would not consider himself as having been chosen to
be, he would not consider his being as having been bestowed, in the way
that a Christian would. His attitude toward the divine would be more like
one of admiration and reverence rather than one of gratitude, because according to his pagan understanding there is something in him that is not due
to the god, something that precedes both him and the god, something for
which the god is not responsible. To some degree the pagan does stand on
his own over against the divine in a way that one who believes in Creation
does not. For the pagan the whole is essentially prior to both the divine and
the rest of being, but for the Christian the divine could be the whole, even
if it is not, since it is meaningful to say, in Christian belief, that God could
be all that there is.

This understanding of the whole has an impact on how we understand
ourselves, since we have such a prominent place in the whole of things; we
are the ones for whom the whole is an issue, and the way we take the whole
will modify how we take ourselves. The issue of Creation is not just a question about things but a question about ourselves as well.

It is interesting to note how the metaphysical and the personal become
blended in this Christian understanding. If the world is understood as possibly not having been, then its being is the outcome of a determination that
selects between possibilities. Before the beginning there was something like
an indeterminate future; before the beginning the world might be, but it
also might not be. Its actual being is then the outcome of something like a
choice, something like the determination of an undetermined situation that
contains possibilities that invite a decision. The play of metaphysical modalities, of possibility and actuality, calls for something like a choice, something
like a personal transaction. Creation is not simply emanation from possibil-

ity to necessity; if it were, it would no longer be Creation. And just as the modes of possibility, actuality, and necessity, when examined on this scale, are only analogous to the modes we experience in our worldly involvements, so also the choice to create is only analogous to what we are familiar with as choices; but there is no word more appropriate for us to use than "choice" as we attempt to speak about the actual but nonnecessitated existence of the world. And because something like choice is involved in Creation, something like gratitude is our appropriate response to it, not just for the being of things, but for our being as well. The fact that we are is the outcome of a personal transaction, not the outcome of chance or necessity, and it calls for a personal reaction on our part.

Finally, it should be apparent that what seemed like a kind of indifference of God toward the world, in the claim that God is not perfected by Creation, is really the condition for a greater generosity and benevolence in Creation. If God is not perfected by creating, then he does not create out of any sort of need, and his creating is all the more free and generous. There is no self-interest and no ambiguity in the goodness and benevolence of Creation. And the pure generosity of Creation tells us about the nature of the giver of this gift. The nature of the action tells us what the agent is like, and, along with the generosity of Redemption, it establishes the context for our own response in charity, first toward God and then toward others.

Creation and other Christian mysteries

Let us now discuss the relationship between the Christian understanding of Creation and some other Christian beliefs. I wish to claim that the final determination of the Christian sense of Creation is achieved as an implication of the Christian understanding of the Incarnation. In the councils of Nicaea, Ephesus, and especially Chalcedon, in response to controversies about the being of the Redeemer, the church stated that Christ was one person and one being with two complete natures, the human and the divine, and that neither of these natures was in any way diminished or changed by virtue of their union in him. Christ was fully human and fully divine. He was one being but two "kinds" of being. In stating these things, the church claimed to be restating the understanding of Christ that is found in the New Testament.

In the natural order of things, a union such as that of the Incarnation is impossible, and to assert such a union would be to state an incoherence or an inconsistency. In the natural order of things, each being is one kind of being. In being what it is, each thing excludes other kinds of being. A human person is not and cannot be a tree; a lion is not and cannot be a diamond. And since the divine as part of the world is one of the natures in the world, in the natural order of things a god, as understood by pagan thinking, cannot be human. A god could become human only by becoming less than a god, or not fully human, or by being only apparently human or only apparently divine, or by becoming some new kind of thing different from both the divine and the human. One being could not be fully human and fully divine. Zeus might appear as a swan, but he could not have become a swan.

The doctrine of the Incarnation, therefore, implicitly tells us something about the nature of the divine. For the Incarnation to be possible, the divine nature must not be conceived as one of the natures within the whole of the world. It must be conceived as so other to the world that the union in the Incarnation would not be an incoherence. Thus the Jewish emphasis on the otherness of God, which provided the background for the life, teaching, and actions of Christ, was ratified and intensified by the belief in the Incarnation.

The doctrine of Creation is also related to belief in the Holy Trinity. First, just as in the Incarnation, the special sense of the divine that the doctrine of Creation introduces opens the possibility of a new union and a deeper communion, the union of one nature and three persons. In worldly being, it would again be incoherent to speak of three persons in one nature or one being, to speak of three persons in one substance. Each agent or person we experience is one being. But when we conceive of God as so different from the necessities of the world that he could exist, with no loss of excellence, even if the world were not, then we cannot say that the Triune God is not possible. The limitations and definitions we are familiar with from our experience of the world and of agency within the world no longer apply without qualification.

Secondly, the doctrine of the Holy Trinity confirms the understanding we have of the transcendence of God through belief in Creation. A pagan religious thinker might raise an objection to the understanding of God that we have proposed, of God as the one who could be all that there is, even without the world. He might object that this is too extreme a projection of unity. It seems to remove the involvement of difference, otherness, multiplicity, relation, and exchange from the highest being, and it seems to remove any sense of community from the divine. It seems to remove the tasks that ought to be involved in being. Unity seems to be carried to excess. It is as though someone were so impressed by the beauty of Plato's One that he wanted to project nothing but the One in sheer isolation. The good seems to be discarded in favor of the best. One aspect of being seems intensified to the exclusion of other principles that are equally necessary, even for the One and the Good to be what they are.

This is an objection that could be made if the divine were merely distinguished from the world and left in solitude. But part of the Christian understanding is that community, exchange, relation, and divergence are to be found within the divine nature, in the life of the Holy Trinity. The exchanges, relations, and divergences, as well as the community, are not the kind we are familiar with, and in no way do they subordinate God to a need for exchanges with the world; quite the contrary. Because of the abundance of the life of the Holy Trinity, God becomes even more independent in his nature of any involvement with anything that is not divine. This independence of nature, of course, does not become indifference; rather, it defines both Creation and Redemption as all the more generous and unnecessitated.

The Christian distinction between the world and God is also important in regard to the doctrine of analogy. Traditionally, Christian theology has claimed that discourse about God is analogous discourse, that is, that a word like *good* or *one* when applied to God is meant in a way that is analogous to its usage in worldly applications. The unity of God is not the same kind of unity as that, say, of a human being or an animal. Rather, there is an analogy of proportion in the two uses. The divine unity is to God as human unity is to a human being, or as organic unity is to a living thing. Such an analogy allows us to say that we know something of what the word means when it is applied to God, and that we can apply the term meaningfully, even though the full and literal sense of the term is beyond our comprehension.

There is no problem with the analogous use of terms within the confines of worldly experience. We find analogous structures everywhere. For example, there is an analogy between the way scales are to fish, and feathers are to birds, and hair is to mammals. There is an analogy between the way the past is presented in memory and the way the past is presented in a historical treatise; the term "the past" is used analogously, not univocally, in the two cases. There is even a rather uncontroversial analogy between, say, the wisdom of the divine principle in the world, and human wisdom, and animal cunning. Even a secular thinker will attribute a kind of ingenuity to evolution that is analogous to human prudence. All these are worldly analogies that possess an intelligibility and provide an illumination peculiar to them as analogies.

But in the Christian distinction between the world and God, a new and more radical analogy is both introduced and required. A new kind of non-worldly difference is introduced, a new distance that a new analogy is supposed to span. This distance becomes so great, and the difference between the worldly and the divine becomes so radical, that at first it would seem that nothing at all could span it. It would seem that nothing coherent could be said about the divine, because the divine is so out of reach of our discourse. However, this extreme of obscurity, this excess of darkness which is an excess of light, is complemented by the belief that the world does have its being from God and that traces of the hidden God will be found in it, and that they support analogous discourse about the Creator.

Language arises as an outcome of our power to distinguish, and the syntax of language arises as we bring back together, into various kinds of wholes, the things and features we have discriminated. The special distinction that occurs in the Christian understanding of God and Creation, the distinction between God and the world, with the special form of negation and affirmation that it implies, gives rise to an appropriately modified language, to the terminology and syntax of theological analogy.

Creation as a distinct dimension

Belief in Creation is not simply belief in a fact or an item of information that is added to all the other things we know and hold as true. Belief in Creation introduces what I would like to call a dimensional difference, a new way of taking things. It introduces a new way in which the world as a whole, and everything in the world, can be interpreted.

There are other forms of thinking that also introduce new dimensions, and if we examine them briefly, we may be helped to appreciate the special character of Creation. Consider, for example, the difference introduced when we learn what names are, or when we learn how to use names. If we learn that things have names, we are not merely given one more fact about the world, one more feature of things. Rather, when we appreciate things as nameable, everything in the world, and even the world as a whole, takes on a new aura. Everything takes on a new mode of being presented, and we ourselves take on a new form, not only because we expect ourselves to have our own name, just like everything else, but because we surface as the ones who use names, who can supply the name of a thing or who can look for its name if we do not know what it is. If things are nameable, it is partly because we or someone like us can give names. The presentational form of being named is a form for things, but a form for us and for our intentionality as well.

Likewise, a dimensional difference is introduced when things are appreciated as measurable and countable. This too is not simply a new fact, but a new way in which things can be presented. Moreover, in introducing measurability and countability, we are not just making a change in our psychological and intellectual powers. We are saying something about how beings can be presented and intended. We are saying something about the being of things and about ourselves as the datives for the presentation of things.

Still another dimensional difference occurs when we appreciate the articulations of time, when we entertain not just what is immediately going on, but the distant future and the past. When this happens, we do not merely annex a future and a past to an unperturbed present; it is not the case that we begin with a complete present and then add two more dimensions to it. Rather, the present itself becomes established as the present in its contrasts with the future and the past.

Now a religious attitude, even a pagan one, also introduces a dimensional difference into the way we take things. A religious attitude is not merely the addition of a divine principle to everything else. It is also a new way of taking the "everything else," a distinctive way of appreciating things. Things, in the religious attitude, are taken as being governed or influenced or known or judged by an agent or a mind that is different in kind from our own. Our own perspective on things becomes contrasted to a perspective that is radically different, and the things we know and experience are appreciated as also known and influenced by the gods.

But the Christian distinction does not simply fit into the religious perspective. It introduces a further dimensional difference into the natural religious understanding. All the things that are, including ourselves, are now appreciated as known and chosen by the God who allowed them to be. The whole context, even the whole religious context, is changed. The gods or the divine are replaced by God, and everything looks different when this happens. What had seemed to be the whole—the whole made up of the gods and the world—is now seen not to be the ultimate whole. God alone could be all that there is. God alone could be the whole. The sense of the whole itself changes.

And this dimensional difference pervades all the other presentational forms, so that language and names, for example, now become activated in a context that is not like that of the context of the world. The names of God, and discourse about God, are not like the speech we use in expressing the things we know in the world. To mention another example, the presentational form of picturing takes on a new dimension, since a depiction of the divine, understood as it is in Christian belief, is not a normal image of an object, nor is it an idol; it is rather an icon, and the theology of icons, with the importance it has had in the Eastern Christian tradition, can be fruitfully developed against the setting of both Creation and Incarnation.

I want to emphasize that unless this new sense of the whole, this rather formal change in the way we take being, is introduced, other descriptions of God and of the relationship we have to God will not be properly understood. For example, we may believe in divine providence, but unless everything is appreciated according to the sense of Creation that we have discussed, the providence of God will not be properly interpreted. The context for what is meant by providence will not have been correctly established, and the difference between the biblical providence of God and, say, the Stoic sense of providence, will not have been secured. Christian discourse about God remains vulnerable to distortion so long as the context of Creation, and the logic that follows from this context, have not been clarified.

The theology of disclosure

The dimensional difference introduced by belief in Creation establishes a new setting within which everything we are familiar with is understood in a new way. Everything is identified within a new set of differences and everything thereby takes on a new tone. Another person, for example, is no longer only our brother or sister or friend, but is someone who exists through the generosity and choice of God. This truth about the person makes us act toward him or her in a new and appropriate way. If the being of other persons is God's gift, other persons are more emphatically understood as ends in themselves than they would be if they had simply the dignity, great as it is, that comes from being rational agents, fellow citizens, members of our family, or neighbors or friends.

Now it is one thing to introduce this dimensional difference and to live in and according to it. That is done by someone who lives in Christian faith. It is another thing to reflect thoughtfully on the new dimension and to think about it, as clearly and systematically as we can. We begin to think about it as a dimension: in the way it comes forward, in the way it differentiates itself from the original and spontaneous religious dimension, in the way it sheds light on things and allows us to appreciate things and persons in a new context, in the way it calls for and legitimates a new analogical language, in the way it changes the sense we have of the whole and the world and the divine, in the way it modifies the modalities of being, the actuality, possibility, and necessity of our experience, in the way it introduces new forms of negation, distinction, and assertion, in the way it calls for an appropriate response in our self-understanding, deliberation, and action, in the way it introduces the possibility of sacraments and icons. To carry out such investigations is to pursue a theology of disclosure, to think theologically about the epiphany of God in our world.

This theology of disclosure is a supplement to the Scholastic theology that has been the dominant form of theology, in Catholic circles at least, since the Middle Ages. Scholasticism reflected on the existence and nature of God, and on the world in its relation to God, but it carried out its work within the horizon set by the Christian distinction between the world and God. It did not examine the emergence of the distinction itself. It took the presence of the distinction for granted.

Furthermore, the theology of disclosure is an appropriate and positive response to issues that have been raised in modern, post-Scholastic thinking. During the European philosophical age set by the late Scholastics, Machiavelli, Descartes, Hobbes, and modern science, the issue of appearances has surfaced as the central philosophical concern. Appearances have been interpreted as coming between ourselves and the things we want to know. We have been led generally to be skeptical of appearances and to separate them as phenomena from the things in themselves, from the noumena, that are known through scientific inference and not directly through perception and received opinion. In religious thought there has been a corresponding tendency to turn within, to find our contact with the divine more through immanence and subjectivity, and not in the world. In this turn to subjectivity the sacramentality of the world has been allowed to fade away.

The theology of disclosure is an attempt to publicize religious appearance. It is concerned with a distinction that occurs in regard to the world, not just with a subjective experience. It seeks to discover an indication of the divine even in the materiality of the world. In doing this it attempts to validate appearance and remove the suspicion we have toward it. It also emphasizes history, whether biblical, ecclesiastical, or secular, as the place in which the Christian distinction occurs, but it interprets this history speculatively. It sees it not simply as information about the past, but as serving the truth that the distinction brings to light.

Thus the theology of disclosure supplements Scholastic ontology by introducing subjectivity and appearance in a more systematic way, and it responds to modernity by thinking about appearance in terms of distinction and being. And the religious issue that it brings to the fore, the central concern that allows it to speak about faith and reason, and grace and nature, and the world and God, is the issue of Creation. The theology of epiphany turns to Creation not as a problem but as light, a light that both itself appears and allows other differentiations to take place, a light whose brilliance is glimpsed by human reason and revealed in the word of God.

4

CHRISTIAN RELIGIOUS DISCOURSE

Christian religious discourse is not the same as religious discourse in general. It would not be accurate, however, to say that the latter is simply a genus for the former. Nor is religion simply a genus for Christianity as a species. The way Christian religion and its discourse differ from religion as such and its discourse is complex, and this difference is based on the way the divine is understood in both cases. Sociologically or anthropologically, natural religion might be considered a genus for Christianity, but it cannot be so considered theologically.

In natural religion, in the religion that exists in human life apart from biblical revelation, god or the gods are understood as the best, most power-ful, and the governing part of the world, but they are understood as being part of the whole. It would make no sense, in natural religion, to say that the divine could be all that there is. The divine is the best and most admirable, but it is necessarily contrasted to that which is not divine.

Christian religion differs from this natural religion not only because it has certain particular beliefs, such as belief in the Incarnation, Redemption, and the Holy Trinity, but also because it has had revealed to it a distinct sense of the divine. In the Christian understanding, God could have been all that there is; it is not necessary that God be part of the whole. God has in fact created the world, and the world does exist as other to God, but in principle it need not have been so. God could have been the whole. For Christian un-derstanding, the world exists "contingently," and it exists as the outcome of a choice made by God. In this understanding, the world does not exist with any kind of contingency but the kind that depends on a choice; and not on any kind of choice but the kind involved in Creation. The logic of parts and wholes, as well as the logic of necessity and contingency, are transposed in Christian belief.

Christian biblical belief is different from natural religion in the way it understands Creation, but even Creation is not the ultimate defining doctrine in Christian faith. Creation itself is profiled against the background of a new understanding of what the divine means.

This understanding of the divine has an impact on the discourse used in Christian religion. Christian discourse must make use of analogy, but the sort of analogy it uses is not like other kinds of analogy. It is only analogous to them. I will discuss the theme of analogy, but before doing so, I will mention several types of speech found in Christian religion; this survey will try to bring out the variety in the ways language is used in Christianity. I will mention seven kinds of speech and will bring out a special point or two about each.

Seven forms of speech in Christian faith

The first kind of speech is prayer, speech which is directed not toward other people nor toward oneself but toward God. It is important to note that not all understandings of the divine imply the possibility of prayer. Aristotle's conception of god as the self-thinking thought, for example, would not imply that we should or even could pray to god, because this divine principle does not know things in the sublunary world and would not be concerned with anything that is not permanent and necessary. The contingent and the particular would not be worthy of his attention. The Christian understanding of God and of the relation of the world to God does establish the possibility of prayer, and it also establishes its necessity. Since the world and everything in it, ourselves included, exist only through divine choice, we cannot not be obliged to be grateful for existence. Not only can we pray, we ought to pray. It would be unseemly not to do so. The possibility and the responsibility of prayer are derived theologically from the Christian understanding of the divine.

The second kind of speech that is prominent in Christian belief is narrative. This form of discourse is called for because in biblical belief, God has intervened in history; first, in his covenants with the Jewish people and his providence over them, then in the Incarnation and the life of the Son of God. Worldly events enter into Christian religion, and these events are not just illustrations of general truths or eternal necessities. These events, in their materiality and their "episodity," are part of what is believed. For the Christian, there is glory to God not only in the heavens but also on earth. Thus, the divine is manifested not only by speculation, which would reach the eternal and the necessary, but also by narration, by the distinctive biblical narration that "collects" the events in which God has intervened in the history of the world. The core of the Bible is narration, not systematic treatise, law, or poetry; the Bible is the holy book because God has acted in the world, and these actions are represented primarily in narration.

There are some other distinctive features of biblical narrative. A treatise calls for understanding, but a narrative calls for belief.[1] The appropriate noetic correlate to a treatise is understanding, and the appropriate noetic correlate to a story is belief. We could understand a story without believing it, but such "mere" understanding is not what the Bible calls for. It must be not only understood but also believed. Also, as a narrative the Bible relativizes itself. It speaks about things that happened and so subordinates itself to the events it recounts. The text cannot become an end in itself. This reference beyond the text is especially vivid in the Gospels because there are four of them and each relativizes the others. Also, the narratives in the New Testament contain an interesting mixture of perspectives. At their core are the actions and words of Jesus, but the narratives also include the actions and the words of those who responded to him in his presence (Mary his mother, the apostles, the disciples, the Scribes and Pharisees, Mary and Martha, Zacchaeus, the unnamed Samaritan woman). Such people have to be mentioned because Christ's actions could not have taken place or been described apart from his involvement with them. But in addition, the New Testament has to mention the actions and words of the people who responded to Jesus in his absence, in his aftermath, so to speak (Paul, Stephen, Cornelius, the Corinthians, Galatians, and Ephesians); they become paradigms for us who have to do the same. The New Testament narratives thus show how Christ can be identified in these multiple forms of presence and absence.

1. This observation was made by Hans-Georg Gadamer during a discussion at a meeting of the Deutsche Gesellschaft für phänomenologische Forschung in Trier in May 1987.

A third kind of speech used in Christian belief is found in the creed. Creeds are not narratives, even though they talk about events. They talk about events more in the form of a simple report, a statement that something happened or that something is the case, a statement that distills what happened and the truth revealed in what happened, but that does not get into the details of the events. The creeds condense the meaning and the substance of the biblical narration. Furthermore, as their very name indicates, creeds explicitly state our belief in the content of these reports. The Bible, as a narrative, calls for belief, and the creed explicitly expresses such belief.[2] It expresses both what we believe and that we believe it.

A fourth kind of discourse is that of preaching or rhetoric. Preaching is related to the belief we have been discussing: if the biblical narrative calls for belief, and if the creed expresses belief, preaching bears witness to and encourages the belief proper to Christianity. Once again, the biblical narrative does not stand alone; just as it needs a creed to distill its meaning, so it needs exhortation to foster the belief that is the noetic correlate to the biblical narrative.

One might say that all religions involve preaching and that this form of speech is not special to Christianity, but there is something distinctive about the way it appears in Christianity: the transmission of the biblical message by "witnesses," by confessors and martyrs, is essential to the spread and continuation of Christian faith.[3]

---

2. It would be theologically valuable to contrast the literary forms of creed and biblical narration. We should also note that a creed is not a treatise; this distinction too could be fruitfully spelled out. Thus, the network of narrative, creed, and treatise provides a worthy theme for theological reflection.

3. In this connection, the story in Francis Bacon's *New Atlantis* of how Christianity came to the island of Bensalem is revealing. The visitors who arrive at the island are surprised to find that the inhabitants are Christian. They desire to know "who was the apostle of that nation, and how was it converted to the faith." They are told that twenty years after the Ascension of Christ, the inhabitants of the island saw a flaming pillar appear in the sky. They went out in boats to investigate it and found in the water a wooden chest containing a Bible and a letter from St. Bartholomew. Thus Christianity was brought to Bensalem through the reading of a letter and a book and through a flaming pillar, not through the living witness of the Church and its missionaries and sacraments. The apostle, "the one sent," was not St. Bartholomew but the letter. The story reflects an emphasis, typical of the Renaissance, on scholarly interpretation as opposed to ecclesial life as the source of Christian truth; the invention and spread of printing must have been essential for this new form of evangelization. St. Bartholomew was the apostle of Bensalem but he never arrived there in person; his letter made him present, but it had to be interpreted by those who could read it. The story also states that the various people on the island spoke different languages

A fifth kind of discourse special to Christianity is the kind of speech used in the sacraments. The sacraments are more than speech, but they involve speech. It is traditional in theology and canon law to distinguish between the matter and the form of a sacrament. The form of a sacrament is the words that are pronounced when it is effected. It would be valuable theologically to investigate the performative nature of sacramental speech and especially to ask who the speaker and the agent are in the case of the sacraments.

A sixth sort of discourse is poetry, as it is found in the psalms, the prophets, and in wisdom literature, and in the epideictic speech and writing composed through the history of the Church. Poetry is especially concerned with display, with making something perceptible, with bringing out the glory or the *doxa* of a thing. Hans Urs von Balthasar's work on the glory of God and the place of aesthetics in Christian faith can be invoked here, and the relationship between the *doxa* of faith and the *doxa* of God's glory can be indicated as a theme to be explored.

The seventh and final kind of speech both underlies and pervades the others. It is the declaration of the truths that are believed in Christian faith, the teaching that corresponds to the hearing that St. Paul says is constitutive of belief: "Faith comes from what is heard, and what is heard comes through the word of Christ" (Romans 10:17). Such teaching was carried on in the Old Testament by Moses, the prophets, and the writers of the sacred books. In the New Covenant it was done primarily by Christ, then by those he commissioned to teach in his name. These truths are reformulated by the Church in her creed, they are the substance of what is preached, and they tell us what prayer is. They are embedded in the biblical narrative and they need to be complemented by the events that the narratives describe, but they serve also to explain what the events mean, that is, they show what is happening in them.

---

and yet were able to read the book and letter. This was a repetition of the miracle at Pentecost but with a difference: it was not the apostles present in person who were enabled to speak in different tongues, but various readers who were enabled to decipher a text. The miracle was in the readers and not in the speakers, and everything was done through the mediation of the written—or the printed—word. Furthermore, there would have to have been something like an "apostolic" tradition in Bensalem to preserve the *reception* of the Bible and the letter (not directly the actions and words of Christ). The tradition would have stemmed from the original witnesses to this reception and it would have handed down the story of the pillar, Bible, and letter. Since readers originally deciphered the Bible and the letter, would readers in subsequent generations be able to reinterpret the texts and events that the tradition was handing on?

These, then, are seven forms of discourse used in Christian faith. I mention all seven to show the wide-ranging use of words in Christianity, so that we will not think that the problem of Christian discourse and analogy applies only to the sciences of theology and philosophy when they speak about God. Analogy applies in all forms of Christian discourse. Throughout all these forms, words such as *God, divine, Creator, Redeemer, goodness, grace, making, response, giving, acting,* and the like are used, and such words are applied both to God in his own life and to the actions he performs in the world. Even the words applied to worldly things become used analogously when the world is understood as having been created in the biblical sense, because the world and everything in it are now seen to be contingent in a new way.

Analogy within natural thinking

Before entering into Christian religious analogy, let us briefly discuss analogy within the worldly setting. As is generally known, Aristotle spoke only of one kind of analogy, the kind the scholastics called "analogy of proportionality." What the scholastics called "analogy of attribution" was not called analogy by Aristotle. He called it "*pros hen* equivocation." Let us first discuss the analogy of proportionality. In this analogy, we have an identity of two ratios: A is to B as C is to D. If we were to take A and C independently, we would not say that they are the same; however, the *ratio* of A to B is the same as the ratio of C to D. The two ratios are the same.

Analogy is not the same as metaphor. Metaphor is a rhetorical trope. It is situational and personal, even highly subjective. As pleasing and illuminating as metaphor might be, it does not have a place in science. Indeed, metaphors, as Thomas Hobbes reminds us, can be a misleading distraction in science. They can make us think there are identities where none exist. Analogy, however, is a form of speech that has a place in science. There are some things that would not be properly understood unless we knew they were analogous to other things. For example, we understand human reasoning better and more fully when we realize that it is analogous to animal cunning, that animals carry out some activities that are analogous to the exercise of human prudence. Animal cunning and human prudence are not only metaphorically related to one another.

Furthermore, the identities that analogies bring out are not mere appearances, as metaphors are. They truly are identities: animal cunning is not the same as human intelligence, but animal cunning is to animals as human prudence is to man. Feathers are not scales, but feathers are to birds as scales are to fish. We can do without metaphor in scientific discourse, but we cannot do without analogy. To bring this out more vividly, take the provocative instances of what we could call emergent analogies, cases in which we are not yet sure if we have "landed" an analogy or not. For example, DNA is said to embody a code, a genetic code; is this expression a metaphor or an analogy? Could we really speak of DNA without using the word *code?* Have we stumbled on an analogous understanding, while perhaps originally using the term in only a metaphorical way? The same question could be asked about artificial intelligence; are expert systems and other computer programs called intelligent only metaphorically or can we discern an analogy at work in the use of this term?

An important aspect of analogy is that it forces us to see things in wider contexts. It helps us resist the tendency of modern thinking to break things down into particles and to think that we have explained an entity when we have gotten to the ultimate pieces of which it is composed. In such thinking, all names are ultimately univocal; things are all boiled down to elements that are the same everywhere. It has often been observed that ratios play an important role in ancient mathematics, and that the importance of ratios was linked to the more geometrical and hence the more worldly and public character of ancient mathematics. The modern mathematics that began with Vietà and Descartes moved away from ratios toward individual numerical values, toward algebra in place of geometry, toward the equation in place of the analogy, toward the algebraicization of nature. This mathematical development was related to the search for elementary particles and for the elementary forces by which the particles are related. The search for the laws of nature replaced the search for the natures of things. If we take analogies as essential and irreducible, however, we will become more sensitive to the forms of things and see things in their fuller context and environments. We will explain the form, say, of birds as analogous to the form of fish; we will see the adaptation of birds to their niche as analogous to the adaptation of fish to theirs. We will be less inclined to explain fish and birds in terms merely of changes in the particles that make them up.

Another feature of analogies is the fact that they are two-edged swords.

If we see that animal cunning is to animals as prudence is to human beings, this insight does not only help us understand what animal cunning is; it also helps us understand human prudence more adequately. We see human prudence as nested in and anticipated by the more basic animal forms of cognition and behavior. Thus, we cannot say that the analogy is directed solely toward the clarification of any one or any pair of the four terms used in it (A, B, C, D). It sheds light on all four.

We should also say a few words about how the analogy of attribution works in the natural order, even though Aristotle did not call it analogy. Here we deal not with four terms in two ratios, but with two, three, or more uses of a single term, all of which are clustered around a single, primary, "focal" meaning (as Joseph Owens has called it). We are all familiar with Aristotle's example of the use of the term *health,* which primarily refers to the good state of a bodily organism, but which can also refer to medicine, exercise, food, and complexion, insofar as they are related to a healthy organism as causes, instruments, signs, or effects of it. This sort of analogy is also not mere appearance, as metaphor is, nor is it mere chance, as simply equivocal terms are. The analogy of attribution, like the analogy of proportionality, has a place in science. We would not understand the health of an organism if we did not also see it embedded in a cluster of things that are related to it and thus allow it to show up in a wider context. Once again, analogy helps us avoid reductionism and a kind of univocal "particle philosophy."

I want to make a special point concerning the analogy of attribution. I draw this point from an excellent article by Gunther Patzig entitled, "Theology and Ontology in Aristotle's *Metaphysics.*"[4] In this essay, Patzig says that Aristotle thinks that in some domains we can "grasp the whole in some one favored part, and only in that."[5] Patzig appeals to Aristotle's remark in the *De anima* that the human hand is the tool of tools.[6] This remark does not just mean, Patzig says, that the hand is superior to other tools, but rather that all tools "are only . . . raised to the status of tools through the activity of the hand. Without a hand to use them, all other tools would no longer properly

---

4. Gunther Patzig, "Theology and Ontology in Aristotle's *Metaphysics,*" in *Articles on Aristotle,* volume 3: *Metaphysics,* edited by Jonathan Barnes, Malcolm Scholfield, and Richard Sorabji (New York: St. Martin's Press, 1979), pp. 33–49. The article was originally written in 1960 and was based on the dissertation Patzig completed in 1950.

5. Ibid., p. 40.

6. Aristotle, *De Anima* III, 8, 432a1–2.

be called tools. Tools are dependent for their status as tools upon the human hand."[7] In like manner, of course, the health of an organism makes it possible for us to call medicine, complexion, and behavior healthy. We *call* them healthy because they are healthy, but they are healthy only in reference to the health of an organism, which lets them both be and be called healthy in an analogous way. Note that if taking the hand as the tool of tools merely meant that it was superior to all other tools, then only the analogy of proportionality would be operating in this case; there would be no causation at work. Analogy of attribution requires not only a primary instance of something, but some sort of causation, some sort of bringing into being that occurs between the primary instance and the derived ones.

Analogy in religious thinking

I wish next to discuss the use of analogy in natural, nonbiblical religion, the religion that arises in human interaction with the world. In such religion, analogy is used to speak about the gods or the divine principle. In natural religion, however, god or the gods are part of the nature of things. The gods of Homer and Hesiod, the divine mind described by Anaxagoras, the god that the Socrates of the *Apology* says he obeyed, Plato's demiurge, the prime mover and the self-thinking thought of Aristotle, the god of the Stoics and the gods of the Epicureans, all these are entities within the whole of things. They are part of the nature of things. They are the most admirable, the best, the most powerful and the governing parts of the whole. As Patzig puts it, we can grasp a whole through its most favored part, and for the world as a whole the most favored part is the divine; therefore all knowledge would be incomplete until it is placed in relation to this highest and best part. Still, for natural religion the divine principle remains a part of the whole and it could not be without the whole.

What we are talking about as the most favored part is not just an issue for ancient myth and philosophy. Something like it is recognized even in our modern, secular, scientific understanding of the universe; people still have a reverence for the ultimate governing principles of things, for the laws of nature, or evolution, or matter-energy. Evolution, for example, is sometimes credited with something like the divine foresight and power of

7. Ibid., p. 41.

Plato's demiurge: it makes something like the right choices for the development of things. Evolution, or the evolutionary force in the universe, is seen as the most favored part through which we can grasp the whole, and our understanding of the whole is colored by whatever we take to be the most favored part.

Two points remain to be made about analogy in natural religion. The first concerns the analogy of attribution. Analogy in regard to the divine principle is different from worldly analogies, because in it we deal with an entity that is the most favored part of the world as a whole. It is the ultimate focal meaning for the term *entity*. Although the divine is still part of the world, it is at the edge of the world. This makes it different from terms such as *healthy*, which are embedded in the world as less favorable parts of the whole. Their partiality is more partial. The second point concerns the analogy of proper proportionality. If one of the ratios in the analogy of proportionality deals with the divine, then the proportions are not exactly the same as those located entirely within the world. The divine is part of the world, but it is at the edge of the world, and so our comprehension of it is less thorough than our knowledge of things that are more ordinary parts of the whole we call the world.

Analogy in Christian thinking

After this brief statement concerning nonbiblical religion, I will discuss biblical religion and the place of analogy in it. As we move into this fourth part of my essay, we will not leave the third part behind. One of the main reasons we discussed nonbiblical religion is that it serves as a foil against which biblical religion can be clarified. The latter is only analogous to the former.

In natural, nonbiblical religion, in pagan religion, the world is divided into two parts, the divine and the nondivine. At times this distinction is formulated as that between the celestial and the sublunary, or the divine and the profane.[8] The divine or the celestial is part of the world and it is experienced as such. It is the domain of the necessary and the independent. We have some experiential and intellectual contact with this divine, eternal, immortal part of being.

8. The contrast between the divine and the profane is very well brought out in Gerhard Krüger, *Religiöse und profane Welterfahrung* (Frankfurt: Klostermann, 1973).

In biblical religion, however, there is a change. The distinction between the celestial and the earthly continues to exist, but the celestial is no longer simply equated with the divine. As von Balthasar has pointed out, in the Bible the heavens are the place where God dwells, but the heavens are not coeternal with God.[9] Both the heavens and the earth are now seen to have been created by God. In the Bible, God's necessity and independence are greater than the necessity and independence of the heavens; a new sense of the necessary and the independent is introduced. In the Bible, God is divine in a sense different from the sense used in nonbiblical religion.

A strategic way of putting this, as we have seen earlier, is to say that the biblical God could be even if the world, both heaven and earth, were not. God could be in complete perfection and goodness even if there were no world. God does not exist primarily as part of the world, nor does he exist primarily as Creator of the world (if he did, he would have to create in order to be as perfect as possible). The biblical God would be God even if the world had not been created. He would be no less perfect if he had not created. This understanding of God sheds light on what Creation is: it is an action done out of sheer generosity and goodness, with no need, no imperfection prompting it. God's perfection is so intense and complete that he is not made better by having created. God's necessity and excellence are different from the necessity and excellence of the divine perfections reached by pagan religion and philosophy. His necessity and excellence are only analogous to them.

This understanding of the divine sets up a new space within which analogy has to work, and it sets up a new space in which the analogy we are familiar with becomes strained. We are dealing with a new sense of analogy, one that is only analogous to the kind introduced by the pagan philosophers and theologians. The biblical sense of analogy has to bridge a gap and cover a difference that is not there in pagan thinking. To adapt Patzig's formulation, God is no longer just the most favored part of the whole; he could be the whole. In biblical religion, it becomes conceivable, even though it is contrary to fact, that God could be all that there is. Even after Creation occurs, it would still not be accurate to say that the divine and the worldly make up

---

9. See Hans Urs von Balthasar, *Theodramatik II: Die Personen des Spiels; Part 1: Der Mensch in Gott* (Einsiedeln: Johannes Verlag, 1976), pp. 155–69; for other references see *Theodramatik IV: Endspiel* (Einsiedeln: Johannes Verlag, 1983), p. 377.

a whole and that the divine is the most favored part of the whole. After Creation we deal with a whole in a new sense, one that transforms the sense of whole found in natural religion. And just as the term *whole* is transformed, so also are the terms *divine* and *world*.[10]

In this new setting, we have to be careful not to let analogy spin out of control. We have to be careful not to let it slip back into being mere metaphor. Christian religious discourse does not just point to a mystery or indicate a transcendence; it also conveys an understanding, or at least the glimpse of an understanding, one that is appropriate to this new context and hence only analogous to the understandings we achieve in the natural setting. The use of analogy was strained even in natural religion, as it was extended to touch that which was at the edge of things; now we stretch it further into that which is beyond the edge, not in a spatial sense, but in the sense that this divinity could be even if it were not beyond the edge of things, that is, even if there were no things for it to be contrasted with.[11]

The special role of distinctions

In the final part of my essay, I wish to make a speculative point concerning the transformation of analogy between natural and biblical religion. The point I will make might sound like something belonging in logic or mathematics, but in fact it does belong in metaphysics and theology.

We stretch natural analogy, we fit analogy for this new Christian setting,

10. In this essay I discuss Christianity in contrast with natural pagan religion but do not speak about the difference between Christianity and the higher religions of Islam and Hinduism. This point was brought out by W. Norris Clarke, S.J., at the meeting of the American Catholic Philosophical Association at which an earlier version of this paper was presented. A thorough examination of this issue cannot be made here, but I would like to mention one important difference between Christianity and Hinduism. The latter seems clearly to recognize that the divine could exist without the world, and in this respect it seems to be similar to Christian faith, but it also seems to deny to the nondivine, to the world, the kind of genuine being that Christianity recognizes in it. Thus, if we were to use the statement, "God is all that there is," as a touchstone to bring out the differences among these religions, we could say that the statement is meaningless in pagan natural religion, it is meaningful but false in Christianity, while in Hinduism it is not only meaningful but also true.

11. One of the changes that occurs in regard to the analogy of proportionality when it is applied to Christian discourse is that the two ratios (A is to B as C is to D) are no longer to be taken as the same, but only as similar. However, the nature of similarity would have to be defined appropriately for this context. I am grateful to W. Norris Clarke, S.J., for bringing to my attention the difference between identity and similarity of ratios in regard to Scholastic uses of the analogy of proportionality.

by the activity of making a distinction. Christian analogy depends on a distinction. The formal logic, the formal syntax of Christian analogy, requires as a background a special distinction. In it, we contrast the world from God by saying that God is not part of the whole, not part of the world. I would like to use the term "the Christian distinction" to name the distinction between the world and God.[12] For this distinction to arise, the biblical sense of the divine must be distinguished from the natural sense of the divine. We could not introduce the biblical sense of the divine without having the pagan sense as a foil, as something against which we draw a contrast. The pagan sense of the divine is needed as a setting. To formulate this in Old Testament terms, the Jewish sense of God could not have arisen except in distinction from the sense of god professed by the Gentiles. The Jews distinguished themselves from the Gentiles because their God, Jahweh, was distinguished from the gods of the Gentiles. In distinguishing the biblical God from the pagan gods, the Jews and later the Christians distinguish the world from God by saying that God could be all that he is even if there were no world.

Making this distinction is an essential prerequisite for analogy as it works in biblical religion. If this distinction is not made, either Christian analogy will fall back into pagan analogy and the divine will be considered as the best thing in the universe, or Christian analogy will turn into metaphor.

Consider, for example, how we speak of divine reason. Suppose we draw the analogy of proportionality and say that divine reason is to God as human reason is to man. In Christian belief the first of these ratios is projected even beyond the reason that Plato attributes to the demiurge and to the world soul, the reason that brings order and beauty to the cosmos. The Christian sense of divine reason is more mysterious; it is not just the reason that orders the world, but the reason that causes things to come to be out of nothing, the reason that brings salvation through the cross, the reason whose depth we could not appreciate if all we had to look at were the order and beauty of the world alone, if we did not also have the word of God revealing to us what St. Paul called "the mystery kept secret for long ages, but now manifested through the prophetic writings . . . and made known to all nations to bring about the obedience of faith" (Romans 16:25–26). We have to keep in

12. On the Christian distinction between the world and God, see Robert Sokolowski, *The God of Faith and Reason: Foundations of Christian Theology* (Washington, D.C.: The Catholic University of America Press, 1995).

mind the double correction operating in Christian analogy: we first have to adjust our human sense of reason to adapt it to the divine cosmic reason, and then we have to adjust this in turn to speak of the reason that could be apart from the world, the reason that "planned" both Creation and Redemption. This double adjustment is necessary, and it always has to be kept alive as we use Christian words, in whatever mode of discourse we use them: in prayer, biblical narrative, creedal statements, preaching, the sacraments, the psalms, or in teaching.

The analogy of proportionality involves two ratios that are related to one another. In the case of Christian theological analogies, one of these ratios deals with the divine nature and its features. It is not the case, however, that only the terms in that one ratio are adjusted when we move into Christian discourse. Rather, the other ratio—the created one, let us say the one that speaks of human reason as related to man—is now seen as profiled against the divine. The created world and the entities in the world take on a new coloration when they are taken in this new setting; or, rather, not just a new coloration but a new meaning. The world as well as the divine is differently interpreted when understood against the background of the Christian distinction between the world and God.

We might think, for example, that analogy works primarily as a way of helping us appreciate something about God, that the vector of analogy works from the created world, with which we are familiar, to the divine, which is mysterious and unknown to us. As we have stated earlier, however, analogies are two-edged swords, and the worldly also takes on a new intelligibility when seen against the background of this new sense of the divine. This is brought out vividly by a passage in St. Paul's letter to the Ephesians, in which he says: "I bend my knees to the Father of our Lord Jesus Christ, from whom all fatherhood in heaven and on earth receives its name . . ." (Ephesians 3:14–15). It is not just that human fatherhood or the human family gives us a glimpse of what the relationship of God to us is like; once God is understood to be Father as Christ revealed him to be, then human fatherhood takes on a different sense, one that could be given only in this context.

I have spoken about the way the distinction between the world and God supports the analogy of proportionality in Christian discourse, but it also works in the analogy of attribution in such speech. As Bernard Montagnes has shown in his classic work on analogy, St. Thomas Aquinas appeals in his later works only to the analogy of attribution when speaking about discourse concerning God, but Aquinas also modifies Aristotelian "*pros hen* equivocals" when he does so.[13] Instead of speaking about the relationship of several terms to one focal meaning, Aquinas speaks about the relationship between one thing and the ultimate cause of its being. He appeals to the themes of causality and participation in doing so, and this development depends on Aquinas's understanding of *esse* as act. The sense of this causation, however, the sense in which things are not just given their form and their substance by God but also their *esse,* the sense in which things are contrasted not with being something else or with being just unformed matter, but with not being at all, with sheer nonexistence—all this takes place only against the background of God understood as not a part of the whole of things. Each and every thing, one by one, is ultimately understood as created out of nothing, and so each thing is now understood in its relation to its creative cause and its *esse* is analogized in this connection. The final, metaphysical context for each entity is no longer the world as a matrix, with each thing embedded within it and related to many other things, including the most favored part of the world; the final context is set by the *esse* that could be all that there is. The new context depends on a special distinction between the world and God.

Let us recall how important distinctions are in establishing meaning and speech. The famous chapter 4, book IV of Aristotle's *Metaphysics* tells us that if we wish to say anything at all we must implicitly make a distinction; we must not only posit some sort of sense but also exclude some other sense. Any positive determination involves a marking off from something else. The negation that is involved in a distinction is required as condition for bringing forward anything positive as a theme for discourse. Such a blend of the positive and negative is at work in a special way, with a distinctive kind of distinction, in all Christian discourse. The logic of this distinction, and its relation to Christian analogy, is a rich theme for further theological and philosophical exploration.

---

13. See Bernard Montagnes, O.P., *La doctrine de l'analogie de l'être d'après Saint Thomas d'Aquin* (Louvain: Publications Universitaires, 1963), pp. 81–114. Aquinas's doctrine of analogy is extensively treated in John F. Wippel, *The Metaphysical Thought of Thomas Aquinas: From Finite Being to Uncreated Being* (Washington, D.C.: The Catholic University of America Press, 2000), pp. 501–75.

PART II

THE EUCHARIST AND
THE HOLY TRINITY

5

PHENOMENOLOGY AND
THE EUCHARIST

The Eucharist calls for two kinds of response from us. It calls for the piety of prayer and the piety of thinking, of theological reflection. It is obvious why the Eucharist makes these demands. In our Christian faith, the Eucharist reenacts the central action that God performed in the world, the redemptive Death and Resurrection of Jesus Christ. This action was performed not only through the power of the divine nature but also through the human nature that the Word of God had assumed in the Incarnation. Redemption was the work of both God and man, a divine and a human accomplishment. This saving event of the Death and Resurrection of Christ is made present again in the Eucharist; it is the substance of the eucharistic celebration. Nothing could deserve our devotion and our contemplation more than this.

The Eucharist and the Church

The Eucharist is the central action performed by the *Church*. In the Eucharist, the Church accomplishes what she has been established to do; she enters into Christ's offering of himself to the Father and she makes Christ present to the world. She joins with him before God the Father, and she manifests him to the world in his most perfect act of obedience and charity. The Church is completed in the Eucharist. More precisely, however, the Eucharist is not just the moment during which the Church acts; it is also the moment when *Christ* accomplishes what he was sent to do, the moment at which he fulfills the mission given him by the Father. The Eucharist is not just the action of the Church but the action of Christ himself. And still more precisely, the Eucharist is the moment during which *God* acts, the moment at which the Creator achieves his second, more perfect creation and reveals to believers and to all the world who and what he is. The Eucharist is the definitive action of the Church, of Christ, and of God. Everything else the Christian does takes its bearings from this decisive sacrament and sacrifice.

The Eucharist tells us about God. It speaks more eloquently to us about God than do the heavens and the earth. The heavens and the earth are the visible signature of God's creative power, but the Eucharist speaks to us about the internal life of God in the Holy Trinity and about the charity that exists in God before and beyond Creation. The Eucharist does this because it represents the redemptive Death and Resurrection of Christ. Speaking about our redemption, Joseph Ratzinger says, "In the pierced heart of the Crucified, God's own heart is opened—here we see who God is and what he is like. Heaven is no longer locked up. God has stepped out of his hiddenness."[1] The created universe, in all its splendor, is no longer the ultimate witness to God's goodness; it is no longer the final expression of his wisdom and power; the created universe now becomes merely the stage where God, in the person of the Son, became part of what he had created, and where he accomplished a new Creation through the redemptive Death and Resurrection of the Incarnate Word. To quote Cardinal Ratzinger again, ". . . Creation exists to be a place for the covenant that God wants to make with man."[2] One reason why the Resurrection is more powerful than the Creation narrated in the book of *Genesis* is that the Resurrection brings being and life not out of nothingness but out of the deeper nihilism of sin and death. This saving action of God, this recreation of the world, brings with it the promise that the resurrected and living Christ will come again at the end of time. It is this redemptive action that is reenacted in the celebration of the Eucharist.

According to the faith of the Church, the Eucharist presents the Death and Resurrection of Jesus, and in performing this action the Eucharist builds

---

1. Joseph Ratzinger, *The Spirit of the Liturgy*, translated by John Saward (San Francisco: Ignatius Press, 2000), p. 48.
2. Ibid., p. 26.

up the community of the Church, the Body of Christ. It is not the case that we are faced with an alternative, that in the Mass we have *either* a sacred action *or* the establishment of a community. The Church is not just any kind of community; she is the society that was born on the cross, through the action of Christ, the action of God, that is embodied again in the Eucharist. When the Church celebrates the Eucharist, she both reenacts the Death and Resurrection of Jesus and confirms herself as the community established by this event.

Furthermore, through the Eucharist, the members of this community are enabled to participate actively in the Death and Resurrection of Christ. They become able to do so because they are adopted into the sonship of Christ and hence into the action that he performs. They form a community because they are incorporated into Christ through the Eucharist as his Mystical Body. This community of the Church, therefore, could not be established except through the real presence of the Lord in the Eucharist and through the identification of the Eucharist with his saving Death and Resurrection.[3] The mystery of the Incarnation is prolonged in human history, not only in the words of Scripture, but also in the action of the Eucharist, and consequently in the witness, the *martyrion,* given by those who participate in the Eucharist. The Church would be a very different thing if she were built up merely through the use of words, without the central action of Christ that gives the words their substance, and without the imitation of Christ in the lives of those who are her members.

The Eucharist and the Incarnation

The Eucharist, together with the Church that is built up around it and provides the context for it, is the prolongation of the Incarnation. The Word of God, the eternal Son of the Father, became man; God became part of what he created. But this work of God was not an event that occurred once and then receded into the past; the Incarnation was meant to change creation and to change history, and to do so in such a way that the change remained palpably present. As St. Leo the Great says in speaking about the As-

---

3. In the Reformation, various Protestant churches developed a different theology of the Eucharist because they adopted a different idea of the Church. Conversely, the Catholic understanding of the Church is related to the Catholic understanding of the Eucharist.

cension of our Lord, "The visible presence of our Redeemer has passed over into sacraments. . . ."[4] The sacramental presence of the Incarnate Word succeeds the physical presence. The Eucharist is not merely an afterthought to the Incarnation and Redemption; there is a kind of teleology and completion in the eucharistic continuation of the presence of Christ in the world. The Eucharist is the sacramental extension of the Incarnation.

To help show how the Eucharist and the Incarnation are related, I will describe a certain trajectory in the many controversies that have surrounded the mystery of the Incarnation. The Incarnation has been greatly disputed since the earliest centuries of the Church. The human mind seems to recoil from the truth that God became man and suffered a humiliating death; the denial of the Incarnation of the transcendent God seems to be the paradigmatic heresy in the life of the Church. People have repeatedly tried to interpret Christ in ways that dilute this mystery. It was the Incarnation and not, for example, the transcendence or the unicity of God that was the subject of the initial controversies in the Church.

Thus the first two general councils, Nicaea in A.D. 325 and Constantinople in 381, addressed the Arian heresy and its variations, which claimed that Christ was less divine than the Father and not a complete human being; the Logos was not fully God and Christ was not fully man. Arius said, therefore, that the true God did not really become man at all, and the councils condemned his teaching and its variants. The next general council, Ephesus in 431, dealt with the heresy of Nestorius, who accepted the earlier definitions and admitted that Christ was truly both God and man, but said that the two natures really did not make up one being; rather, the divine nature was merely joined to the human; it dwelt in the human as in its perfect temple. Once again, God did not really *become* man; once again, the stark reality of the Incarnation, of God's truly becoming a human being, was denied. The Church condemned the teaching of Nestorius and insisted that Christ was truly one person, one being. The next step was the monophysite heresy, which admitted that God took on a human nature in Christ but said that this human being was completely transformed into the divine nature and did not continue to exist along with the divinity. This teaching was treated in the fourth general council, that of Chalcedon in 451.

4. St. Leo the Great, "Sermon II on the Ascension," in Migne, Patrologia Latina, vol. 54, p. 398.

The Council of Chalcedon is often taken to be the last of the great Christological councils, and certainly it provided the most definitive teaching on the Incarnation. However, further issues arose in the Church that continued to threaten the integrity of this mystery. In the seventh century a heresy arose that admitted the two natures in Christ, divine and human, but claimed that there was only one will and one mode of activity, the divine. Because this teaching claimed that there was only the divine will and no human will in Christ, it was called the heresy of monothelitism. This position was something like a rear-guard action still being waged by the human mind in its resistance to the "scandal" of the Incarnation; it was condemned by the sixth general council, which was held at Constantinople in 680–681.

But even at this point, the controversies did not come to a halt. In the next century, the eighth, there occurred in the Eastern Christian Church the great and important movement of iconoclasm. It was the next expression of this persistent inability of the mind to take in the truth that God became a human being. It dealt not with Christ himself, but with the images that we might make of him. It spoke not only about Christ's own being but also about his representation in an icon. The controversy arose in a public and dramatic way in 726, when the emperor Leo III issued an edict condemning icons; he subsequently removed and destroyed the icon of Christ that had been placed over the gate to the imperial palace in Constantinople.[5] The next emperor, Constantine V, argued for the destruction of icons of Christ by saying that the person of Christ was divine and therefore could not be circumscribed or captured in a physical, visible manner. In 754 an iconoclastic synod called by the emperor claimed that the Church had fallen back into idolatry by making images of Christ, and it condemned St. John Damascene and others who defended the icons. The controversy lasted about 120 years, and almost all the icons in the Eastern Church were destroyed. Only in 843 did the conflict end, with the restoration of icons on the first Sunday of Lent that year. Iconoclasm was an offshoot of the monophysite her-

5. See Alain Besançon, *The Forbidden Image: An Intellectual History of Iconoclasm,* translated by Jane Marie Todd (Chicago: University of Chicago Press, 2000), pp. 115, 123–24. See also Christoph Schönborn, *God's Human Face: The Christ-Icon,* translated by Lothar Krauth (San Francisco: Ignatius Press, 1994), p. 151. For some sources concerning icons, see St. Theodore the Studite, *On the Holy Icons,* translated by Catharine P. Roth (Crestwood, NY: St. Vladimir's Seminary Press, 1981), and St. John of Damascus, *On the Divine Images,* translated by David Anderson (Crestwood, NY: St. Vladimir's Seminary Press, 1997).

esy. In a subtle and indirect but important way, it denied the full truth of the Incarnation. It admitted that Christ had a divine and a human nature, but when it denied that an icon could represent Christ, the Son of God, it also denied, by implication, that the divine nature and the divine person were so embodied in the human being of Christ that the further embodiment in an image could represent the God who had become man. The connection between the Incarnation and the icon is expressed by Cardinal Schönborn in his book *God's Human Face:* "In Christ, our human existence is to be made divine, while it does not cease to be 'human flesh and blood.' The icon, depicting Christ in his human likeness, serves as a final assurance, a kind of imprinted seal, of this belief."[6]

Iconoclasm was a heresy in the Eastern Church. Some 200 years after the iconoclastic crisis in the East, a controversy arose in the West concerning the Eucharist. It was provoked by the ideas of Berengarius of Tours, who lived in the first century of the new millennium; he died in 1088. There had been earlier controversies about the Eucharist in the ninth century, and Berengarius revived them. He claimed that the presence of Christ in the bread and wine of the Eucharist was only symbolic or figurative; the words of Christ in the institution of the Eucharist were to be taken metaphorically, not literally. The teachings of Berengarius did not find a following and were rejected by theologians and by the Church, but they can be seen as precursors of disputes about the real presence of Christ in the Eucharist that came to the fore during the Reformation. One could say, perhaps, that the controversies about the Eucharist—and hence about the Church that is established around the Eucharist—were the way in which the resistance to the Incarnation was carried on throughout the second millennium of the Church's history.

There is a single trajectory in the controversies concerning the Incarnation. At first, in Arianism, you deny that the Logos is fully divine and that Christ is fully human; once the Church asserts the full divinity and humanity of Christ, you say, with Nestorius, that the divine and the human natures do not make up one being, one person; once the Church says that they do make up one person and one being, you say that the divine nature absorbs the human; once the Church says that both natures remain intact, you deny

6. Schönborn, *God's Human Face,* p. 216.

that the human nature has its own will and activity; once the Church says that there is a human will in Christ, you deny that there can be an image or icon of the Incarnate God; once the Church says that Christ can be imaged, you deny that he is truly present in the Eucharist, you deny that the Eucharist extends the Incarnation in a sacramental way. Controversy about the Eucharist is thus related to controversy about the Incarnation, and I would add that disputes about the Church and about the Blessed Virgin are so related as well.

It would follow, then, that a loss of faith in the Eucharist—a loss of belief in the real presence of Christ in the sacrament, and a loss of the belief in the identity of the Eucharistic sacrifice and that of Calvary—leads to a loss of faith in the Resurrection, which leads to a loss of faith in the Incarnation, which leads to a loss of belief in the Holy Trinity. If you deny the truth of the Eucharist, you begin the drift toward Unitarianism. I wonder also if the trace of iconoclasm in the Church in recent decades—the removal of statues and pictures, the movement toward abstraction in architecture and decoration, the antipathy toward the Holy Father and the Vatican, the "anti-Roman affect," as it has been called—does not also raise difficulties in regard to faith in the Incarnation.[7] The human mind seems persistently unwilling to accept the intense nearness of God incarnate, which confirms Creation and makes everything truly real.[8]

Phenomenology

We have been speaking about the Eucharist and its relation to the Church and to the Incarnation. What shall we say about "phenomenology,"

7. One of the main points in Besançon's brilliant book *The Forbidden Image* is that abstract expressionism is a modern form of iconoclasm; see chapter 8, entitled "The Russian Revolution," which treats the work of Malevich and Kandinsky.

8. The thought about the nearness of the incarnate God is from Francis Martin. There is a Neoplatonic tendency in Christian thought to resolve things into their intellectual or spiritual forms and to explain human cognition not by the natural powers of the soul but by inspiration. This movement toward the spiritual is a reflection of the more general human tendency, found in Plato and corrected by Aristotle, to deny the entity or substance of material objects. On the latter point, see the excellent study by Wolfgang-Rainer Mann, *The Discovery of Things: Aristotle's "Categories" and Their Context* (Princeton: Princeton University Press, 2000). Cartesian immanence and German idealism are modern versions of this perennial propensity. For a literary statement of the reality of the Incarnation, and a critique of the mythological and purely spiritualistic understanding of religious things, see Evelyn Waugh's novel *Helena*. Perhaps the reason why the human mind tries to escape from matter and flee to ideas is that it loves itself inordinately.

the other term in the title of my essay? What relation does it have to the theology of the Eucharist? What is phenomenology?

Phenomenology was the most significant continental European philosophical movement in the twentieth century; it dominated European thought for at least the first two thirds of the century. Husserl, Heidegger, and Scheler were some of its major figures in Germany, and Sartre, Merleau-Ponty, and Marcel were among its leading representatives in France. It continues to be an active and important philosophical tradition. It is a form of philosophy that pays close attention to the way things appear. It insists that different kinds of things offer us different patterns and structures of appearance. It also claims that one of the major tasks in philosophy is to describe these patterns and structures, to describe the different ways in which things manifest themselves. Appearances are part of the being of things; they are not merely subjective impressions. It is true that things have natures and essences and that philosophy should try to formulate definitions that capture the essentials of things (as it does in scholastic philosophy, for example), but there is also a philosophical intelligibility in the way things manifest themselves, in the way they come to light, and phenomenology attempts to bring out this intelligibility of disclosure. It also pays attention to the human subject, the one to whom things appear; it attempts to describe the human being in his rational activity, which is, of course, the activity that defines him as a person.

Phenomenology is often interpreted as being highly subjectivist and relativistic, as claiming that we never get to the reality of things but remain *only* with appearances, and that these appearances are merely the way things *seem* to *us,* not the way they are in themselves. Some writers in this movement may accept this interpretation, but I do not think that phenomenology needs to be understood in this subjectivist manner. Quite to the contrary, I would claim that we can interpret phenomenology in such a way that it can be used to counteract the subjectivism and relativism of much of modern thought. It provides an alternative to the excesses of postmodernism and deconstruction. For example, I think that phenomenology successfully overcomes the understanding of experience found in the British empiricists and that it also overcomes the radical Kantian distinction between phenomena and noumena. Phenomenology claims that the noumenon, the thing in itself, does become a phenomenon, it does become given to us in its own way. I think, and I have tried to show by example, that phenomenology can revive the kind of realism that marked ancient and medieval philosophy, and that it can do so while taking modern science and even modern political philosophy into account.[9] Phenomenology studies the human being as what I would like to call "the agent of truth," which, I believe, is a good paraphrase for the definition of the human person.

I would like to offer a few examples of the kind of things that phenomenology investigates. It addresses the important philosophical distinction between words and images: words express things and images depict things, and the manner in which each of them works is different. It is interesting to explore this difference, to show how images contain the presence of what they depict without having the thing itself there, while words refer to things without seeming to contain them in the way that images do. There is a more radical absence and transparency in words than in images. Both words and images, of course, must be contrasted with the direct perception of the thing itself, with the presence the thing has when it is directly experienced. These philosophical explorations show how the various kinds of presence and absence interweave with one another to constitute the recognizable identity of an object that can be given through all of them: one and the same object can be directly experienced, can be imaged in a picture or a drama, and can be referred to and articulated in speech. Such contrasts among words, images, and direct perception were developed in a strategic way in Husserl's first major work, *Logical Investigations,* and they have remained prominent themes in phenomenology ever since.[10] The philosophical treatment of words and images, furthermore, has important theological implications. In the theology of the Holy Trinity, the Son is called both the Image of the Father and the Word that the Father expresses.[11] How have the concepts of word and image been transformed to apply to this new theological context? Furthermore, the treatment of words and images also comes into play in eucharistic theology, because the Eucharist obviously engages both language and representation.

9. For examples of the descriptions phenomenology can offer and for an argument for its realism, see Robert Sokolowski, *Introduction to Phenomenology* (New York: Cambridge University Press, 2000), and *Pictures, Quotations, and Distinctions: Fourteen Essays in Phenomenology* (Notre Dame: University of Notre Dame Press, 1992).

10. For the interplay of perception, images, and speech, see Edmund Husserl, *Logical Investigations,* translated by J. N. Findlay (Routledge: Humanities Press, 1970), Investigation VI, §§4–10.

11. Schönborn uses the work of St. Athanasius to speak of the Eternal Son as the image of the Father; in *God's Human Face* (p. 11) he says, "Through the revelation of the mystery of the Trinity, a new dimension of the meaning of *image* has opened up."

One might object that other philosophers and theologians have talked about words, images, and things. In the iconoclastic controversy, for example, John Damascene, Nicephorus of Constantinople, and Theodore the Studite wrote about the nature of icons, and Aristotle and the Stoics wrote about the use of words in human reasoning. What is so special about phenomenology's treatment of these topics? I think that phenomenology restores the validity, the truth function, of such forms of presentation. Since the turn to the subject in Descartes and Locke, things like pictures and words and sensory impressions have been reduced to merely psychological impressions. They have been turned into subjective states that only hint at the real things "out there." But these things—words, pictures, percepts—have a certain ontological status; they have their own way of being. Their primary affinity is with logic, not with feelings or mental states. They are ways in which things manifest themselves, and they have a role in the activities of reason. Phenomenology restores their function in the truth of things, the function that they had, for example, in the work of Plato.

Another important contribution of phenomenology is its description of the manner in which syntactic structures work in human thinking. When we speak and think about things, we articulate them into parts and wholes, and these structures in the manifestation of things are expressed in the grammar of our speech. Speech and syntax can become extremely refined and complex, with all sorts of subordinate clauses, modalities, metaphors, arguments, inferences, and insinuations. All such complexities, however, circle around the elementary and central activity of predication, when something is asserted about something, when S is said to be p. Predication is the basic syntactic structure. The convolutions we find in speech, however, are not ends in themselves; they are all subordinated to the manifestation of things, to bringing things to light, to the exchanges that occur between speaker and listener, and even to the activities that take place within the mind of a person who is trying to make things clear to himself in solitary thought. Every articulation is a disclosure. Husserl develops this study of language and syntax in the *Logical Investigations* under the rubric of categorial intentionality.[12]

One more example of what phenomenology contributes can be found in its analysis of the human subject. It provides a subtle and detailed descrip-

12. On categoriality, see Husserl, *Logical Investigations,* Investigation VI, §§40–52.

tion of the identity of the human person. The rational human being is described as the agent of syntax, as the one who articulates things in words, and
who, in doing so, takes on the responsibility of being truthful in speech and
other forms of expression. The human person is also described in his temporal structures, the structures of remembering, imagining, and anticipating:
when I remember experiencing something—when, for example, I remember seeing a car run a red light—I do not just have a kind of moving picture in my mind of something that happened earlier. Rather, I displace myself into the past; I, here and now, reactivate the perception I had there and
then. I reenact that perception, and I "duplicate" myself into the one who
remembers and the one who is remembered. My present self and my past
self are played off against one another in memory, and my own self is really
the identity between these two profiles. Also, when I imagine or anticipate
something that will happen later, I carry out the same kind of displacement
of myself, but now it is projected into a possible future. If I am considering
buying a house, I imagine myself living in it; I imaginatively "try it on for
size." As conscious persons, we live always in the past and in the future as
well as in the present; we are interwoven through time, and our conscious
identity is established through these temporal displacements. It is *this* self,
established through time and founded on a bodily identity, that can then experience things and make judgments, and take upon itself the responsibility
of letting things appear, of telling the truth.

Such an analysis of the human being is interesting and illuminating on
its own terms, but it can also be valuable in many of the current debates that
have arisen concerning the human person, especially those associated with
biology, such as the controversies concerning brain science and human ge-
netics. Phenomenology can help show that when I make a claim, when I say
that something is true, or when I deliberate about what course of action I
should take, I carry out such activities as a human person; it is not my brain
or my genes that do so. Such a philosophy can help defend the human being
as a responsible agent of truth.

Phenomenology of the Eucharist

Phenomenology can also be used in a theological reflection on the Eucharist, where it can help us clarify how the Eucharist, and the redemptive
action that is performed in the Eucharist, appear to us. I would like to use

the term "theology of disclosure" to name this kind of reflection, because the more obvious term, "phenomenological theology," is so cumbersome. This theology would bring out the appearances that are proper and specific to the Eucharist and to Christian things generally. It would bring out the patterns and structures of appearance that are essential to the sacramental presence that follows in the wake of the Incarnation. Two particular themes deserve investigation.

First, according to the faith of the Church, the sacrifice that occurs in the celebration of the Eucharist is the same sacrifice that was achieved by Christ on the cross. There was only one sacrifice that redeemed the human race and made it possible for man to become adopted into the Sonship of Christ; it was the sacrifice on Calvary. Each Mass is also a sacrifice, but it is so not by being a separate, independent action. Rather, it reenacts, it makes present again, the one sacrifice of Christ. But how can this occur if the death of Christ occurred centuries in the past? How can a past event, in its individuality, be made present again? Worldly historical events are fixed at their moment in history. They can be commemorated but they cannot truly be made to happen again. We can publicly remember and celebrate the founding of our nation, but we cannot make that founding occur once again here and now; we cannot truly reenact it. Time is relentless and inescapable, and it leaves events behind.

The sacrifice of Christ, however, was not merely a worldly historical event. It *was* such a worldly event, it happened in human history, but its true meaning, its substance, what happened when it occurred, was not just a worldly occurrence. It was a transaction, an exchange, between Christ and the Father. Although it took place in time, it touched eternity as did no other event in history. It did so because of the person who achieved it and also because of what was done. It was the perfect sacrifice offered to the Father, the perfect act of obedience of the Son, different from all the other actions he performed in his life on earth. Because the sacrifice of Christ touched eternity in this way, it was not just a historical event: it took on the kind of presence that marks the eternal moment, the moment out of time: "For Christ did not enter into a sanctuary made by hands . . . but heaven itself, that he might now appear before God on our behalf" (Hebrews 9:24).[13] The

13. In the Old Covenant the sacrifice was made repeatedly "as the high priest enters each

sacrifice of Christ is eternally present to the Father; the Lamb in the Apocalypse appears as having been slain (Revelation 5:6–12) and the wounds of
the passion remain in the Risen Lord.

When the Eucharist is celebrated now, it is not turned merely to the
historical past. Its primary focus is not on the past but on the eternal present of God. The entire Eucharistic Prayer, the Canon of the Mass, is directed
toward God the Father. This setting is established by the Preface and the
Sanctus, in which the congregation, the Church assembled at this particular
time and place, enters into the company of the angels and saints in heaven
and sings God's praise with them, in words taken from the beginning of the
book of the prophet Isaiah. The Eucharistic prayer then continues to be directed toward God the Father, and it enters into the redemptive sacrifice of
Christ as it is being presented to the Father in that eternal moment. The reenactment of Calvary in the Eucharist enters into the presence of Calvary
to the Father, and the real presence of Christ in the sacrament is that of his
glorified Body and Blood eternally presented to the Father.[14] It is because
God is so transcendent, because he is so radically beyond time and beyond
Creation, that the Eucharist can be the reenactment of the redeeming Death
and Resurrection of Christ. The Eucharist can reenact an event from the
past because it joins with that event in the eternal present of God. This contact with the eternal moment is expressed in the Eucharist by the fact that
the eucharistic prayer is addressed to God the Father.

The second thing I wish to do in this brief theology of the Eucharist
is to study more closely the words of consecration. The Eucharist reenacts
the redemptive Death and Resurrection of Jesus, but it does so in a manner
that is very complicated. It does not immediately refer to Calvary, it does
not relate to Calvary in a straight line, so to speak; the Eucharist is not like a
Passion Play that depicts or directly recalls that event. Rather, it approaches

---

year into the sanctuary with blood that is not his own" (Hebrews 9:25). The priests' actions were
subject to the necessities of history. In the New Covenant each Eucharistic celebration may be
a distinct temporal event, but the thing celebrated is always one and the same: the one sacrifice
of Christ, achieved through his own blood, a sacrifice that could not be repeated and is forever
present to God.

14. On the issue of the Real Presence and Transubstantiation, see Robert Sokolowski, "The
Eucharist and Transubstantiation," chapter 7 below. For related topics, see Sokolowski, *Eucharis-
tic Presence: A Study in the Theology of Disclosure* (Washington: The Catholic University of America
Press, 1994), and "Praying the Canon of the Mass," chapter 6 below.

the death of Christ by a kind of detour, if I may use the term, by first reenacting the Last Supper. At the Last Supper, of course, Christ anticipated his own death. He *pre*enacted his sacrificial offering; he looked ahead to it and accomplished its substance as he instituted the sacrament of the Eucharist. Because Christ anticipated and preenacted his Death and Resurrection, the Church can reenact it afterward. The Eucharist looks back to the sacrifice on Calvary by going still further back to the Last Supper and looking forward with Christ to the sacrifice on the cross. The consecration in the Mass weaves together these forms of presence and absence; it composes the past, the present, and the future, as well as the moment of eternity, into an intricate and highly sophisticated structure, one that elevates the mind as well as the heart. These complexities in presentation help make the Eucharist into what the first eucharistic prayer calls an *oblatio rationabilis,* a rational sacrifice.

The Last Supper is called up, of course, in the brief narrative, the institutional narrative, that introduces the words of consecration. This narrative in turn is embedded in the eucharistic prayer. Consider how the narrative and consecration are placed within the entire eucharistic prayer.

The eucharistic prayer begins with the Preface and continues after the Sanctus. As the prayer proceeds, it gives way to the epiclesis, when the celebrant, in the name of the Church, calls on the Holy Spirit to descend on the gifts. The epiclesis gives way to the institutional narrative: "The day before he suffered, he took bread into his sacred hands.... He broke the bread, gave it to his disciples, and said." This narrative, in turn, gives way to the words of consecration: "Take this, all of you, and eat it: this is my body, which will be given up for you." There is an elegant sequence in the forms of speech spoken by the celebrant: we begin with prayer, the prayer gives way to epiclesis, which gives way to narrative, which gives way to the words of consecration. As this sequence unfolds, there is a striking change in the personal pronouns that are used by the priest. The first three of these forms, the prayer, epiclesis, and narrative, explicitly or implicitly, all use the first-person plural. The priest says "we" or "us" or "our," because he speaks as a representative of the Church. He speaks in the name of the Church, both the Church as a whole and the Church assembled here and now in this place. But in the words of consecration, the priest begins to use the first-person singular: he says, "*my* body" and "*my* blood," and "do this in memory of *me.*"

At this moment and in these words the priest speaks no longer simply in the name of the Church, but in the name of Christ, in the person of Christ. Both grammatically and spiritually, he speaks in the person of Christ. To put it another way, he now lets Christ become the speaker and the agent. He lets Christ take over the action that is being performed. At this central part of its most central action, the Church recedes and no longer speaks in her own name; she lets Christ take over and accomplish what he accomplished at the Last Supper. She lets him do whatever he did there, by simply allowing him to speak in his name, not her own. It is by virtue of the literary form of a quotation that the Church allows Christ palpably to take control of her liturgy. Of course, it is somewhat inappropriate to say that the priest or the Church "lets" Christ speak, as though he or she gave him permission to do so; rather, the entire liturgy is being performed under the guidance of Christ. The priest and the Church merely provide the bodily vehicle by which Christ reenacts what he did at the Last Supper, and thereby reenacts his own offering to the Father. And yet, Christ does need and use the Church and the voice and gestures of the priest to become present sacramentally in the world, as he once used the words and the body of the Blessed Virgin Mary to become present in the humility of the Incarnation.

When the priest recites the words of consecration, he quotes the words of Christ. Moreover, not only the words of consecration but also the gestures associated with them—taking up the bread, looking up to heaven, bowing to show thanks and praise—are also quotational. The words and the gestures are quotations; they are not part of a drama. The priest does not suddenly perform a little play that depicts the Last Supper before the congregation. The words and gestures are quotational and not dramatic. This is an important phenomenological difference, a distinction in the mode of presentation. Quotation is a distinct form of manifestation. In quotation, we allow our voice to be the vehicle for the thinking and the display that have been performed by someone else. We allow another person to articulate the world through our voice. We subordinate our speech to the authority of someone else, to his authority as an agent of truth. This is precisely what happens at the consecration: the authority of Christ comes into play explicitly, as *he* becomes the grammatical speaker of the words, and *he* achieves what is being done. He is the person speaking. The Church expresses herself in a palpable way as the Mystical Body of Christ when she enables him to speak and to act at this central point of the Eucharist. Christ offers himself not only to us but to the Father at that moment.

The presence and authority of Christ would not come to the fore in this powerful way if the priest were to understand himself as an actor in a drama, as someone who is *depicting* Christ at the Last Supper. If the priest were to take himself as an actor, he would assume a greater authority than he should, and he would not be as transparent as he ought to be. It would be the priest's interpretation of the drama that came to the fore, not the action of Christ. To consider the priest as engaged in a drama would also, I think, detract from the fact that even in the consecration the primary focus of the Eucharist is still toward the Father. To see the action as a drama would turn the focus toward the congregation as the audience or the participants in this drama. In the traditional liturgy, when the altar did not face the congregation, there was no tendency to take the words of consecration as a theatrical reenactment of the Last Supper. It is true, of course, that the words of consecration do also address the community at the Eucharist; the body of Christ will be given up and the blood will be shed *"for you,"* but this is not the primary and exclusive focus, and it should not be made to override the presentation of these actions to God the Father. One could say that the priest celebrating the Eucharist continues to address God the Father, but that Christ speaking through the priest addresses the community, as he did at the Last Supper. The complexities of quotation permit these two forms of address.

Concluding remarks

Our discussion of the Eucharist has made use of many themes in phenomenology: the temporal patterns of present, past, and future, profiled against the background God's eternity; the presence and absence of the one action of Christ in these various temporal and presentational contexts; the contrast between words and pictures. We have made extensive use of the phenomenon of quotation and we have distinguished it, phenomenologically, from drama. Our remarks do not counteract anything in patristic or scholastic theology, but they do add a dimension that may have been underplayed in them, one that is especially appropriate for theology in the cultural situation in which it finds itself now, whether that situation be called modern or postmodern.

Finally, the fact that God became man in Christ, that he took on the weakness and suffering of the human condition, and that he even becomes our food in the Eucharist, does not diminish his transcendence and power. In fact, these acts of humility enhance his majesty. They show that God can do these things and still remain the all-powerful Creator of the world, the one who creates not because of necessity or any kind of need, but out of sheer generosity. The generosity of Creation is made more evident to us precisely by the majesty of the new Creation, which was accomplished by God in humility and suffering when he became the servant of those he created, the one who took upon himself the most painful and degrading of all human tasks. In this action of Death and Resurrection, it is not only God's power and glory that are manifested to us, but also the generosity of his own divine life, the life of the Holy Trinity. The Eucharist brings us into this action and into this life, and it displays, until the end of time, the one saving action that is the point of the created world.

6

PRAYING THE CANON OF THE MASS

The priest celebrating Mass should try to fit his thoughts and sentiments to the words that he says. His internal dispositions should match the external expressions of the liturgy. In addition to the words, however, the structure of the Eucharist also provides a pattern to which the priest's thoughts and sentiments can be conformed. In this essay we will discuss several structural elements in the Canon of the Mass that should be kept in mind, by both the priest and the people, during the celebration of the Eucharist.

The Preface and Sanctus

The Eucharistic Prayer begins with the Preface. The celebrant addresses the congregation and invites them to lift up their hearts and give thanks to the Lord our God. From that exchange onward, until its close at the Great Amen, the Eucharistic Prayer is addressed to God the Father. It is important for the priest and the people to keep this focus in mind.

The Preface recalls the saving action of God and emphasizes some aspect of it that is appropriate for the feast of the day: Advent or Lent, the Christmas or Easter season, a commemoration of the Blessed Virgin or one of the saints. Then, the final sentences of the Preface place us, even while we remain here on earth, in the company of the angels and saints. It is with them that we recite the Sanctus, the prayer derived from the vision of the prophet Isaiah. In chapter 6 of the Book of Isaiah the song of praise, "Holy, Holy, Holy, Lord God of hosts," is chanted by the seraphim; in the Preface it is presented as being sung by the heavenly host, by the angels and saints, and we join our voices with theirs. The Sanctus ends with a reference to the Messiah: "Blessed is he who comes in the name of the Lord," drawing from the words of Christ in Matthew 23:39, which in turn are drawn from Psalm 118:26. The celestial glory of God has been brought to earth in the Incarnation, and God is manifest not only in the heavens but also on earth.

Thus, the Preface and especially the Sanctus draw us into the divine presence in heaven, in company with the angels and saints. The Sanctus should be said deliberately and its impact should remain with us throughout the Eucharistic Prayer. It provides the setting within which the entire Eucharist is to be celebrated. The Mass is our participation in the celestial liturgy.

Structure of the consecration

After the Sanctus, the Eucharistic Prayer continues with praise and petitions made to the Father. When the time comes for the consecration, however, the structure of the prayer changes in two ways. First, there is a change in literary form: the prayer gives way to the epiclesis, the calling down of the Holy Spirit, which in turn gives way to the institutional narrative, which in turn gives way to the words of consecration, the quoted words of Christ. The literary form changes from petition to invocation to narrative to quotation. Each of these steps should be distinctly registered when they are made, not only for the devotion of the celebrant but also for that of the congregation. They should not be rushed through or blurred into one another.

Second, the grammatical form of the words being said by the priest changes. The *we,* the first-person plural of the prayers and epiclesis and narrative, gives way to the *I,* the first-person singular of the quoted words of Jesus during the words of institution. The two changes in linguistic structure, in the literary form and in the grammar of the pronouns, are expressions of deep theological aspects of the Eucharist.

In both the faith of the Church and the structure of the rite, the Eucharist reenacts the Last Supper. The priest repeats the words of Christ over the bread: "Take this, all of you, and eat it: for this is my body, which will be given up for you." He also repeats the words of Christ over the wine: "Take this, all of you, and drink from it: for this is the cup of my blood, the blood of the new and everlasting covenant. It will be shed for you and for all so that sins may be forgiven." Then, as a closure to these words, he says, "Do this in memory of me." In these words, and in the gestures he makes as he takes up the bread and the chalice, the priest reenacts the words and gestures of Christ at the Last Supper.

However, the Last Supper was not just an event enclosed in itself. At the Last Supper, Jesus anticipated his passion and death, and in the faith of the Church the Eucharist ultimately reenacts not the Last Supper but the redemptive death of Christ. The Church sacramentally reenacts the sacrifice of the cross because Christ preenacted that sacrifice at the Last Supper. When the Church identifies her present action with that of Christ at the Last Supper, she also identifies her action with the sacrifice of the cross, because the Last Supper anticipated that sacrifice. The one sacrifice of Christ is presented through a structured manifold of appearances: as anticipated by Jesus and as remembered and reenacted by the Church.

This action of the Church, however, is carried on before the eternal Father in the setting provided by the Preface and Sanctus. The one sacrifice of Christ was primarily an action by the incarnate Son before the Father and it is eternally present to the Father, transcending the temporal limitations of worldly time and history: "But [Jesus], because he remains forever, has a priesthood that does not pass away. Therefore, he is always able to save those who approach God through him, since he lives forever to make intercession for them" (Hebrews 7:24–25). The Mass too is achieved before the eternal Father, and for that reason the Church's sacrifice can blend with that of Calvary. It is by virtue of its presence before God's eternity that the Mass overcomes the exclusions of "now" and "then" and present, past, and future that occur in respect to all historical events. In the Mass we enter into the same sacrifice achieved once and for all by Christ. The identity of the sacrifice achieved before the Father permits such a sacramental identity for us here on earth.

Grammatical changes

The priest says the prayers of the Canon of the Mass in the first-person plural. In doing this he prays in the name of the Church. He says that "we" ask God to accept and bless the gifts we bring, that "we" offer these gifts for the holy catholic Church, and he asks that God remember all of "us" gathered before Him. The epiclesis, the invocation of the Holy Spirit on the gifts, is also expressed in the same grammatical form: the priest asks that God bless and approve "our" offering, and that he let it become for "us" the body and blood of the Lord. The institutional narrative is also said under the aegis of what "we" say, even though the pronoun is not explicitly used in it.

In the words of institution, however, in "this is my body" and "this is the cup of my blood," the priest speaks in the first-person singular because he speaks no longer in the name of the Church but in the name of Christ. He allows Christ to be the speaker of the words; or, to put it more appropriately, Christ elevates the voice of the priest, through sacramental quotation, to become the vehicle for his own speech; the priest is enabled to speak *in persona Christi*. At this central point of her sacred liturgy, the Church renounces any verbal initiative of her own and lets the words of Christ himself achieve the sacred action, the reenactment of his own redemptive death.

The priest does this while remaining within his own historical context, in his own world and time, with the cares and needs of the Church and the people around him; but while focused on the sacrifice of Calvary, he echoes the words and actions of the Last Supper, and he also stands within the celestial liturgy in which the Son, the Lamb of God slain for our sins, is eternally present to the Father. All these temporal and eternal dimensions are engaged in the words that are said and the gestures that are made during the institutional narrative and consecration. All these dimensions can be present to the minds of the priest and the people at this point in the liturgy.

Quotation and not dramatic depiction

There is an interpretation of the Eucharistic Prayer that would draw us away from the context in which the liturgy is performed before God the Father: we may be inclined to think that the consecration is rather like a drama, a play performed before the congregation. We may even tend to think that the congregation is involved in the play, as depicting the disciples at the Last Supper: the priest takes the role of Christ and the congregation the role of the apostles. To this way of thinking, the words and gestures of the priest are seen as dramatic depictions of what Christ did and said at the Last Supper.

Such a dramatic interpretation of the Mass would not be appropriate. It is more fitting to think of the words and gestures of the priest as quotational, not dramatic. The priest quotes the words and gestures of Christ; he does not perform them in the manner of an actor. There are several reasons why quotation is a more fitting presentational form for the consecration than drama.

First, to see the consecration as a drama would shift the focus of the liturgy from its relationship to God the Father to an axis between the priest and the people. The liturgy would cut away from its presence before God, which had been established in the Preface and Sanctus, and it would be centered on the dramatic impact of the priest acting before the congregation as audience or participants. Second, such an interpretation would highlight the Mass as representing the Last Supper, but would diminish its reenactment of the redemptive death of Christ. The Mass would be seen as a sacred meal and not a sacrifice. Third, this interpretation would place the liturgical emphasis on the person of the priest as the performer; drama highlights the present actor, whereas quotation takes us away from our present context and lets someone else speak through us. If Lawrence Olivier is depicting Hamlet, we think of *Olivier*, not primarily Hamlet, as taking center stage; but if we quote what someone says we subordinate our voice and especially the content of our speech to that other person. We let someone else speak through us and we subject our responsibility to his. Christ is more palpably the speaker when we take his words as being quoted than if we were to take the priest as dramatically representing him. Christ, the one who is quoted, speaks with the authority of the incarnate Son of God, as one who has the power to bring about what he declares in his words. Fourth, in the old rite the possibility did not arise that the priest was dramatically depicting the Last Supper before the congregation; the focus was entirely toward God the Father.

The difference between quotation and dramatic depiction is also relevant to the prayerful attitude of the priest. If the priest sees his words and his gestures as quoting those of Christ, he can more appropriately see himself as the servant of both Christ and the Church, the person who is there to hand on to others the message and the achievement of Christ the Lord. If the priest were to see himself as a dramatic actor, his own persona and style would come to the fore in an inappropriate and probably intrusive way. His would be the primary agency. Quotation affords a salutary anonymity to the priest in his sacramental ministry. It also relieves the priest of a burden that actors have, that of finding ever new ways of making their performance interesting to their audience. The priest is not there to perform; he is there to accomplish the liturgy as it is written in the Roman Missal. He is there as the servant of Christ and the Church, a servant who becomes quotationally transparent in the words and gestures of the consecration. Christ is the ultimate minister of the Eucharist, and his activity is perceptibly manifest when his words and gestures are quoted at the center of the Church's offering.

The Church's quotation of the words and gestures of Christ is done primarily before God the Father. Christ's speech comes to life in an address before the eternal Father, expressing the eucharistic action of the Son toward the Father. However, at the Last Supper the words of Christ were directed toward the disciples ("Take this, all of you, and eat it: for this is my body, which will be given up for you"). Certainly an overtone of such an address spoken by Christ, now directed toward the people, remains in the words of consecration, but the primary focus of the celebrant toward God the Father is never interrupted. When the priest recites the words of consecration, he will quite naturally tend to take them as being spoken to the faithful, but he should not let the theocentric focus of the Church's prayer be lost.

The institutional narrative

As a final remark regarding eucharistic quotation, we must say a word about the institutional narrative. As we mentioned earlier, there is a sequence of four stages in the literary form of the consecration: from prayer to invocation to narrative to quotation. The place of the institutional narrative is especially important in this sequence.

The institutional narrative sets the stage for the quoted words of consecration: "On the night he was betrayed, he took bread and gave you thanks and praise. He broke the bread, gave it to his disciples, and said. . . ." These words refer us to another time and place and they record certain events and actions. The verb "said" then introduces the quotation. We have stated that the four stages of this sequence should not be rushed and the distinctions among them should not be blurred; to avoid such haste and obscuration, it is especially helpful to bring the narrative to the fore and to be conscious of it as a narrative. If the priest pays attention especially to this part of the Eucharistic Prayer, the other parts fall more easily into place. The narrative, which is accompanied by the quoted gestures of Christ (taking the bread, taking the cup, looking up to heaven), prepares both the priest and the people for the voice of Christ.

It is interesting to observe that all quotation needs at least a little narrative to introduce it. Quotation needs at least a phrase such as, "he said," which displaces us from our present time and place and signals that what is to follow is someone else's speaking. In the eucharistic narrative we are displaced into the context of the Last Supper and its anticipation of the redemptive death of the Lord. The priest, by drawing attention to the narrative as such, can provide an immediate preparation for the words that follow and the action performed in them. He can articulate more reverently the stages of the eucharistic consecration, both for himself and for the people assisting at Mass.

The elevation and acclamation

We have emphasized the fact that the Eucharistic Prayer is recited, in the company of the angels and saints, before God the Father. The elevation of the host and the chalice can also be seen in this context. It is true that historically the elevation was introduced to allow the people to see and worship the consecrated species. This reverence toward the presence of Christ, however, can take on a deeper meaning if the elevation is seen also as a presentation of the consecrated bread and wine to the eternal Father. We worship Christ not only as the Incarnate Word come down among us, but also as the eternal Son, as present within the Holy Trinity. The bread and wine are profiled against the eternal Eucharist between the Son and the Father, and we are allowed to glorify and participate in that sacred exchange. The consecrated bread and wine are presented to the people, but in conjunction with their presentation by the Church to the Father.

The acclamation following the consecration, which is usually addressed to Christ in the sacrament ("Lord, by your cross and resurrection, you have set us free"; "We proclaim your death, Lord Jesus"), can also be seen in this setting; we address Christ in glory, not only present in the bread and wine but as eternally present to the Father. Thus, the trinitarian and celestial setting remains in force during the elevation and acclamation; we do not turn away from it simply to what is present before us at the altar.

To see the elevation and acclamation in this trinitarian context would avoid a difficulty that many liturgists have raised. The claim has been made that both the elevation and the acclamation, with their focus on Christ, disrupt the continuity of the Eucharist Prayer, which is directed toward God the Father. No disruption would occur, however, if in the elevation and acclamation the priest and people were directed toward the Redeemer in the life of the Holy Trinity, in the presence of the eternal Father. On the contrary, the focus of the prayer toward the Father would acquire a deeper dimension as it moved through Christ the Savior in the Father's presence.

Thus, the three points that punctuate the Eucharistic Prayer—the Sanctus, the consecration and its elevation, and the doxology and its "minor" elevation before the Great Amen—can be seen as variations within the prayer addressed by the Church to God the Father. In the Sanctus the Church addresses the Father and anticipates the coming of the Son when she prays, "Blessed is he who comes in the name of the Lord." In the concluding doxology the Church expresses the honor and glory due to the Father and presents the Son, who is now sacramentally part of the creation that was achieved through him, the eternal Word of God. The Son is no longer anticipated; he has come among us, and now through him, with him, and in him, in the unity of the Holy Spirit, all glory and honor is given to the Father. In the elevation and acclamation after the consecration, the Church addresses the Son, in both his sacramental presence and his presence before the Father, *in sinu Patris.*

This focus of attention toward the Father and the Holy Trinity does not detract from the attention due to the congregation in the liturgy. The Mass is for the people, but it is not done by the priest toward the people. Both priest and people are directed toward God in the Eucharistic Prayer. The people join their offering of the sacrifice to that of the priest, to that of Christ who speaks through the priest, and as they do so they are turned toward God the Father, under the guidance of the Holy Spirit. Their share in this sacred action, their "active participation," as the Second Vatican Council expresses it (*Constitution on the Sacred Liturgy* §11, §14, §27, §30), elevates them sacramentally to the eternal life and presence of God. The focus of their attention is not on the priest himself but on the Father and the Son their Redeemer.

Prayers before and after the Eucharistic Canon

After the Canon of the Mass has been concluded at the Great Amen, the priest and the people pray the Our Father. The Our Father is also said from within a special context, one that is different from the context of the Eucharistic Prayer. The setting for the Eucharistic Prayer was provided by the Preface and Sanctus, which placed us among the angels and saints. The context for the Our Father is set by the sacramental presence of Christ in the community of the Church on earth. Now that Christ has become present among us in the sacrament, we are able—we are emboldened—to call God *our* Father; the previous uses of the term *Father,* in the Preface and Canon, would have referred primarily to him as Father within the Holy Trinity and as the origin of all things. The context for the Our Father, set by the presence of Christ among us as our savior and brother, is contrasted with the celestial context set earlier by the Preface and Sanctus. After the Great Amen we return to earth, so to speak, to the place of the Incarnation, with Christ now sacramentally present with us, and we begin to prepare for our individual communion with him by reciting the prayer he taught us to say.

If the Our Father follows the Eucharistic Prayer, the offertory prayers precede it. In them we take bread and wine out of their normal usage and dedicate them to God as our offering of the fruits of the earth, to be transformed by him into the presence of Christ. In the traditional liturgy it was customary to sing a Marian hymn at the offertory, a practice that was highly appropriate, since the Blessed Virgin is the supreme instance of the dedication of our own nature to the service of God, to become the instrument of his presence among us. Mary's fiat is echoed in the offertory of the Mass.

I would like to close these reflections on the prayers of the priest by making a suggestion for thanksgiving after Mass. In the old rite, the prayer called the Placeat and the Prologue to St. John's Gospel were said toward the end of Mass, before and after the final blessing and dismissal. This prayer and gospel are not used in the new rite, but they can well be recommended as private prayers of the priest after Mass is over. In the Placeat the priest prays that the sacrifice he has just offered be pleasing to the Holy Trinity and that it be beneficial for himself and those for whom it was offered. In the Prologue to St. John's Gospel we recall the preexistence of the Word as God with God, the coming of the Word as life and light for men, the acceptance and rejection of the Word, the contrast between John the Baptist and Jesus, and the Incarnation of the Word among us. These prayerful and biblical thoughts are appropriate as part of the priest's thanksgiving after the sacrifice of the Mass and the reception of communion. The fact that they were included in the Mass in the old rite shows that their suitability for the Eucharist was recognized in earlier ages. Using them as prayers of thanksgiving will remind us of the continuity between the old rite of the Mass and the new.

7

THE EUCHARIST
AND TRANSUBSTANTIATION

Christian theology is reflection on the faith of the Church. The Church, under the guidance of the Holy Spirit, receives and teaches her faith and when necessary defines it. Theology reflects on this faith, in a manner analogous to the way in which philosophy reflects on prephilosophical life and conversation. Theology is the exercise of reason within faith, and scholastic theology is reason's self-discovery within faith.

Theology helps bring out the intelligibility of the deposit of faith. The intelligibility is already there in faith and revelation, and theology helps to make it manifest. It performs this service for the benefit of the Church and the faithful, and also simply for the distinctive understanding that faith can bring.

Two theological issues regarding the Eucharist

When we reflect on what the Church believes concerning the Eucharist, two theological issues come into prominence: the identity of the sacrifice between Calvary and the Mass, and Transubstantiation or the Real Presence of Christ in the sacrament.

Regarding the identity of the sacrifice, the Church holds that one and the same sacrifice is offered on Calvary and in the Eucharist, first in a bloody and then in a sacramental manner. The two ways in which the sacrifice is offered do not mean that two sacrifices are offered; rather, a single sacrifice is offered by the incarnate Son of God to God the Father. As regards the temporal structure of this mystery, we can formulate the identity between Calvary and the Eucharist in two ways. We can begin with the sacrifice of Calvary and say that it is reenacted when the Church offers the sacrifice of the Eucharist (that is, we can say that the past sacrifice is brought forward to the present moment). Conversely, we can begin with the present liturgy and say that in the sacrifice of the Mass the participants are brought into the presence of Calvary (that is, the present community is brought back to the past moment). We can say either that the past becomes present or that the present is brought to the past. Both ways of speaking are equivalent, but both obviously are paradoxical or "beyond belief" when viewed within the horizon of human history. Clearly, the belief in the singularity of the sacrifice does raise a problem, since the temporal distance between the two historical events (the death of Christ and the celebration of the Eucharist) seems at first glance to exclude the possibility of a single action. We will have more to say later concerning this topic.

The second theological issue in the Church's eucharistic faith is that of the Real Presence of Christ in the sacrament. This is the issue of Transubstantiation, according to which the bread and wine are changed into the body and blood of Christ, while retaining the appearances and the natural characteristics of bread and wine.

The identity of the sacrifice and the question of Transubstantiation are two different issues, but they are closely related: how could the Eucharist be the same sacrifice as that of Calvary if Christ were not truly present to offer himself to the Father? Without the Real Presence of Christ, the same event or the same action could not take place.

Both issues are present in St. Thomas Aquinas's treatment of the Eucharist, but in his work by far the greater emphasis is placed on the theme of the Real Presence. Most of Thomas's discussion in Questions 73–83 of Part III of the *Summa Theologiae* is concerned with the question of how the matter of the sacrament is changed: how the substance of the bread and of the wine become the body and blood of the Lord, while continuing to appear and to react as bread and wine. Thomas also gives much attention to the effect the sacrament has on those who receive it. He gives relatively little space, however, to the question of the identity between the sacrifice of the Eucharist and the sacrifice of Calvary. Indeed, when he addresses this topic, he says simply that "the celebration of this sacrament is a certain representative image of the passion of Christ, which is the true immolation of him," and this representative function of the Eucharist is compared with the representation provided by the figures of the Old Testament.[1] It is even compared with the altar as representing the cross on which Christ was sacrificed.[2] Thomas insists that there is only one sacrifice, that of Christ himself,[3] but he speaks of the Mass more as an image of that sacrifice than as identified with it.

We find a contrasting emphasis in the eucharistic theology of the twentieth century, in the type of thinking begun by Dom Odo Casel, O.S.B. Here, the issue of the identity of the sacrifice comes to the fore. The event of the Eucharist is seen to be somehow the same event that took place in the redemptive Death and Resurrection of Jesus. When this theme becomes prominent, however, the issue of the Real Presence seems to fall into the background. We may insist that the Eucharist reenacts the death of Jesus, but then what are we to say about the Real Presence, apart from the event of the Eucharistic celebration? In this perspective, does Transubstantiation have any role?

I would claim that the two issues are closely related, and that we cannot have the one without the other: no Transubstantiation without identity of sacrifice, and no identity of sacrifice without Transubstantiation. Both issues are essential, but emphasis will be placed on the one or the other depending on the theological approach we use. It may be that a more ontological approach will emphasize Transubstantiation, while a more phenomenological approach will emphasize the identity of the sacrifice.

The celestial focus of the eucharistic action

A feature of the Eucharist that is important for both issues is the focus of the central prayer of the Eucharist, the Eucharistic Canon, which extends from the Preface to the Great Amen. This entire prayer is directed toward God the Father. The Preface speaks to the Father and recalls his saving actions in a manner appropriate to the feast of the day. The Sanctus is especially important for determining the direction of the prayer. It places us among the choirs of angels, as we repeat the song of the Seraphim cited in chapter 6 of Isaiah. The last part of the Preface, which leads into the Sanc-

---

1. St. Thomas Aquinas, *Summa Theologiae* III, q. 83, a. 1.
2. Ibid., III, q. 83, a. 1, ad 2.
3. Ibid., III, q. 83, a. 1, ad 1.

tus, often mentions the articulated ranks of angels and it also mentions the saints. As we say the Eucharistic Canon, we join the angels and saints and take part in the celestial Eucharist, the glory given to the Father by the Son who redeemed the world, the Lamb presented in heaven as slain, the Mystic Lamb, so profoundly depicted by Jan van Eyck in the Ghent Altarpiece. Our worldly Eucharist joins with the celestial. Dr. Eric Perl, who is a member of the Orthodox Church, once said that he was asked by a student in a religion class whether there would be a Eucharist in heaven; he said that he answered, "There won't be anything else." The angels and saints in heaven participate in the action of the Son toward the Father, and we now in our Eucharist join in their participation; in the Roman Canon we pray to Almighty God, "that your angel may take this sacrifice to your altar in heaven." This celestial focus, established by the Preface and Sanctus, continues till the Great Amen, where Christ, now present on the altar, reconciles the entire created world in a return to the Father: "Through him, with him, in him, in the unity of the Holy Spirit, all glory and honor is yours, almighty Father, forever and ever. Amen." The Sanctus and the Great Amen should be taken as directing us toward the celestial Eucharist and associating us with it. This focus and direction are somewhat masked when the priest faces the congregation, because it then appears that his words are being directed toward the people and not toward God the Father, and care must be taken to make this focus clear in the celebration of the Eucharist.

This participation in the heavenly Eucharist is of great importance for both the identity of the sacrifice and Transubstantiation. The celestial Eucharist is beyond time and world history. It touches history because the saving action of the Son of God took place in time, but his action was not just a temporal event. His obedience to the Father, his acceptance of the cross for our redemption, was an action in time that was related to the eternal Father. It occurred in time but touched eternity. It changed the relationship between creation and the Father. The celestial Eucharist is the eternal aspect of the death of Christ; it is not just a memorial or reminder of that event.[4]

---

4. One might ask whether the other sacraments do not also transcend time in the same way as the Eucharist; there is a difference, however, in that the other sacraments do not reenact any particular action of Christ. A baptism, for example, does not reenact any particular action performed by Christ, but the Eucharist reenacts both the Last Supper and the sacrificial death of Jesus.

His Resurrection witnesses to the eternal aspect of this action; the Risen Lord bears forever the wounds of his passion. In our present Eucharist, we join with the action of Christ not simply as a past historical action, but as the transaction between Jesus and the eternal Father, the transaction and exchange, the *commercium*, between time and eternity, which subsists in the celestial Eucharist. It is because of this action that we can join in the Great Amen, in which the created universe is brought back to the Father through the Son, who was the point of creation, the Word through whom the universe was created.

Only because the action of Christ touched eternity can it be reenacted as the very same action now. The identity of the sacrifice, the fact that the Eucharist reenacts an event from the past, the fact that we now are made present to a past event, is made possible because of the nature of that original and singular action. We cannot recover events in worldly and human history. Once done and past, they cannot be redone in the present; they can only be remembered or commemorated. But the action of Christ was not just an action in worldly and human history; it was an action before and toward the eternal Father, it had an eternal aspect, and so it can be reenacted now.

This celestial focus helps us understand the possibility of the Church's faith in the sameness of the sacrifice in the Eucharist and on Calvary. However, we can look at the same state of affairs from another perspective. The Church's faith in the sameness of the sacrifice is itself a witness to the celestial character of the Eucharist. Our belief that the Eucharist reenacts something from the past implies that the action of Christ was not finished once and for all, but that it is alive now and always. Our belief in the identity of the sacrifice implies that the sacrifice was not just a historical event. The Eucharist does not just remind us of what happened in the past—the Death and Resurrection of the Lord—but proclaims the eternal aspect of that event. It proclaims the fact that Christ, the incarnate Son of God, with his glorified body and blood, lives eternally before the Father.

It seems clear, then, that the celestial focus of the liturgy clarifies for us the sameness of the sacrifice. It helps us bring out the intelligibility of that sameness. But what does this focus have to do with the issue of Transubstantiation?

The bread and wine of the Eucharist become the body and blood of the Lord, but they become specifically his resurrected and glorified body and blood. Transubstantiation should not be taken as a mere substantial change in the natural order of things. It is not as though we were to claim that a tree became a leopard but continued to look and react like a tree, or that a piece of cloth became a cat but still seemed to be cloth. I think some of the objections to Transubstantiation come from an implicit belief that such a worldly change of substance is what is being claimed. Rather, it is not simply the worldly substance of the body and blood of the Lord that are present in the Eucharist, but his glorified body and blood, which share in the eternity of the celestial Eucharist. The bread and wine are now the vehicles for the presence of the eternal Christ, the eternal Son who became incarnate for us, died and rose from the dead, and is eternally present to the Father. The ontology of the Holy Trinity is part of the Church's faith in Transubstantiation.

In fact, does not the glorified Christ *need* something like the eucharistic presence in order to allow his death to be present to the world? The teleology of the Incarnation moves not only to the sacrificial Death and Resurrection, but also toward the Eucharist, in both its celestial and its worldly forms; the Incarnation finds its end and completion in the Eucharist, which allows the risen Christ to be "scattered" throughout the world even while he subsists within the Holy Trinity. The glorified body of Christ is present to the Father and to the angels and saints, and it is this body and blood that are the substance of the bread and wine in the sacrament of the Eucharist. Through the eucharistic continuance of the Son's act of obedience, glory is given to the Father not only in the heavens but also on the earth. We might suggest that this eucharistic presence of Christ is in fact a more fitting expression to the world of his glorified life than continued resurrection appearances would have been.

I would even venture to raise the following question: Does not the denial of the Real Presence of Christ in the Eucharist bring in its train a dilution of our trinitarian faith? Does it not make us drift toward a unitarian understanding of divinity? If we question whether the Son is truly present in the Eucharist, are we not led to question whether he was truly present in the Incarnation, and then whether he is truly distinguished from the Father? If we begin to think this way, do we not begin to take the sacraments as images and metaphors of a single divine principle? It is true that there are other presences of Christ—in the Church, as his mystical body, in the words of Scripture, in the believer, the confessor, and the martyr—but all these depend on his primary presence, achieved by his own action and through his own words, in the Eucharist.

The Christian tradition of the East, with its strong focus on the celestial liturgy, encounters less difficulty with the true presence of Christ in the sacrament than does the West, precisely because of this focus and the correlative belief in the eucharistic presence of the glorified Christ. We in the West tend to think primarily in terms of human psychology and worldly history, and these concerns make us raise problems that may be less likely to arise in the East.

I have one more point to make concerning the manner in which the Eucharist represents and reenacts the Death and Resurrection of the Lord. The issue is often formulated in the following way: we ask how the celebration of the Eucharist can represent the death of Christ *to us*. But to pose the question this way is to begin at a derivative stage, not at the true beginning. First and foremost, the Eucharist represents and reenacts the death of the Lord *before the eternal Father*. The Eucharistic Canon is directed toward the Father, and even the representation of the Last Supper, in the institutional narrative and words of consecration, is directed first and foremost to him. Now, can we truly think that this representation before the Father of the death of the Lord is only an image, only a commemoration, only a human remembrance? God does not remember in the way we do, and the past is not lost to him the way it is to us. The redemptive action of the Son is eternally present to the Father, and this action is carried out by the person of the Son in the Eucharist. The identity of the Eucharist and Calvary before the Father secures its identity before us. The Mass and Calvary are the same before the Father, *and therefore* they can be the same for us.

Matter and spirit

I would like to develop more fully the idea that the Eucharist embodies and presents the glorified body of Christ. To do this, I must comment on how matter and spirit are related in the world. I will distinguish three different points of view.

In the first viewpoint, one that is typified by a darwinian understanding, what we call spirit is an epiphenomenon of matter. All we have in the universe is matter in motion. Matter may be very mysterious, and in its development it gives rise to marvelous kinds of bodies, such as plants, animals, and even human beings, but all these apparently "higher" things are really congelations of matter and material forces. Most of the writers in cognitive science, those who try to reduce consciousness and rational processes to the activities of the brain and nervous system, would subscribe to this understanding. In this viewpoint, of course, spirit and personality are simply complex forms of matter. I have recently seen this reductionist viewpoint expressed in the following way: it is not that God has created the heavens and the earth, but the heavens and the earth have created God, because through evolution they have brought about the human organism, which in turn projects the idea of a divine being.

The second viewpoint is an Aristotelian or Stoic understanding, one that is a rather spontaneous, natural way of looking at the world. It is not reductive, but holds that matter and spirit are mixed in the universe. There are purely material levels of being, but there are also more spiritual and rational levels of being, and each interacts with the other. The spiritual dimension shapes matter and brings about complexities and intelligibilities that sheer matter could not. The existence of life and thinking beings bears the imprint of spirit. Most attempts to refute the Darwinian, reductive point of view aim at reestablishing this kind of understanding of the complementarity of matter and spirit.

The third viewpoint, which is biblical and creationist, holds that the spiritual or the personal dimension of being precedes the material. Matter exists, but it has come into being through a personal action of God. "Before" there was matter, there was and is God, who is spirit and life. The personal dimension, in this viewpoint, does not arise from matter, nor does it merely accompany the impersonal and the material, but rather it brings it into being. Matter and all created being might not have been, and they exist because of something like a personal choice. The eternal in some sense "precedes" the temporal and causes it to be. In this biblical understanding, the divine choice to create was carried out in sheer generosity or charity, under no pressure and under no need for improvement. The generosity of Creation is the backdrop for the humility of the Incarnation and the charity of the Eucharist. In this third viewpoint, then, the personal or spiritual dimension precedes and causes the material.

Faith in the Eucharist as embodying and presenting the glorified Christ clearly can be held only against the background of the third understanding of matter and spirit. It would not be possible in the first two viewpoints, not even in the one that mixes matter and spirit as two necessary components of the world. The Eucharist must be seen against the setting of Creation, which in turn becomes a context for the Incarnation, in which the eternal and almighty Creator enters into what he has made and becomes a part of it. He then continues his presence in this creation in a eucharistic and sacramental manner. The time and the space of the Eucharist are established by the entry of the eternal and transcendent into the created world. The Eucharist itself, because it would not be possible except against the background of this understanding of spirit and matter, is a perpetual reminder of the transcendence and power of God, which manifested themselves most fully not by spectacular cosmic effects but by the life, Death, and Resurrection of Jesus the Lord.

The Real Presence in the Eucharist is therefore not just the concealed presence of one worldly substance under the appearances of another, but the presence of the full mystery of God's being and his work, the mystery hidden from all ages and now made manifest to us, the point of the universe and of creation. It is this presence, this glory, that is the substance of the Eucharist and the core of the doctrine of Transubstantiation. Furthermore, the presence of eternity and transcendence in the Eucharist are not merely a presentation of abstract divine attributes, but the presence of the eternal Son, the Logos, who accomplishes two things in the sacrament: he gives glory to the Father and shares his life with us.

Perhaps some of the difficulties that arise in regard to the Real Presence stem from the way we understand spirit and matter in the world. We may unconsciously subscribe to the first or the second understanding that we have listed above: that of reductive materialism or of a Stoic or Aristotelian mixture of matter and spirit. If these two ways of understanding the world remain in the background for us, we will not be able to accept the idea of Transubstantiation. If we propose to interpret the Eucharist in a manner that will speak to a culture that accepts the Darwinian universe, one that accepts only a materialist and technological sense of being, it will be impossible for us to conform to the Church's faith in this mystery.

But we should not think that it is inevitable that a materialist view of nature will triumph; we ought not fear that the studies of life and cognition will reduce life, consciousness, and thinking to mechanical processes. Instead, we should look at the issue in the other way: we have every reason to marvel at the fact that matter enters into life and rationality, that it is assumed into living organisms and into human consciousness and human exchanges, such as moral actions. Matter enters into the realm of spirit and reason. Matter is already spiritualized when it is elevated into life and rationality.

The Eucharist extends this trajectory into a still greater spiritualization of matter, one that could not have been anticipated by our study of natural phenomena. The Logos through whom the world was created becomes part of creation, not only in the Incarnation, when he became united with a human nature, but also in the Eucharist, under the appearances of bread and wine. Matter is elevated into a new condition in the Eucharist, in a way that expresses its exaltation in the glorified body and blood of Christ.

I believe that the Gospel of St. John, and especially the Prologue to the Gospel of St. John, provides an admirable context for the eucharistic celebration and for eucharistic devotion. The Real Presence in the Eucharist calls to mind our belief in the God who was in the beginning and the Word who was with God, who was God, even in that beginning, "before" there was matter. The Eucharist steers us in that direction and into that context; it is a perpetual reminder of the transcendence of God, both when it is celebrated and overcomes the confinements of time and history by reenacting in the present the sacrifice of Christ, and in the tabernacle, where the saving event is not immediately reenacted, but where Christ is present for our contemplation and prayer. St. Thomas expresses this dimension of the Eucharist when he draws on Aristotle and says, "It is the law of friendship that friends should live together." He goes on to say that Christ "has not left us without his bodily presence in this our pilgrimage, but he joins us to himself in this sacrament in the reality of his body and blood."[5]

Transformation of matter

In the Blessed Sacrament, matter becomes a vehicle for the presence of the transcendent God. Can we reflect on how this occurs?

5. St. Thomas Aquinas, *Summa Theologiae* III, q. 75, a. 1.

One of the points made repeatedly by St. Thomas in his discussion of the Eucharist is the contrast he draws between the Eucharist and the other sacraments. In the other sacraments, the material element—the water in baptism, the oils used in anointing—is set apart or consecrated simply for the use that is made of it. These sacraments terminate in the application made of the matter (for example, water is used in baptizing). In the Eucharist, in contrast, the matter itself is transformed: the sacrament finds its completion in the change of the material element.[6] The bread is not only used to nourish us but is changed in its substance. The Eucharist involves Transubstantiation while the other sacraments do not. The baptismal water and the oils used in anointing remain water and oil.

To bring out the meaning of such a change in matter, let us examine another way in which matter is elevated into a higher use. Consider the kind of elevation of matter that occurs when something material is made into a human symbol. A piece of cloth is made into a flag. When this occurs, the cloth becomes more than cloth. Within the human context, the cloth truly is a flag and certain responses become appropriate while others are inappropriate and even provocative. No one cares if you burn a piece of cloth or stomp on it, but people do care if you burn a flag or trample upon it. Would this paradigm be helpful in speaking about the Eucharist? To make the case stronger, suppose we said that the Eucharist is a more substantial symbol than a flag, because the transformation is brought about not simply by human agreement but by the declaration made by Christ, with divine authority. The bread is the body of Christ not simply by human convention but by divine assertion, and therefore it would remain so even apart from the continued agreement of believers. The bread and wine of the Eucharist would take on a new sense, a paradigmatic sense, within a community of shared meaning.

But this model fails, because the logic and the being of such symbols is not adequate to the Church's eucharistic faith. Even though a flag truly is a flag, it also remains cloth, while the bread does not remain bread. This fact is brought out by a remarkable comment of St. Thomas, who observes that in the Eucharistic Prayer Christ is quoted not as saying, "*This bread* is my body,"

---

6. Ibid., III, q. 73, a. 1, ad 3; q. 74, a. 2, ad 3; q. 78, a. 1.

but "*This* is my body." If Christ had said "this bread" was his body, then the thing referred to would still be bread, but the simple demonstrative pronoun "this" without a noun implies that it is not bread any longer.[7]

Furthermore, to say that in the Eucharist the bread and wine remain what they are but acquire a new signification would contradict the logic of the Incarnation. Christ was not simply a prophet who pointed out the way to the Father; he *was* the way to the Father. He did not just communicate the truth about God, he was the Word of God. The believer comes to the Father not by the way and the truth that are signified by Christ, but through Christ himself, who is the way, the truth, and the life. Analogously, if the bread and wine were to remain bread and wine, they would point us toward the Death and Resurrection of Christ and toward the Son of God, they would signify him and what he did, but they would not *be* his presence and the presence of his action among us. The Eucharist would fail to continue, sacramentally, the form of the Incarnation, and we would be deprived of the presence, the bodily presence, of the way, the truth, and the life. The Incarnation would have been withdrawn from the world.

The Eucharist continues the Incarnation, but there are important differences between the two mysteries. In the Incarnation, when the Word became flesh, the divine nature did not transubstantiate the human nature. It did not take the place of the human being. To say that it did would fall into a monophysite interpretation of the mystery. To understand the Incarnation as a transubstantiation would imply that the human nature ceased to be but only appeared to be when united with the divine. Instead, the human substance, soul and body, is integrally present in the Incarnation. In this respect, the human substance in the Incarnation is different from the substance of bread in the Eucharist. The human substance, soul and body, remains intact, but the substance of the bread does not.

Indeed, it is the very material and bodily quality of the Incarnation that calls for Transubstantiation in the Eucharist. If Christ is to be present in the sacrament, he must be present in his divine and human natures; if his human nature is to be present, it must be present in both soul and body. And if his body is to be present, the bread cannot be. The one thing cannot be two material substances, both bread and a human body, not even the glori-

7. Ibid., III, q. 78, a. 5; cf. q. 75, a. 3; q. 75, a. 8.

fied human body of Christ. If it is the one it cannot be the other. The two bodily natures exclude one another, and it is the bodily presence of Christ that is specifically emphasized in the words of consecration. The body of Christ is not *with* the bread but takes the place of the bread in the change we call Transubstantiation. If we deny this change, we deny the bodily presence of the glorified Christ, and hence we deny the presence of Christ. Without Transubstantiation the sacramental presence of Christ would not occur.

In the Eucharist, therefore, it is the radical *worldliness* of the Incarnation, its materiality, that calls for Transubstantiation in the Eucharist. It is the *incarnate* divinity, the Word made flesh and not simply the divine nature, that is present in the Eucharist. If I may use the terms, the body of Christ, because it is material, "displaces" or "dislodges" the bread. Whatever matter may be, it takes place, it is located. Through Transubstantiation, the bodily presence of the transcendent divinity, in the person of the Son, takes its place among us in a manner that follows upon the Incarnation, and it does so by replacing the substance of bread and wine.

However, not everything of the bread ceases to exist in the Eucharist. As St. Thomas says, "the accidents, which are the proper object for the senses, are genuinely there."[8] The accidents and natural characteristics of bread are truly there; we should not think of the species of bread and wine as merely images in our minds. They are part of the world and they provide the place where Christ is present. St. Thomas says that these accidents serve as a kind of subject for the presence of Christ: "Strictly speaking, there is no subject in this change. . . . All the same, the accidents which remain do bear a certain resemblance to a subject."[9] The sacramental presence of the Word occurs here in this place and at this time, and it thus bears the signature of the Incarnation. The visible and tangible forms of bread and wine, the forms present to the senses, remain as they are, but the substantial form, the form present to the understanding, does not: the body of Christ is now present to the understanding, but to an understanding enlightened by faith, an intelligence guided not by vision, touch, or taste, but by hearing. We recall also that the Eucharist directs us toward the celestial liturgy and our future participation in it, where no sacramental presence, no appearance of bread and wine, will be needed, and where the same God who is now an object of faith will be

8. Ibid., III, q. 75, a. 5, ad 2.
9. Ibid., III, q. 75, a. 5, ad 4.

present to vision. In that celestial liturgy the bread and wine are no longer required for the presence of Christ, but his human being, the fruit of the Incarnation, does remain. For our present state, however, the bread and wine are a worldly expression of the glorified body of Christ that is present to the Father, a worldly expression that we return to the Father in the Great Amen of our Eucharistic Prayer.

Transubstantiation, Incarnation, and Creation

We have discussed the way in which the logic of the Incarnation leads on to Transubstantiation, but more can be said about the interplay between these two mysteries. They should not be seen as separate truths; they are interrelated, and the two should be profiled theologically against one another. The intelligibility of each is clarified by bringing out the identities and the differences between them.

In the Incarnation, both the divine and the human substances are present, and the actions of the incarnate Word are theandric, the actions of God and man. As many of the Church Fathers claim, if the actions of Christ were not those of both God and man, our salvation could not have been achieved. We had to be saved by one like us if *we* were to be saved, but we had to be saved by one greater than us, by God himself, if we were to be reconciled with God and allowed to share in his life. The act of salvation sheds light on the agent who accomplishes it.

The Eucharist reenacts the same theandric action, the action of God and man, but the substance of the bread does not enter into this action. It is not the case that in the Eucharist there is the sacramental action of God, man, and also bread. If this were the case, the eucharistic action would not be the same as that of Calvary; it would be something new and different. The bread and wine must give way and not enter into the substantial action. The bread and wine do not act, and so sacramentally they are not there to act. It is true that the bread and wine are consumed and nourish our bodies, but this physical achievement belongs to the species of the Eucharist, not to its substance. It is fitting that we receive the bread and wine as an expression of the life that is given in the sacrament, but their effect on our person, though necessary as a condition, is accidental to the sacramental action. The bread and wine do not enter into the action in the way that the human substance of Christ enters into the action of the incarnate Word. Furthermore, they are not present in the celestial liturgy, while the human nature of Christ is present and effective there. They are simply the worldly expression of that liturgy.

The term *substance* does not name a merely passive substrate. It expresses what a thing is, not only as a being but also as a source of action. We say that the substance of the Eucharist is the body and blood of Christ because the action being reenacted is that which occurred in the separation of his body and blood, in his redemptive death, and this action was defined by being the achievement of his divine and human natures. Both natures are present in the act of salvation and in its eucharistic reenactment. This divine nature, furthermore, is the one nature of the Holy Trinity, even though it is present, in the Incarnation and the Eucharist, in the person of the Son. The divine substance is the power by which the world was created; it entered into creation when the Word became man, and in the Eucharist we worship it as the origin of all things and the source of our Redemption. In the Eucharist the Creator becomes immanent in his creation not just by his causal power but also by his localized presence.

This presence of the divine nature in the Eucharist is such as to exclude the danger of pantheism from Christian belief. The concentrated presence of the Creator in the Eucharist makes it clear, by way of contrast, that God is not present in the world as the universal force and highest entity, as the Stoics understood the divine nature to be. If God becomes part of the world, he does so in the manner of the Incarnation and the Eucharist, not as a spirit or intelligence that is the governing part of the world. The Eucharist bears witness to the radical transcendence of the Christian God.

We have seen earlier that the bodily aspect of the Incarnation makes Transubstantiation necessary; because the body and blood of Christ become present, the substance of bread and wine cannot remain. While the material character of the Incarnation makes Transubstantiation necessary, it is the divine aspect of the Incarnation, the presence of the divine nature in the Incarnation, that makes Transubstantiation possible (and the possibility is prior to the necessity). Only because the divine substance becomes present in the Eucharist, as the ultimate source of the action being reenacted there, can Transubstantiation occur.

When we claim that the presence of the divine nature is a condition for the possibility of the Eucharist, we do not appeal simply to the omnipotence of God; it is not just that God as Creator is all-powerful and could bring about the kind of change that occurs in the Eucharist. Rather, the point is that the Eucharist represents the action of the transcendent God: the redemptive Death and Resurrection of Jesus is the work of God (his primary work, greater even than Creation, revealing more profoundly who and what he is), and hence the reenactment of that action is the work of the same divine nature, the work of the transcendent Creator who recreates the world he has made. The risen Christ reveals the kind of life that is given by God and the kind of life that is lived by him. If this is the work being done, and if the divine nature is there to do it, the natural substance by which this action is represented dare not remain, even though the human nature with which the action was accomplished must remain. The bread and wine are substantially emptied out to clear a place for the action of God. If the bread and wine were still there they would continue to act and so would intervene in the single divine performance. We would not be drawn by the Eucharist toward the one action achieved on Calvary, but would partake of something simply happening now.

If the Eucharist is truly the action of God, the bread and wine cannot remain in their substance. However, if one were to claim that the Eucharist is primarily the action of the community (and not of the priest speaking in the person of Christ), then the bread and wine would remain what they are. Transubstantiation would not occur; instead, the bread and wine would become symbols of the gifts the people offer. In such an interpretation, it would not be Christ who speaks the words of consecration but the community, whether the assembly gathered here and now or the one that is said to have originally compiled the ritual and the words. Transubstantiation depends on whose action the Eucharist represents.

Both the Incarnation and Creation provide the background for the Eucharist. This relationship can be clarified by a contrast between Christ and the Blessed Virgin. The glorified body of Christ is present in the Eucharist, but the sanctified body of the Blessed Virgin could not become present in a worldly substance. The reason for the difference is that the Eucharist expresses the action of salvation, while the Blessed Virgin was and is its primary and paradigmatic recipient. It is true that her action in the *fiat* was part of her salvation and ours, but it was so in a manner different from the way the active obedience of the man Jesus was part of our salvation. Christ redeemed but was not redeemed, while Mary was the first of those who were redeemed. The Assumption and Coronation of the Virgin express her perfect receptivity to grace, while the glorification of Christ expresses his action and victory, which is ultimately the action and victory of God himself, the work of the divine nature. It is this action that is present in the Eucharist, in such a manner that the bread and wine that are its expression cannot remain as a part of the achievement.

The revelation that occurs in the Eucharist

As the central action in the life of the Church, the Eucharist continuously discloses the mysteries of Christian faith. The action of the Eucharist complements the words of Scripture and the teaching of the Church. It reveals the Resurrection, bearing witness to the fact that Christ is alive now and a source of life and light for us. By revealing the risen Christ, the Eucharist discloses the Incarnation, since the Resurrection confirms the presence of God in Christ. Through the Incarnation, the Eucharist discloses the mystery of Creation, the fact that the God who became incarnate was also the one who created the world out of the sheer generosity we call charity. By revealing the mystery of Creation, the Eucharist reveals the divine nature as transcendent to the world and yet acting in it, both giving it being and recreating it through the mystery of Christ. Finally, the Eucharist reveals the truth that the divine nature is present to us in the person of the Son, and that therefore the life of God is trinitarian.

The Eucharist is at the center of a series of transformations that converge from two directions, from God and from the world. God, in his infinite charity and in his wisdom and art, created the world and transformed elements of it into man, into a body that lives a rational and spiritual life. God then assumed a human substance and entered into his creation in the hypostatic union. This transformation was perfected by the Death and Resurrection of Jesus, the action that reconciled the whole of creation to the Creator. God sanctified his creation by becoming united with part of it, and he redeemed it and gave it a new form by what he accomplished in that union: "If anyone is in Christ, he is a new creation; the old has passed away, behold, the new has come. All this is from God" (II Corinthians 5:17–18). These transformations, from Creation to Redemption, were accomplished by God. From the other extreme, from the created world, material substances, wheat and grapes, become transformed by human art into bread and wine. These substances are again transformed in the Eucharist, when they become involved in the re-enactment of God's redemptive action, the continued representation of his presence and activity in the world. The bread and wine, the work of human hands, are our humble gift to God. As Mary offered the human body to the Word, we offer him our bread and wine. He becomes united with them, but in a manner different from his union with a human substance in the Incarnation. In the Eucharist, the transformation is a Transubstantiation, in which the bread and wine give way entirely, except in appearance, to the presence of God, the Creator and Redeemer. The Eucharist in turn is the pledge of future glory for those who partake of it, transforming them into the image of the Son: "Beloved, we are God's children now; what we shall be has not yet been revealed. We do know that when it is revealed we shall be like him, for we shall see him as he is" (I John 3:2).

The logic of the Incarnation leads to the change of substance in the Eucharist. Let us conclude by turning to a particular moment of the Incarnation, to the Transfiguration, the transformation of Christ that took place, on the mountain, before Peter, James, and John. The Eucharist is a reversal of the Transfiguration. When Christ was transfigured, his substance remained the same but his appearance changed. In the Eucharist the opposite occurs. The appearances of bread and wine remain the same, but what they are has changed. They look no different, but they are now understood to be the presence of Christ and his act of Redemption. Both the Transfiguration and Transubstantiation express Christ's glory, the one to the eye and the other to faith, the one before his Passion, the other afterward. The splendor of the vision is contrasted with the humility of the bread and wine. These differences notwithstanding, it is fitting for us, as we participate in the Eucharist, to respond as did Peter, James, and John: to be moved by gratitude and fear of the Lord, and to sense the meaning of his Passion and Resurrection, the meaning they have before the Father and for us.

8

THE IDENTITY OF THE BISHOP

A Study in the Theology of Disclosure

Our conference is dedicated to the theme of ecclesiology in the light of the Second Vatican Council, and the specific topic I was asked to speak about is the identity of the bishop.[1] I think we all are familiar with the concepts of ecclesiology, the episcopal office, and the Council. However, the title assigned to me also mentions something called the theology of disclosure. This is a term we may not be familiar with, so let me begin with a few remarks about it.

Theology of disclosure

I would like to define the theology of disclosure as a form of theological thinking that makes use of phenomenology. Why should theology make use of this philosophical form? Not just in order to connect theology with a recent and contemporary type of philosophy—in other words, not because it might seem to be the fashionable thing to do—but because something important can be achieved by this kind of thinking. Christian theology has always been given a certain style by the philosophy it has incorporated into itself. Patristic thinking was marked by Neoplatonism and Stoicism, and

---

1. This paper was originally given at a conference held at the John Paul II Cultural Center in Washington, D.C., in November 2003. The conference was entitled *The Call to Holiness and Communion: Vatican II on the Church*. It was sponsored by the Sacred Heart Seminary of the Archdiocese of Detroit.

scholastic theology showed the imprint of Aristotelianism. The theology of disclosure would reflect the concern with appearance that is central to modern philosophy.

The theology of disclosure tries to reflect on the way the things of our Christian faith come to light, how they are manifested to us. It tries to reflect on the appearance of Christian things. It does not, however, take these appearances to be merely subjective or psychological or even just historical. It attempts to get to essential structures of disclosure. It tries to examine the structures of appearance, for example, in regard to the sacraments, especially the Eucharist; in regard to the Church herself; in regard to the theological virtues of faith, hope, and charity, as well as prayer; and most fundamentally, in regard to the God revealed to us in Christian faith and teaching. It tries to show what is specific and distinctive about these and other Christian things and how they are disclosed to us. It tries to show how these things must appear if they are what the Church declares them to be.

By paying attention to appearances, and by stressing the fact that appearances are public and verifiable and not merely private and subjective, the theology of disclosure comes to terms with many of the problems that modern philosophy and culture have raised in regard to Christian faith. Everyone agrees that there is a tendency in modern culture to privatize Christian faith, even to sentimentalize it, to deprive it of any truth value. The theology of disclosure aims at countering this tendency and tries to reemphasize the publicity of Christian belief, to restore the conviction that a person could not be a Christian without publicly proclaiming the truth of that faith. As Francis Slade says, when discussing Jacques Maritain and Richard Rorty, "Christianity cannot live in the privacy of the heart. It is the religion of publicness. To cease to profess it publicly is 'to lose the Faith.' This is because Christianity is the religion of truth."[2] Truth is public, not private; Christianity reveals the truth of things and so it cannot be confined to merely internal, private sentiment. It also becomes incumbent on Christianity to show what kind of truth it deals with, and the theology of disclosure can help it to do so.

The value of the theology of disclosure is not exhausted, however, in its effort to counter the modern tendency to privatize or psychologize Chris-

2. Francis Slade, "Was Ist Aufklärung? Notes on Maritain, Rorty, and Bloom. With Thanks but No Apologies to Immanuel Kant," in *The Common Things: Essays on Thomism and Education,* edited by Daniel McInerny (Washington, D.C.: The American Maritain Association, 1999), p. 52.

tian faith; it has a further positive value in itself. It allows us to appreciate more deeply the things revealed to us in Christian faith. It complements, I believe, the more purely ontological style of scholastic theology, and it recovers some of the themes of patristic thought, which also spoke about the way Christian things come to light for us. Thus, the theology of disclosure comes to terms with modern problems, but it also contributes to the positive contemplation and understanding of Christian truths.

A simple and intuitive way of describing the theology of disclosure is to say that it tries to show how Christian things are distinguished from the natural things that provide their context. Most fundamentally, the theology of disclosure would attempt to show how the God revealed in Christian faith is to be distinguished from the divinities that pagan culture and thinking arrived at.[3] It would try to show how faith, hope, and charity are to be distinguished from the natural virtues of temperance, courage, justice, prudence, and friendship; it would show that they are a different kind of virtue. The theology of disclosure would try to show how the sacraments are to be distinguished from natural religious celebrations. Things are manifested when they are distinguished from things that are like them, from things that provide their context, and the theology of disclosure speaks about such distinction and manifestation in regard to what is revealed in Christian faith.[4]

The bishop as teacher

The documents of the Second Vatican Council frequently repeat the refrain that the office of the bishop involves three tasks: teaching, sanctifying, and governing.[5] *Lumen Gentium* devotes three distinct sections to this triad

---

3. I would like to observe that pagan attitudes and pagan "gods" are not merely a matter of ancient times; they return perennially, and they are no strangers to the modern scene. Two of the ways they appear now are to be found in New Age religion and in the aestheticism that often goes along with modern rationalism. It was quite astonishing to see the widespread criticism provoked by *Dominus Jesus,* the instruction of the Congregation for the Doctrine of the Faith; many people, both within and outside the Church, did not seem to realize the distinctiveness of the understanding of God and Redemption taught by the Church.

4. We might call the theology of disclosure a kind of "theology from below," because it begins with the natural human context and distinguishes Christian realities from it; however, it would not have the anthropological character so often associated with this phrase.

5. Citations from the texts of the Council will be taken from *The Documents of Vatican II,* edited by Walter M. Abbott, S.J., and Msgr. Joseph Gallagher (New York: Guild Press, 1966).

of teaching, sanctifying, and governing (§§25–27), and it goes on to say that priests also share in these tasks as they represent the bishop in the particular parishes of the diocese (§28; see also §32). The three functions are presented as the essential obligations bishops have in their role as shepherds; the document says, "With their helpers, the priests and deacons, bishops have therefore taken up the service of the community, presiding in the place of God over the flock whose shepherds they are, as teachers of doctrine, priests of sacred worship, and officers of good order" (§20).

Lumen Gentium also notes that these tasks and this authority are given to bishops as successors of the apostles, whose mission in turn reflected the mission of Christ himself from the Father: ". . . Jesus Christ, the eternal Shepherd, established His holy Church by sending forth the apostles as He Himself had been sent by the Father. He willed that their successors, namely the bishops, should be shepherds in His Church even to the consummation of the world" (§18). We should notice the sequence in this action of Christ. He did not first establish a Church and then appoint its leaders, nor did he simply allow the membership to elect their rulers; after living with his disciples and forming them, he sent the apostles as the ones responsible for shaping the Church from the beginning, under the guidance of the Holy Spirit. There was no Church until it was formed around the apostles; the Church is apostolic by definition. The apostles are not an afterthought to the Church but are constitutive of it, and the way they exercise their decisive role in the Church is through teaching, sanctifying, and governing. The central role of the bishops in the Church reflects the extraordinary prominence of the apostles in the four gospels and in the Acts of the Apostles.

The triplet of teaching, sanctifying, and governing is found throughout *Lumen Gentium*. It also appears in the *Decree on the Bishops' Pastoral Office in the Church,* where it is again related to the role of shepherd. The Council says, "They [the bishops] feed their sheep in the name of the Lord, and exercise in their regard the office of teaching, sanctifying, and governing" (§11). This triplet is classical, of course, and is based on the authority of Christ as prophet, priest, and king. The identity of the bishop is defined by his role of teaching, sanctifying, and governing.

Let us look more closely at these three tasks and the relationships among them. They are not a random collection of duties. There is an order to them, and each has its own kind of priority.[6] For example, the sanctification of the Church, which is expressed in the eucharistic liturgy, is primary in the sense of being the final cause, the activity in which the Church is most perfectly herself. The role of governance or shepherding is primary in the sense that it is the bishop, in union with the college of bishops and the pope, who is given the authority to make the critical decisions concerning the life of the Church, to determine how the Church will be ordered, in keeping with God's revealed word. I would, however, like to concentrate on the primacy of the role of teaching, of declaring the truth of God's revelation, which in its own way is fundamental to the other two functions. Apostolic teaching establishes the possibility of sanctifying and governing, and it gives these other two tasks their sense. Teaching is related to sanctifying and governing in a way analogous to the way the theological virtue of faith is related to hope and charity. Faith opens up the whole domain of Christian life; it opens the space in which hope and charity can occur. Likewise, apostolic teaching opens the possibility for Christian life and for the Church. It establishes the space in which sanctification and governance can take their place, and it makes clear what the sanctification and governance truly are. Apostolic teaching is fundamental for the manifestation of the other two tasks.

This teaching role in the Church is described in another document from the Second Vatican Council, *Dei Verbum,* the Dogmatic Constitution on Divine Revelation, which says that the original preaching of the apostles "was to be preserved by a continuous succession of preachers until the end of time" (§8). It says that "the apostles, handing on what they themselves had received, warn the faithful to hold fast to the tradition which they have learned either by word of mouth or by letter." The document goes on to say: "This teaching office is not above the word of God, but serves it, teaching only what has been handed on, listening to it devoutly, guarding it scrupulously, and explaining it faithfully by divine commission and with the help of the Holy Spirit . . ." (§11). This theme is, of course, a paraphrase of the great statement of St. Paul who, in writing to the Corinthians about the

---

6. In his comments on my paper, Fr. Earl Muller, S.J., brought out the reciprocal priorities of the three roles of the episcopal office and showed that my original draft did not adequately take them into account. I am grateful for his remarks and hope that the present draft is more satisfactory.

Eucharist, the central act of sanctification in the Church, begins by saying, "For I received from the Lord what I also handed on to you" (II Corinthians 11:23). Earlier in the same letter, when he addresses a number of problems in regard to the liturgy, he begins his exercise of governance by saying, "Be imitators of me, as I am of Christ. I praise you because you remember me in everything and hold fast to the traditions, just as I handed them on to you" (II Corinthians 11:1–2).

The deposit of faith is something we receive and assent to, not something we construct. It is not a work generated by our minds, not a theological opinion, not something we think out on our own, not a personal belief that some people have. It is the faith of the Church and it is entrusted to the bishops.[7] The most basic reason why the deposit of faith is not the product of our own intelligence is that it involves a revealed understanding of God, one that transcends human reason.

The duty to hand on the faith of the Church, which is ultimately the teaching of Christ, is the most fundamental task of the apostles and the bishops in the sense that it establishes the possibility of the other two. The office of teaching shows that sanctification is possible, and it also shows how and why the governance is authorized. The truth revealed by God has to be declared and preserved, and the Eucharist and sanctification of men are to be achieved, *and therefore* the apostles and bishops are invested with authority to provide for the good order of the Church. The apostles and bishops do not have their authority simply because the membership and the goods of

---

7. There is a passage in the *Commonitorium* of St. Vincent of Lérins that expresses very well the role of the bishop in handing on the faith. In a commentary on St. Paul's remarks to Timothy, in which Paul exhorts Timothy to preserve the deposit of faith, St. Vincent writes, "What is 'The deposit'? That which has been intrusted to you, not that which you have yourself devised: a matter not of wit, but of learning; not of private adoption, but of public tradition; a matter brought to you, not put forth by you, wherein you are bound to be not an author but a keeper, not a teacher but a disciple, not a leader but a follower. . . ." St. Vincent continues by exhorting the bishop to present the inherited truths in a fresh and beautiful way, but always to teach what has been received, not his own innovations: "[E]ngrave the precious gems of divine doctrine, fit them in accurately, adorn them skillfully, add splendor, grace, beauty. Let that which formerly was believed, though imperfectly apprehended, be clearly understood as expounded by you. Let posterity welcome, understood through your exposition, what antiquity venerated without understanding. Yet teach still the same truths which you have learned, so that though you speak after a new fashion, what you speak may not be new." This translation is taken from *A Select Library of Nicene and Post-Nicene Fathers of the Church*, Second Series, volume 11, St. Vincent of Lérins, *Commonitorium*, chapter 22. The translation has been slightly amended.

the Church have to be organized in some way or other, and someone has to be given the task of carrying out such organization. The Church is not a society that arises spontaneously in human affairs, and then quite naturally determines its own rulers. Rather, governance in the Church is based on a revealed truth. From a human point of view, it is based on an explanation or an argument.[8] The governing role of the bishop is defined by the teaching he hands on, and so the identity of the bishop rests primarily not on his governing role but on the fact that he is commissioned to receive the tradition of the Church, in her teaching and her liturgy, and to hand it on to the people entrusted to his care. Because he must hand on the truth and grace of Christ, he must also govern. Without the teaching, the legitimacy of his ruling is called into question.

For the sake of contrast and definition, let us try to imagine another idea of the role of the bishop, another "model," if you will, of the episcopal office. Suppose that the bishop were understood to be primarily a mediator among various groups in the Church; his task would be to bring about a consensus among them, to allow them to live together and thus preserve the unity of the Church. Among the members of the Church, there are different and often differing groups. All such groups in their diversity claim to be Catholic, and it would be the role of the "overseer" to keep them all in the fold, to mediate among them and let charity prevail. Such an image of the bishop would take his governing role as primary, but it would leave him without any compass, and as a sheer mediator he would be purely formal, without any definition, without any identity. The only thing that could save him from this sort of deconstruction is a return to the tradition that he inherits and is commissioned to hand on; unity in the Church is based on the truths of Christ, not on social consensus. That tradition, as the truth of Christian teaching and liturgy, defines the bishop as well as the Church. It authorizes and also guides him in his role of governing. In other words, all the decisions that the bishop has to make are to be made in the light of the truth that he teaches, not simply on his own practical judgment.

8. It would be interesting to examine whether the modern state was conceived in imitation of the Church as a society. Premodern political societies were understood to be natural human developments that did not require a theoretical justification, but the modern state is the result of philosophical argument. It is brought into being and justified by words and arguments, not by gradual social agglomeration. Hobbes is the first large-scale theoretician of the modern state and Machiavelli is the one who discovered it.

What kind of teaching?

Let us examine the teaching that is so central to the identity of the bishop. When we use the word *teaching,* we tend to think it signifies an academic activity. The kind of teaching demanded of the bishop, however, is based on the prophetic role of Christ, who is prophet, priest, and king. The teaching in question is not scholarly or academic, but the handing on of the inherited teaching of the Church, displaying the faith of the Church. The bishop, in his formal identity as such, no longer has the right to his personal opinions; he is authorized and commissioned to represent what the Church believes.

This teaching does not occur only in what the bishop alone says and does; it also implies, obviously, that the bishop will see to it that his priests are formed in the true faith during their seminary education, and that the preaching and catechetical instruction in his diocese is orthodox. He is the teacher of teachers in his diocese. The bishop should remind his priests, deacons, and catechists of the importance of Catholic doctrine in the life of the Church. Orthodox teaching is not something to be trifled with; everything is thrown into turmoil when it is neglected. The exercise of the teaching office also means that the bishop will ensure that the liturgy will be properly performed, since the liturgy serves not only to sanctify the people but also to educate them in the faith. How could one convey a sense of what the Eucharist really is, how could one teach the truth of the Eucharist, if the liturgy were to be celebrated in an inappropriate and unworthy manner, one that makes it seem to be something other than it is? How can the Church convey a sense of God's power, majesty, and love if the tone conveyed by the liturgy is more that of a social gathering than a prayer and sacrifice offered to God? Episcopal supervision—which, incidentally, is a redundant term—is especially centered on the teaching and the liturgy that are carried on in the diocese. Who will ensure the authenticity of teaching and liturgy if the bishop does not do so?

The core of what is to be taught is simply the Church's credo, her profession of faith: that the world we live in is not all that there is, that it is not ultimate, but has been created by God who is so perfect and good that he created it out of sheer generosity and abundance, not out of any need to create; that God lives a triune life, of Father, Son, and Holy Spirit; that this God, in the person of the Son, was born a man of the Virgin Mary and suffered and died to redeem us, then rose from the dead and now lives with the Father and is present in his Church until he comes in judgment; that he brought us forgiveness of sin and shares his resurrection and life with us; that God knows and loves each of us, and has called us, each and all, to eternal life with him; that our lives are led under God's providence. There are many other things in the Catholic tradition, of course, but these are the core, the creed, the epitome of the gospel, and these truths are as fresh and new and illuminating now as they ever were. They are truths about God and about ourselves that God himself has revealed to us in Christ. The world looks different to us, and we look different to ourselves, when these truths are received. The teaching role of the bishop is to hand on this understanding, just as the first apostles did. All the other truths and practices in our Catholic faith take on their meaning by their relationship to these fundamental articles of faith.

I would like to take a moment to stress the importance of the creed as an element in the teaching of the Church. We are all well aware of the significance of the Scriptures and the consequent value of biblical studies. The Church has highlighted the reading of Scripture in the Liturgy of the Word, and she has taught that homilies should be based on the biblical passages that have been read. But it is still true that the creed is recited, or prayed, just after the homily (appropriately enough, to put things back in perspective). The creed marks the transition between the Liturgy of the Word and the Liturgy of the Eucharist. In the liturgy and in the Christian life, the creed makes present the mind of the Church, expressing the tradition along with the Scriptures. The creed is the recapitulation of the gospels. There are creeds within the New Testament, as in the first chapter of the Letter to the Colossians, where St. Paul brings the community back to the essentials of Christian revelation.[9] When the creed is neglected and all the focus is on the Scriptures, the danger arises that the study of Scripture will be reduced to being a merely historical science.

9. I am grateful to Brother Owen Sadlier, O.S.F., for some of these ideas about the creed. I might also add an anecdote about this matter. In a recent conversation, I expressed some thoughts about the importance of the creed in the liturgy, and someone recalled being with a community that omitted the creed from the Mass. When this person asked why they did so, they replied that for them the creed was "divisive." The importance of the creed has recently been underlined by Luke Timothy Johnson in his book *The Creed: What Christians Believe and Why It Matters* (New York: Doubleday, 2003).

It is absolutely essential to the episcopal teaching office that the articles of faith expressed in the creed not be lost from view. They are so basic that we often take them for granted and may not talk enough about them, but we need constantly to be reminded of them. Basic truths like these need to be repeated over and over again, "in season, out of season" (II Timothy 4:2). It makes a great difference if they become a deep part of a person's life and the life of a community, but they can be lost, and when they are, people will not see how the Church is different from any other religious organization, or why we should make a distinction between Jesus Christ and other profound figures in human history. I think that if the bishop of a diocese brings these truths to mind in an effective way and stresses their importance, the clergy and catechists will do so as well.

I would like to say a few words about what kind of truths these are and how they come to light for us, how they can be taught. They are not just items of information; they make a difference when they are registered for us. We might illustrate this by drawing an analogy. Suppose a young man has been brought up in circumstances in which the people involved in his life were selfish and abusive. He has developed in the same way. At some point, someone speaks to him about human friendship: what it is, how it is exercised, how it is a moral perfection of human beings, a great human good. The words may be only words for him; they don't really register anything. He does not see friendship or benevolence as a human possibility. But then suppose circumstances change, perhaps some people act differently toward him, or perhaps through his own intelligence he begins to see the possibility of friendship. Suppose this truth of human nature registers for him, perhaps gradually, perhaps suddenly. This event is not merely the truth of correctness; the man does not merely find out that certain claims made by others are indeed true. Rather, what occurs is the truth of disclosure. The reality, the truth of friendship itself becomes manifest to him. Friendship becomes distinguished for him. It is not a matter of merely matching a judgment to a fact but a matter of letting something portentous come to light. Something becomes revealed or distinguished.[10]

---

10. A valuable contribution of phenomenology is the distinction between the truth of correctness (in which we simply match a judgment to a fact) and the truth of disclosure, in which something originally comes to light. See Edmund Husserl, *Formal and Transcendental Logic,* translated by Dorion Cairns (The Hague: Nijhoff, 1969), §46.

This is the kind of truth we deal with when we come to realize, whether gradually or suddenly, that our lives are led under God's providence, that we and the world we live in have been created by an infinitely merciful God, who took on the burden of human life and redeemed us, who showed his power over death, and who calls us to eternal life. This is not just information that is confirmed but truth that is disclosed, and it makes all the difference to us. The teaching role of the bishop is to keep that truth alive in the local Church given to his care, and to ensure that his priests, deacons, and catechists strive to do so as well. The Church, especially the apostolic part of the Church, must make this truth available so that people can respond to it. Clearly, to convey such truth engages not only words but also a way of living that bears witness to this truth; but it *does* involve words as well, along with the understanding that the words convey. Words are necessary to explain why we live as we do when we strive to live as followers of Christ. To convey such truths is already to work for the sanctification of people, and it justifies the governing authority of the bishop. Canon law, with its rights and duties, flows from this teaching office.

Teaching about nature as well as about grace

We have been discussing the way in which the bishop is the primary teacher, the apostolic teacher, of the things revealed in our faith. God's grace, however, is not only *elevans* but also *sanans:* his grace enables us to participate in his divine life, but it also heals our human nature. The teaching of Christ and the teaching of the Church shed light on what we are in our natural way of being. Thus, the encyclical *Fides et Ratio* declares that the mission of the Church in the modern world is not only to proclaim the faith, but also "to restore faith in reason,"[11] to show people that their own rational powers are capable of attaining truth about the world, about themselves, and even about God. It should be noted that this encyclical was addressed primarily to the bishops of the Catholic Church; the Holy Father seemed to be inviting them to look more closely at this aspect of their teaching office.

This exhortation does not mean, of course, that the bishops have to

---

11. The phrase "restoring faith in reason" has been used to describe a project undertaken in England in response to the encyclical *Fides et Ratio.* The first volume of studies in this project is *Restoring Faith in Reason,* edited by Laurence Paul Hemming and Susan Parsons (London: SCM Press, and Notre Dame: University of Notre Dame Press, 2002).

become professional philosophers or scientists, but it does mean that they should help people not only to accept God's revealed word but also to discover or rediscover their own natural dignity, the truth about their own nature and the nature of the world in which they live. Such a recovery of true human nature is part of the Christian gospel. Grace builds on nature, and if nature is left in need of repair, it is difficult for grace to build on it. Consider, for example, the truth about human sexuality and the family. The Church must present not only its revealed message, say, about the sacrament of marriage, but must also clarify the nature of sexuality, its *telos*, how it finds its perfection and its excellence as a human good. Human sexuality does not disclose itself in what people call "sex," but in a network of human relationships, between husband and wife and parents and children. That is where its truth is manifested, where we see what it really is.[12] The nature and the good of sexuality must be brought to light. Only in reference to this nature and this good can the distortions and sinful uses of sexuality be defined; only in reference to the good do the prohibitions and commandments make sense. If the good is first clarified, it becomes more obvious why the aberrations are wrong and sinful. Prohibitions against an evil should always be correlated with exhortations toward the good. In this instance, how could the Church's teaching on sexual matters be presented without bringing out the natural definition of sexuality? And the natural meaning of sexuality is certainly not commonly understood in our culture; think of the way it is presented by popular music, television, and movies, in which the distinction between love and lust is almost never made. Nature itself needs to be restored.

There are many other natural truths that need to be revived if grace is to be built on them. Human friendship, social relations, the common good, political life, war and peace, human labor, human action and human responsibility, the natural virtues, even the sense of the world as having meaning and of living things as having their own integrity. Human reason itself needs to be put back into perspective. It is not just the theological and the supernatural that needs to be proclaimed, but the natural as well. And once again, as in the case of the truths of Creation and Redemption, it is liberating for a person to have such natural truths registered for him when they

---

12. Sexual hedonists are often presented as being "realistic" about human desire, but in fact they live in delusion.

had been previously concealed. A person who had confused sexuality with lust is given greater human freedom when he discovers that there are forms of sexuality that are not equivalent to lust. Nature itself is healed by the gospel, and one of the ways in which the truth of the gospel is made evident to people is found in the way the gospel restores nature to what it ought to be. Such a recovery of natural goods can play an important part in Christian apologetics.

A beautiful doctrinal illustration of the way grace confirms nature can be found in the dogma of the Immaculate Conception, in which Mary's humanity is preserved as what humanity should be. In the Blessed Virgin we have, not wounded nature healed, but, to use a phrase of Francis Slade, innocence elevated by grace.[13] In revelation and grace the natural comes forth in its proper integrity; they allow us to see the real character of nature.

Problems related to the teaching role of the bishop

In this final part of my paper, I will mention a few ways in which the teaching office of the bishop might be undermined.

First, the bishop might think that so many intellectual problems have arisen in regard to Catholic faith in the academic and scholarly world that he, the bishop, is no longer sufficiently equipped to hand on the faith. He may be intimidated in the exercise of his office. The issues have become too complex; we now have to defer to experts in theology, Scripture studies, catechetics, perhaps even psychology and history; such people would be better able to master the state of the question and determine the true content of faith. This alienation of the bishop's teaching authority, the devolution from the bishop to the scholar, is a legacy of the Enlightenment. It follows from the understanding of reason that was introduced by thinkers such as Machiavelli and Descartes some five hundred years ago, in which not prudence and tradition but scientific method is taken to be the proper avenue to truth. It is interesting to note that Spinoza, who wrote in the immediate wake of Descartes, emphasized the historical relativism of the Scriptures and implied thereby that the true custodians of the Scriptures were the historians and

13. I am grateful to Francis Slade for these observations about the Immaculate Conception, and for many other remarks that I have used in this paper.

philologists and not the Church.[14] But the kind of truth that is taught by the bishop is not the kind that academicians and scholars are primarily responsible for. The Church's profession of faith is determined not by scholars but by the Church, primarily by the apostles and their successors, and ultimately by Christ.

Some churchmen may feel a sense of inferiority before the academy. Indeed, anyone would be awestruck by the spectacular success of science, technology, and medicine. Their methods seem almost to guarantee truth and to move us unstoppably toward more and more discovery. How can anyone compete with this? How feeble it may seem, in contrast, to simply repeat something inherited from the past. But still, science, technology, and medicine are human achievements, and to be expert in them does not guarantee that one will use them well; another kind of truth is required for that, one based on a knowledge of both nature and human nature, and it is this kind of truth that Christian faith addresses, in the realms of both nature and grace. Furthermore, the humanities and social sciences, which deal more directly with human goods, have not enjoyed the same unquestionable success as the hard sciences; in fact, it is not unreasonable to say that they are in a particularly confused state right now, so much so that the academy would be one of the last places one would look to for guidance on important human questions. I should also add that there is a very strong bias against Christianity in the Western intellectual and academic world, even within Catholic institutions, and the Church should not be naive about this hostility. This world has practically declared war on Christianity and it specifically attacks its claims to truth, and as we move into the domain of human biological and social engineering the conflict will probably get worse.[15]

14. Baruch Spinoza, *Theological-Political Treatise,* chapters 7–10, discusses the authorship of the books of the Old Testament.

15. Kenneth Minogue has described the sharp conflict between modern rationalism and Christianity: "At both the popular and the elite levels, American secularists are becoming increasingly hostile to Christian believers. The same is true in Europe, where such hostility is even more puzzling because there is a strong feeling among European rationalists that they have already 'won the argument.'" "Religion, Reason, and Conflict in the 21st Century," *The National Interest* (Summer 2003): 131. He says that "Western secularism," which is "entrenched in the universities," takes pains "to assail Christianity . . . with everything from rational argument to satirical mockery" (p. 128). He observes that secular thinkers do not show the same hostility toward other religions, because they see them as expressions of culture, while Christianity makes claims to truth that compete with modern rationalism. This article by Minogue is a review of Phillip Jenkins, *The Next Christendom: The Coming of Global Christianity* (New York: Oxford University Press, 2002).

The bishop should have confidence that the faith of the Church bears witness to itself if it is persistently and confidently proclaimed. Certainly the teacher of the faith and the members of the Church must testify to the gospel by their own way of living, but Christian truths also bear witness to themselves; in themselves they shed light on human existence and on the nature of things, to anyone who is willing to come into this light. There is no reason for the Church or the bishops to be intimidated by academic experts. What Christ has taught us about our destiny as human beings does not need to yield to the pictures presented by our intellectual elites.

I should also add that the bishop does not need to be a great writer or a television star to fulfill his teaching role, nor does he have to address crowds of thousands. It is a matter of persistent and consistent restatement of basic truths. The apostles, after all, spoke to small groups. St. Thomas Aquinas says that direct oral teaching is superior to written because it imprints the teaching on the hearts of the hearers.[16]

Secondly, the bishop's teaching role may be given over to the various committees and offices within the diocese or within national Church conferences. The bishop may think it necessary to defer to their expertise, much as he might be inclined to trust the judgment of scholars over his own. He may defer to the bureaucracy. Of course, councils, committees, and offices may be very helpful to the bishop and even necessary, but they do not take the place of the apostles, and they too must be subordinated to the essentials of the Church's faith. We can't really imagine a committee making a report at the Areopagus, and it was the apostles and Peter who spoke at Pentecost, not their staffs. The bishops run the risk of losing control over their institutions, especially their educational institutions, if they trust the experts more than their own judgment.[17]

The third and final challenge to the identity of the bishop that I wish to mention is more in the realm of ideas. It is the substitution of a religion of humanity for the Christian faith. We often think of Marxism or scientism as the main challenges to Christian thought, but I would claim that the greatest popular influence on our contemporary Western culture has been exercised by John Stuart Mill and Auguste Comte, both of whom lived in the

16. St. Thomas Aquinas, *Summa Theologiae* III, q. 42, a. 4.
17. On Catholic colleges and universities and their task of handing on the faith, see Robert Sokolowski, "Church Tradition and the Catholic University," below, chapter 18.

middle of the nineteenth century, and both of whom thought that Christianity had outlived its time and should be replaced by a religion of humanity. They respected Christianity and wanted to accept its teaching of charity, of benevolence and peace, but they also thought that such benevolence should be based on a love of mankind, not on doctrines about God and not on the hope for eternal life. As Nietzsche said about them, they wanted to "outchristian Christianity" by demanding that we sacrifice everything for others, for humanity at large, and that we do so without any hope of salvation for ourselves, that is, that we should do so with no self-interest whatever. They call for charity without hope for redemption. In Nietzsche's words, "The more one liberated oneself from the dogmas, the more one sought as it were a *justification* of this liberation in a cult of philanthropy: not to fall short of the Christian ideal in this, but where possible to outdo it, was a secret spur with all French thinkers from Voltaire up to Auguste Comte: and the latter did in fact, with his moral formula *vivre pour autrui,* outchristian Christianity."[18] Nietzsche clearly shows that it is specifically the truth of Christianity, the dogmas, that the religion of humanity wishes to deny, and that it does so while claiming to possess an even more noble sense of Christian charity. This point is often shown in a practical way: our secular culture will often accept and even praise the Church to the extent that she is serving the religion of humanity, but it will become hostile to the Church when she publicly presents her own teaching, her own faith.[19]

But Christian charity is not just an amplified human benevolence. Christian charity is based entirely on the belief in God as the supremely charitable Creator and Redeemer, the one whose trinitarian life is even more intensely generous than are his actions of Creation and Redemption. It is because God is the way he is, it is because of the way God has revealed himself to

18. Friedrich Nietzsche, *Daybreak,* translated by R. J. Hollingdale (New York: Cambridge University Press, 1982), §132, p. 82.

19. It is true that the Christian message involves, as an immediate inference, concern for the poor; St. Paul in the Letter to the Galatians describes the Council of Jerusalem and says that he and Barnabas were commissioned to preach to the Gentiles, with the following provision: "Only, we were to be mindful of the poor, which is the very thing I was eager to do" (Galatians 2:10). Concern for the poor follows from the Christian message. In the modern alternative, concern for the poor becomes primary and the message is seen as an ideological contribution. But when this reversal occurs, the concern for the poor becomes more like a partisan political exercise of what Aristotle called democracy, or else an implementation of the modern state.

us, that we are called to Christian charity. You cannot have the theological virtues without the theological truths. We hope for eternal life not because of some striving we experience in ourselves, but because we have been told that God is life, and this life is the light for men, and this light has shone in the darkness. To the Christian, the world looks the way it does, and the human person looks the way he does, because God is the way he is. Christ has revealed this to us, and the Church, through the apostles, hands on this understanding and this living presence of God; she makes it known to all men and confirms it in those who already believe. The identity of the bishop is determined by the mission given him by Christ in the Holy Spirit, to teach these truths about the Father, and to sanctify and govern the Church that is built upon them.

I would like to close with a more general comment on the Second Vatican Council. It may seem trivial to say this, but I think it needs to be said: The Second Vatican Council was not the only ecumenical council in the history of Church. Regrettably, what became known as "the spirit of Vatican II" gave the impression that this council somehow negated all the others, or at least that it was different from all the others and provided a unique interpretation on all the rest. If I may use a metaphor from football, the impression was given that the tradition of the Church was not a continuous handing on, through the centuries, of something received; it was more like a long pass from the apostolic age to the Second Vatican Council, with only distortions in between, whether Byzantine, medieval, or baroque. But in fact, the Second Vatican Council is only one council among many, and all the others—including the First Vatican Council and the Council of Trent—as well as the tradition of the Church retain their force and importance. I think the sudden and radical change in the liturgy of the Western Church contributed to this popular idea of the uniqueness of the Second Vatican Council. One of the greatest challenges to the Church is to reestablish the continuity between the present Church and the Church throughout the centuries, to revalidate the tradition of the Church. This is a challenge for all the educational institutions in the Church, from elementary catechetics to colleges to seminaries to universities and research centers, but it is a challenge for the bishops most of all, since they are entrusted with preserving the definition of the Church. Indeed, as Kevin White once put it, it may be necessary for the entire papacy of some future pope to be devoted to a single goal: the comprehensive restoration of tradition and especially the liturgy, to make it obvious that the changes in the liturgy and in theology begun in the 1960s were not the radical break they are so often taken to be. Without episcopal teaching in continuity with the apostles and with Christ, there is no sanctification and government, and there can be no Catholic Church.

THE REVELATION
OF THE HOLY TRINITY
A Study in Personal Pronouns

In this essay, I wish to use the theology of disclosure to reflect on the mystery of the Holy Trinity. The theology of disclosure is a form of theological thinking that makes use of phenomenology. It may seem strange to invoke phenomenology to speak about the Trinity, because this mystery is certainly beyond any human perception and experience; in what way can the Holy Trinity be a "phenomenon" for us? We cannot have a phenomenology of the Trinity in the way we might have a phenomenology of artworks, or political things, or even religion. But although we may not have a natural perception of the Triune God, his being was revealed to us and we are directed toward the Trinity in our prayers and expressions of belief. It is not inappropriate, therefore, to reflect on how the Holy Trinity was and is manifested to us.

Some comments on method

To bring out what a theology of disclosure can do in this regard, let us contrast it with what St. Thomas Aquinas does in his theology of the Holy Trinity. Aquinas discusses this mystery in the First Part of the *Summa Theologiae,* questions 27 to 43. He presents what we could call the metaphysics or the ontology of the Holy Trinity, using terms such as *person, nature, relation, essence, property,* and *subsistence.* Thomas describes the mode of being of the One God and the Three Divine Persons. He shows, for example, how the persons of the Trinity are established by the relations of paternity, filiation, spiration, and procession. This kind of reflection is typical of scholastic theology, which aims to define the substance of things and determine their principles and causes.

The theology of disclosure carries out a different kind of reflection. It tries to show how this mystery was and is manifested to us. In contrast with scholastic theology, which tries to discuss the being of the Trinity "in itself," the theology of disclosure would reflect on the being of the Trinity both "in itself" and "for us." It tries to show how the "in itselfness" of this truth is given to our faith and our thoughtful acceptance.

Now, one way of showing how the Holy Trinity has been revealed to us would be to trace the history of its manifestation: to show the Old Testament background and anticipations of this doctrine, to show how the four gospels, the Acts of the Apostles, the New Testament epistles, and the Apocalypse speak of the Father, Son, and Holy Spirit, and to show how Church teaching, theological reflection, religious controversies, and conciliar decisions contributed to the mystery and the understanding we have of it.[1] This sort of thinking would be biblical and historical theology; it is often called "positive" theology in contrast with the "speculative" theology of the scholastics. The theology of disclosure, phenomenological theology, is different from such historical theology. It would, of course, accept the findings of

1. There have been many recent studies concerning the Holy Trinity, building on the "classical" twentieth-century work of writers like Barth, von Balthasar, Rahner, and Lonergan. Some recent books, listed chronologically, are Jürgen Moltmann, *The Trinity and the Kingdom* (New York: Harper and Row, 1981); William Hill, O.P., *The Three-Personed God* (Washington, D.C.: The Catholic University of America Press, 1982); David Brown, *The Divine Trinity* (La Salle, IL: Open Court, 1985); Thomas F. Torrance, *The Trinitarian Faith: The Evangelical Theology of the Ancient Catholic Church* (Edinburgh: T&T Clark, 1988); John J. O'Donnell, *The Mystery of the Triune God* (New York: Paulist Press, 1989); Thomas F. Torrance, *Trinitarian Perspectives* (Edinburgh: T&T Clark, 1994); Thomas F. Torrance, *The Christian Doctrine of God: One Being Three Persons* (Edinburgh: T&T Clark, 1996); Alan J. Torrance, *Persons in Communion: An Essay on Trinitarian Description and Human Participation, with Special Reference to Volume One of Karl Barth's "Church Dogmatics"* (Edinburgh: T&T Clark, 1996); Colin E. Gunton, *The Promise of Trinitarian Theology* (Edinburgh: T&T Clark, 1997); Robert W. Jenson, *Systematic Theology*, Volume I: *The Triune God* (New York: Oxford University Press, 1997); David S. Cunningham, *These Three Are One: The Practice of Trinitarian Theology* (Malden, MA: Blackwell, 1998); Stephen T. Davis, Daniel Kendall, S.J., and Gerald O'Collins, S.J., eds., *The Trinity: An Interdisciplinary Symposium on the Trinity* (New York: Oxford University Press, 1999); David Coffey, *Deus Trinitas: The Doctrine of the Triune God* (New York: Oxford University Press, 1999); Bruce Marshall, *Trinity and Truth* (Cambridge: Cambridge University Press, 2000).

both the history of revelation and the scholastic exposition, but it would also provide something else. It would try to show what is distinctive and essential in this manifestation, what is special about it. The Divine Nature, because of what it is, appears to us in a manner different from the way the world and things in it appear, and the theology of disclosure would try to reflect on this appearance. It would try to reflect on the truth of the Holy Trinity, on its manifestation.

Thus, the theology of disclosure would differ from scholastic theology in focusing on how the Christian mystery comes to light and not on its definition, and it would differ from historical theology by focusing on structural necessities and not primarily on matters of fact.

Instead of talking further *about* this theology, let us move directly *into* it. I will try to get immediately to the heart of the matter by turning to a particular contribution the theology of disclosure can make. I will try to show what it can do, and I hope that this illustration will convey a sense of what kind of theology it is.

How Christ spoke of himself

The revelation of the Holy Trinity took place first and foremost in the words and actions of Jesus Christ. To reveal this mystery, Christ used human language. This language allowed him to use the word *I*. By using this word and its variants, Christ was able to express himself as the speaker responsible for what he was saying. A responsible speaker, someone who can say "I," is a person. Because Christ spoke the way a person speaks, he was able to reveal the Trinity to us; he was able to express himself as someone distinguished from the Father and yet intimately related to him; he was able to express himself as a person different from the Father. The first-person singular of Christ's speech is not a mere grammatical feature of the language he spoke, but an essential element in his revelation of the Holy Trinity. The first-person singular must be noted in the theology of disclosure.

Scholastic theology accepts the definition of a person that was formulated by Boethius. In that tradition, a person is defined as an individual substance of a rational nature. Persons are individuals who possess reason. What makes them persons is their rationality; they are rational agents. The rationality of persons is shown not only by their ability to think universal truths, but also by their ability to articulate things through their speech, and their ability to declare themselves as the ones responsible for the thinking, speaking, and acting that they carry out.

Rational agents disclose the truth of things; they can reveal the way things are. In doing so, however, precisely in revealing the way things are, they also disclose themselves as the ones who hold the opinions or manifest the things they express. They disclose themselves as agents of rationality, agents of truth. Persons cannot manifest the truth of things without also manifesting themselves as such, as agents of truth.

Every language provides many ways for a speaker, an individual substance of a rational nature, to manifest himself within and behind the speeches and disclosures that he carries out. The language may have particular nouns or pronouns to express the first person, or it may have special forms of verbs, or it may have certain placements of words. A person is someone who can make use of these resources of language; he can say "I," "me," and "mine" in the special manner that expresses a rational agent. The fact that languages have first-person expressions is due not just to the accidents of linguistic evolution, but more fundamentally to the nature of the being that uses language and the power of disclosure with which that being is endowed. There is pressure on the language to develop a first-person singular because a person is speaking the words of the language.

Jesus asserts many things about the Father. He also asserts many things about himself in relation to the Father. However, the mere fact that he is speaking, the mere fact that he is acting as a person and that he can say "I," shows that he is differentiated from the Father, that he is another person than the Father, even while being one with him. The fact that Christ said *I* showed that in God there is another person besides the Father, another rational agent, someone who is "with" God and who is God from the beginning. The Holy Trinity was revealed in the very fact that Christ spoke and used the term *I* to express himself in his personality, in his Sonship. Christ is a human being but a divine person, and this personality is expressed in his use of the first-person singular.

Another way of making this point is to say that the Holy Trinity could not have been revealed in the third person. It could not have been revealed, say, through a prophet who spoke about the Trinity "from without." The Holy Trinity could only have been revealed "from within," by a speaker who indicates the differentiations within the Trinity not only by what he says but also by his very act of speaking. God could and did use Moses and the prophets to reveal himself in the Old Testament, because there he was revealed in his relationship to the world and to his people, but he could not have used Moses or the prophets to reveal his own internal life. If a prophet were to have spoken about the trinitarian life, it would be hard to know whether his words ought to be taken literally or metaphorically; no such obscurity occurs when the speaker himself has come from that life and speaks about it. God had to accomplish this revelation by himself, in his own voice, through a speaker who was part of the divine life and not someone chosen to speak about it. The Incarnation is an essential part of the disclosure of the Holy Trinity. When Jesus spoke and acted the Holy Trinity was being revealed to the world. As Thomas F. Torrance writes, "In sharp contrast with every other religion, Christianity stands for the fact that in Jesus Christ God has communicated to us his *Word* and has imparted to us his *Spirit,* so that we may really know him as he is in himself, although not apart from his saving activity in history. . . ."[2]

We will explore all these claims at greater length, and will supply the many additions and qualifications that they call for. My major initial point is to claim that the Holy Trinity was manifested to us, and had to be manifested to us, by a speaker who could say *I* while expressing both the mystery itself and himself as part of that mystery. I hope that it is already clear that this sort of observation is different from the findings one comes to in biblical and historical studies. It is more speculative, but it is speculative in a different way from scholastic theology, because it deals with structural elements of manifestation, with the things that belong essentially to disclosure, and not with the definition of what is disclosed.

Declarative and informational uses of the first person pronoun

We must spell out more carefully the way in which a speaker makes use of the word *I* to express his personhood. There are two ways in which the pronoun *I* can be used. First, it can be used in what I would like to call an *informational* way. We can use the word like any other noun or pronoun, simply to identify and say something about ourselves. For example, suppose we are

2. Torrance, *The Christian Doctrine of God,* p. 3.

in a room with several people and someone asks who is over fifty years old, and I reply, "I am over fifty." In this statement I use the word as an ordinary noun just to pick out and describe myself. I do not specifically express my personality by this use of the word *I*. Instead, in my speech, I treat myself as an ordinary object of discourse and describe some feature that I have. The same sort of usage would occur if I were to say, "I am six feet tall," "I am tired," "I am wearing a new suit," or "I arrived here yesterday."

Secondly, however, the word *I* can be used in what I would like to call a *declarative* manner. Suppose I say, "I trust you," or "I promise that I will come back tomorrow," or "I know that Napoleon was born in Corsica," or "I must protect my children." These remarks are not just reports about myself, as were the informational remarks we examined a moment ago. When I say, "I trust you," I am not just stating a fact about myself; I am not treating myself as an object and predicating something about myself. Rather, I am making a commitment and I am expressing myself as doing so. I declare myself as acting rationally. This use of the word *I* expresses the speaker as a person, a rational agent. Moreover, it expresses the rational agent as actually exercising his rationality at the moment he uses the word. This use of the term *I* reveals the person of the speaker in its actual exercise, in its being-at-work as a person.

A person, a rational individual, does not do things the way a nonhuman animal does them. In St. Thomas's phrase, a person does not just act but also has dominion over his acts.[3] This means that a person does not simply behave in one way or another; when he acts, he can also explain why he did what he did, and he can evaluate his actions—as well as the reasons behind them—and say whether or not they were the effective and the proper thing to do.[4] He exercises mastery over his actions, and therefore can be held re-

3. That a rational being has "dominion over its action" is a frequent refrain in Aquinas. In *Summa Theologiae* I, q. 29, a. 1, it is related to the concept of person.

4. Alasdair MacIntyre makes use of Aquinas in showing how the practical intentions of human beings differ from those of animals; see *Dependent Rational Animals* (Chicago: Open Court, 1999). He admits that higher animals have both beliefs and intentions, but shows that they cannot evaluate and reconsider them, as human beings can: "... without language an animal cannot evaluate that which moves it into action" (p. 53). He says, "[Human infants] go beyond the reasoning characteristics of dolphins when they become able to reflect on and pass judgment on the reasons by which they have hitherto been guided" (p. 57). Finally, "... the child moves beyond its initial animal state of *having reasons for acting in this way rather than that* towards its specifically human state of *being able to evaluate those reasons, to revise them or to abandon them and replace them with others*" (p.

sponsible for them in a way that a nonhuman animal cannot. A person is a being that can dispose of his acts, and the declarative use of *I* expresses not just this ability, but its actual exercise.

It is true that there are many limitations on our personal responsibility; there are unconscious and social pressures, ignorance, confusion, and immaturity, but there remains withal a nucleus of rational responsibility, which can be present to a greater or lesser extent. This responsibility, which lurks in some degree within every human discourse, is reflected in the declarative use of the term *I* or whatever other sign-design is used for this purpose in the language the person is speaking.[5] Such a declarative use of the pronoun *I* engages and expresses the person who is using the language.

I have used the term "an agent of truth" to say what a person is. This phrase has a double meaning, and both senses are relevant to the issue at hand. A person is an agent of truth because he is able to achieve truth, to bring it about, in the way that an agent of change is able to bring about some mutation in things. But a person is also an agent of truth in the sense that his actions are carried out on the basis of truth. His agency, his way of acting, is based on truth. What he does is done because he can discover what things are. He can find out the truth of things and act accordingly. He can also fail to do so; he can act in error, illusion, deception, confusion, or irresponsibility. In either case, whether he succeeds or fails, truth is an issue when he acts. A person is an agent of truth in both knowledge and conduct, and his declarative use of the term *I* expresses his engagement in truth. To act as an agent of truth is to act specifically as an individual substance of a rational nature, and to use the term *I* in a declarative way is to express oneself as acting in that fashion.

The declarative use of the word *I* thus expresses our personhood, our rational agency, in its active exercise. It expresses us as exercising dominion over our actions and our thoughts, as engaging our responsibility in them. It expresses not primarily our human nature but our person.

91, italics original). We might add that only a being that has such a reflective distance to its own intentions and understandings can use the term *I* in a declarative manner.

5. The phrase "sign-design" is used by Thomas Prufer as a synonym for linguistic tokens. See his "Quotation and Writing, Egos and Tokenings, Variables and Gaps," in *Recapitulations* (Washington, D.C.: The Catholic University of America Press, 1993), pp. 59–60.

Christ addresses the Father

Let us turn to the gospels. The relation between Christ and the Father is most vividly expressed in those passages in which Jesus directly addresses the Father and thereby formulates the difference between "I" and "you," between himself and the Father. Such passages are surprisingly few in number. In St. John's gospel there are three: Christ's prayer to the Father at the close of the Last Supper discourses (chapter 17), the prayer of thanks he made before raising Lazarus from the dead ("Father, I thank you for hearing me. I know that you always hear me; but because of the crowd here I have said this, that they may believe that you sent me" [John 11:41–42]), and the brief prayer, "Father, glorify your name," which he uttered after his entry into Jerusalem[6] (John 12:28). In the Synoptics there are five places in which Christ addresses the Father, and no single gospel has all five. First, there is the passage in which Jesus says, "I give praise to you, Father, Lord of heaven and earth, for although you have hidden these things from the wise and the learned you have revealed them to the childlike. Yes, Father, such has been your gracious will" (Matthew 11:25–26; see Luke 10:21). All the rest of the passages deal with the passion. Thus, the second is the prayer in the Garden of Gethsemane (Matthew 26:39–44, Mark 14:36–39, Luke 22:42). The third is the cry on the cross, the citation from Psalm 22, found in Matthew (27:46) and Mark (15:34), in which Christ addresses not the Father but God. Fourth and fifth are the words from the cross as recorded by Luke, "Father, forgive them, they know not what they do" (23:34) and "Father, into your hands I commend my spirit" (23:46).

In these passages Jesus obviously uses the term *I* and its variants in the declarative sense, as when he says, "I give praise to you, Father." He is not merely reporting about his relationship to the Father but engaging himself in that relationship. Furthermore, Christ also uses the term *I* and its variants declaratively in the many passages in which he speaks not *to* the Father but *about* his relationship to him. Examples of such usage are found in the statements, "I did not speak on my own, but the Father who sent me commanded me what to say. . . . So what I say, I say as the Father told me" (John

6. One has the feeling that there are many passages in the gospels in which Christ addresses the Father, but this impression might come from chapter 17 in St. John's gospel, which is so splendid and memorable.

12:49–50), and "My Father is at work until now, so I am at work" (John 5:17), as well as the statement, "The Father and I are one" (John 10:30).

Christ also says that his disciples must address God as their Father, and he often uses the term "*your* Father." Whenever he speaks to his disciples in this way, he always distinguishes between the way they are related to the Father and the way he is: he never uses the first person plural to speak about God as both his Father and ours; he never puts us on a par with himself. The distinction is brought out in the statement Jesus makes to Mary Magdalene after the Resurrection, when, in words that both distinguish and unite, he says, "Go to my brothers and tell them, 'I am going to my Father and your Father, to my God and your God'" (John 20:17). God is the Father of Jesus in a different, more radical way than he is our Father, and we can call God our Father only because Christ has done so first. His Sonship is primary and privileged, ours is secondary and derived. It is through his Sonship that we become sons of God. Through his life, Death and Resurrection we become his brothers *and therefore* his Father is our Father, his God is our God. Even after we have been adopted into Sonship with him, a distinction remains between the way God is his Father and the way he is ours.

The reason for this difference, of course, is the fact that Jesus as a person was with the Father for all time, before Creation and before Abraham came to be. Christ was not chosen the way Abraham, Moses, and the prophets were. He was sent, not chosen, and he could be sent because he was with the Father from the beginning. All the patriarchs and prophets were chosen by God at some moment in their lives—the call to Abraham, Moses at the burning bush, Isaiah at the vision in the temple, Amos the herdsman and dresser of sycamore trees; even John the Baptist was called while he was in the womb of Elizabeth. But Christ was never chosen in that way; he did not need to be chosen because he came from the Father. From the moment he knew who he was, he was aware of having been sent by and from the Father. The incident in which he was lost in the temple is illuminating in this regard (Luke 2:41–52). At the age of twelve, Christ knew that he belonged in the temple, doing the work of his Father, and he used the first-person singular to express this: "Did you not know that I must be in my Father's house?" Jesus did not have to be told any of this by his parents. He knew better than they who he was and what his mission was. Indeed, his parents were bewildered by the incident and by what he said to them; his understanding was better than theirs and better than that of the teachers in the temple. It is true that he "advanced in wisdom and age and favor before God and man," but he never needed to be told that he was sent by and from the Father.

Christ as man is related to the Father because he, in his person, is eternally related to the Father as the Son. As St. Irenaeus says, "The Son of the Father has revealed [him] from the beginning, because he was with the Father from the beginning."[7] His worldly, incarnate Sonship reflects his eternal filiation. Many passages in the gospels that talk about the Sonship of Christ have a fruitful ambiguity: they can be taken to express both the worldly relation and the eternal. When Christ says, "Everything that the Father has is mine" (John 16:15), he can be referring to the perfection of the Father's presence in him as our Redeemer, but he could also be referring to the condition in which the Father eternally gives himself—everything that he has, his nature as God—to the Son in the life of the Holy Trinity. The Father does not give only what man and creatures can receive; he also gives eternally in a generosity beyond our measures. Another passage that enjoys the same ambiguity is the one in Matthew in which Christ says, "All things have been handed over to me by my Father. No one knows the Son except the Father, and no one knows the Father except the Son and anyone to whom the Son wishes to reveal him" (Matthew 11:27). The knowledge in question is that which is possessed by the man Jesus, but it is also that which is possessed and reciprocated by the eternal Son. The man Jesus can respond so perfectly to the Father because he is the same agent of truth who responds to the knowledge and gift that the Father eternally shares with him.

The unity between Christ and the Father finds another linguistic expression in the "I am" sayings of Jesus, which echo the "I am" of Jahweh revealing himself in the Old Testament. As Thomas F. Torrance says, "We must remind ourselves again of the oneness between the majestic 'I am' of Jahweh and the gracious 'I am' of the Lord Jesus, between the Being of God and the Being of Christ."[8] When Christ says things like, "Before Abraham came to be, I am" (John 8:58), he uses the personal pronoun in a supremely declarative sense, to express himself not only as knowing or promising something,

7. St. Irenaeus, *Adversus Haereses,* Book IV, chapter 20, paragraph 7; see Ante-Nicene Fathers, vol. 1 (Peabody, MA: Hendrickson Publishers, 1994 [reprint]), p. 489.
8. Torrance, *The Christian Doctrine of God,* p. 133. The issue is treated by Torrance in pp. 118–35.

but simply as being. The fidelity of both Jahweh and Christ is made possible by the manner in which they exist.

"No one knows the Father except the Son, and anyone to whom the Son wishes to reveal him": we too can come to know the Father, provided the Son reveals him to us. The Father, and the relation between the Son and the Father, are not displayed to us simply to show us what God is like. This relationship is displayed in order to allow us to enter into it. The Holy Trinity is revealed to us not as a spectacle but as an involvement. The Father is revealed to us by the Son so that we too can call God *our* Father. We then ourselves can use the first person, whether plural or singular, in a declarative way, to express our engagement as children of God: the revelation calls forth a declaration, an act of faith. We in our rational natures can become agents of truth not only in regard to science and human prudence, but also in manifesting the glory of God, in bearing witness to him. The Father's glory was revealed in Christ, but it can now be seen in his disciples, in those who do not impede his presence in them. Christ himself prayed to the Father, "Consecrate them in the truth. Your word is truth. As you sent me into the world, so I sent them into the world. And I consecrate myself for them, so that they also may be consecrated in truth" (17:17–19). The truth in question is not only correspondence with the way things are, but also disclosure: the disciples do not only receive the true teaching but also serve to manifest it.

The person before God

When Jesus speaks about his Father and our Father, he is not talking about a limited, particular relationship, not even one as profound as the relationship one might have to one's parents or one's people. He is not talking about one relationship among many. To put it in terms that may be somewhat inappropriate, Christ is speaking about his and our relationship to the first principle of the universe, the one on whom everything depends. As Jesus said to the Jews, "It is my Father who glorifies me, of whom you say, 'He is our God'" (John 8:54).

Every human being has a relationship to the first principle of the universe, and Christ modifies that relationship. Christ reveals the truth about the origin of things. For this reason, what he says about his Father has significance for everyone. Christ's words about his Father engage everyone because every human being, as a rational being, is involved with the whole of things and with the first and ultimate principle of the whole. Everyone has some sort of opinion about the cosmos, the whole of things, and also about whatever is the highest and best, the first and the ultimate, in that whole. The first principle might be understood as a providential God, or as a deistic power, or as the laws of nature, or as evolution, or even as accidentality, but every person has a sense of the whole and of what is first in it. Having such an opinion is part of being rational.

The pagan world surrounding the biblical events contained, as its first principles, the gods of poets, the gods of philosophers, and the gods of the city. Homer and Hesiod presented many gods, and Plato, Aristotle, the Stoics, and the Epicureans demythologized those gods, making them into rational principles rather than anthropomorphic agents. These gods or principles did not demand an act of faith. One could quite easily go back and forth between the different kinds of gods, appreciating the insights and aspects that both the poets and the philosophers offered concerning them. The gods of the poets and the gods of the philosophers cannot easily be kept apart. A thoughtful philosopher might be quite sure that the stories of the gods are fanciful and contrived, and his inquiries might lead him to a more worthy understanding of what encompasses the world, but then again in moments of reflection he might well realize that Zeus and Apollo and Artemis do express something true about the way things are. Such a person really did not have to make a decisive choice for or against these divine principles. He has allegiances to his gods, but they are flexible and appropriate to the gods in question.

The Jewish world was very different. Jahweh is not one god among many, nor is he even the first and best of the gods; he is God in a sense different from the "gods" of the Gentiles, who are now shown not to be gods at all; in the Bible, the meaning of divinity is changed. God is not just the best and most powerful being in the cosmos. He is beyond the cosmos, and the cosmos depends on him for its very being; through his power and choice, he creates the world and man. He is also the one who reveals himself to his people in a covenant, and these people are then faced with their own choice of either responding to him or turning away. They cannot believe just more or less, and they cannot drift from this God to other gods and back again, as the pagans might in regard to their gods; they either believe or they do not. The people called by God must declare themselves before God, and their use of the terms *I* or *we* acquires a dimension that was not found among pagan speakers. A human being can now become an agent of truth, an agent of fidelity, in a way that was not possible in response to the pagan gods. The Old Testament is a history of the way the Jewish people, both individually and corporately, declared themselves before the God who declared himself to them.

The psalms, for example, articulate in rich detail the various declarative responses that the believer was able to make before this God: "I cry aloud to the Lord, and he answers me from his holy hill. I lie down and sleep; I wake again, for the Lord sustains me" (Psalm 3:4–5); "I love you, O Lord, my strength. The Lord is my rock, and my fortress, and my deliverer, my God, my rock, in whom I take refuge, my shield, and the horn of my salvation, my stronghold. I call upon the Lord, who is worthy to be praised, and I am saved from my enemies" (Psalm 18:1–3); "Make me to know your ways, O Lord; teach me your paths. Lead me in your truth, and teach me, for you are the God of my salvation; for you I wait all the day long" (Psalm 25:4–5); "O Lord, rebuke me not in your anger, nor chasten me in your wrath! For your arrows have sunk into me, and your hand has come down on me" (Psalm 38:1–2); "For I know my transgressions, and my sin is ever before me. Against you, you only have I sinned, and done that which is evil in your sight" (Psalm 51:3–4); "I have chosen the way of truth, I set your ordinances before me, I cleave to your testimonies, O Lord; let me not be put to shame!" (Psalm 119:30–31). No pagan poet could have expressed such sentiments before the gods he honored, because his gods were nothing like Jahweh, and his gods did not address him in the way that Jahweh spoke to those he had chosen.

When Jesus spoke of God as his Father, he modified the understanding of God that had been revealed to the Jews. Jesus could not have revealed the Father within a pagan setting; he could not have said "Father" to a pagan divinity. Only within the context set by the Old Testament could the Fatherhood of God been revealed. By calling God his Father, and by claiming to have been sent by the Father, Jesus showed that the God who is the source of the world through Creation is also the source of a differentiated life within himself, a life in community. God did not only give of himself to the world when he created it; he did not only give of himself to his people when he called them; he also gives himself to the Son in a form of giving that is independent of the world. God is shown to be a "first principle" not only for the world and for salvation, but also within himself, as the Father of the Son, in the unity of the Holy Spirit. God's further giving in Creation and in the mission of his Son can then be seen as reflecting the immanent gift within the Holy Trinity. The charity to which we are called not only participates in God's generosity in Creation and his greater generosity in the Incarnation; it also reflects, more deeply, the donation of the Father to the Son. This eternal gift finds its perfect worldly response in the sacrificial gift of Christ in his death on the cross, which was revealed, ratified, and completed by the Resurrection, and reenacted and distributed in the Church's Eucharist.

The Jewish understanding of God changed and rejected the sense of the divine that was possessed by the pagans. Christ's words and actions did not reject the Jewish understanding but they did deepen it. Jahweh is the same God as the Father of Jesus Christ, but he is that same God revealed and understood more profoundly, revealed and understood as the origin of trinitarian life. In contrast, the Father of Jesus Christ is not the same God as Zeus or Apollo, but he is what the Gentiles were looking for in their gods; he is, as St. Paul says, their Unknown God, known to them more as a blur than as a definite agent with a name (Acts 17:16–32). Only under this title can he be identified with the Father who gave us his Son. Because the pagans can recognize God in at least this way, they have a context in which to accept the gospel, and the distinction between Gentile and Jew, a distinction introduced into the world by God himself, can be overcome in Christ.[9]

The Holy Spirit

Our discussion of the revelation of the Holy Trinity has concentrated on the relationship between the Son and the Father, because the drama of the gospels occurs primarily between those two persons. What shall we say about the Holy Spirit, the third person in the Trinity, "the Spirit of truth that proceeds from the Father" (John 15:26)? The Spirit is often mentioned in the New Testament, but he is rarely described as speaking or as spoken to. With few exceptions, the Holy Spirit, who bestows the gift of tongues, does not himself say anything. He teaches us what to say but remains silent himself.

9. I am grateful to Francis Martin for the concept of the division in humanity introduced by God himself.

He works not as a speaker but as a force, in the form of a dove at the baptism of Christ, a cloud at the Transfiguration, a driving wind and tongues of fire at Pentecost. The sound of the rushing wind is unarticulated and hence not spoken; there is no syntax to it. Even when St. Paul says that "the Spirit itself intercedes" for us, he says that the Spirit does so "with inexpressible groanings" (Romans 8:26), that is, without syntax and without any first-person pronoun. The grammar of the Spirit's discourse is found not in his own words but in the speech of those whom he inspires to speak. It is the Church that gives voice to the Spirit.

There are two places in the Book of Revelation where the Holy Spirit speaks in his own voice, but without using the first-person pronoun. In 14:13, the narrator says, "I heard a voice from heaven say, 'Write this: Blessed are the dead who die in the Lord from now on.' 'Yes,' said the Spirit, 'let them find rest from their labors, for their works accompany them.'" Here the Spirit speaks about the final condition of those who die in the Lord; he assures us that what they do will be with them after their death. They will be defined for eternity by the acts they perform in this life. The second passage is found near the end of the same book and hence at the end of the entire Bible. In 22:17 we read, "The Spirit and the bride say, 'Come.'" This word is addressed to Christ in glory, whom the Holy Spirit and the Church invite to come at the end, at the transformation of time. This word of the Spirit is a suitable rejoinder to Christ's promise to send the Spirit; closure is achieved at the end of history as the Spirit, together with the Church that the Spirit animates, invites the Son to return, the Son who had sent the Spirit to guide the Church through her history. These two passages, these two verbalizations of the Spirit, deal with two forms of the end of time: with the conclusion of our own lives and the conclusion of worldly life itself.[10]

The Holy Spirit remains somewhat anonymous and undeclared in his present activity, because there is no further divine person to reveal him. The Son reveals the Father and the Holy Spirit reveals the Son, but there is no "fourth" to reveal the Holy Spirit. This anonymity of the Spirit is some-

---

10. There are also two passages in the Acts of the Apostles in which the Spirit speaks in his own voice and uses the first-person pronoun. In Acts 10:19–20, the Spirit instructs Peter to welcome the centurion Cornelius and his companions ("because I have sent them"), and in Acts 13:2 we read, "The Holy Spirit said, 'Set apart for me Barnabas and Saul for the work to which I have called them.'"

how necessary; there must be someone with the authority to reveal the Son and, through the Son, the Father, but that person must remain hidden and ought not declare himself. As Jesus said, "He will not speak on his own, but he will speak what he hears . . ." (John 16:13). He is, after all, the Spirit and not the Word; he is an agent of truth in a manner different from the Son. The Son has said everything that needs to be said, but the Spirit brings it to life. If the Spirit were to speak on his own and thus bring himself into the foreground, he would detract from the declaration of the Son. The action between the Son and the Father, the essential action of the gospels and the Church, would be relegated to the background. The Holy Spirit expresses and seals the unity between Son and Father; he does so in the trinitarian life, in the incarnate life of Christ, and in the life of the Church. In sanctifying us, he brings us into the exchange between the Son and the Father. If the Holy Spirit were to declare himself and to speak at length in the first-person singular, his work would no longer enjoy the transparency that befits it. As Dom Anscar Vonier, O.S.B., states, the gift of the Spirit is "essentially a completion of the Incarnation" and not "an addition to it."[11]

The Holy Spirit has the authority to reveal the Son and the Father, and to possess this authority he must share their life. He proceeds from them as the Son proceeds from the Father, not as the world proceeds from God. Like the Son, the Spirit is sent and not chosen.

Our reflections on the Holy Trinity have centered on the manner in which Christ the Son of God uses human language, and specifically the declarative form of the word *I,* to reveal the Father and to reveal himself as the Father's Word. We have tried to show how human speech, when spoken by the Incarnate Son and confirmed by the Holy Spirit, can serve to express the eternal life of the Triune God.

---

11. Dom Anscar Vonier, O.S.B., *The Spirit and the Bride,* in *The Collected Works of Abbot Vonier* (Westminster, MD: The Newman Press, 1952), vol. 2, p. 88. On p. 9, Abbot Vonier contrasts the glorious, manifest, public coming of the Holy Spirit at Pentecost with the silent and hidden coming of the Son in the Incarnation. He also observes that the Incarnation was gradually and progressively manifested, while "the advent of the Spirit is as complete at the first Pentecost as will be the coming of the Son of God in the glory of the Father at the end of the world. . . . The Spirit at once shows his fullest measure of presence, whilst the Son begins with a minimum."

Postscript

The Latin prayer *Te Deum Laudamus* uses the second-person pronoun in an exquisite way and I thought it would be appropriate to conclude my essay on the Holy Trinity by examining this usage. The prayer begins by twice using the pronoun in the accusative case to address God, and in the third line it specifically addresses the Father, with the same word. The pronoun is placed at the beginning of the prayer and the beginning of each line, for emphasis and for honor. The praise in this section comes from "us" and from the earth (from all creation):

> *Te* Deum laudamus,
> *Te* Dominum confitemur.
> *Te* aeternum Patrem, omnis terra veneratur.

The next three lines each begin with the pronoun in the dative case, and the praise in this section comes from the ranks of heavenly beings:

> *Tibi* omnes angeli,
> *Tibi* caeli et universae potentates,
> *Tibi* Cherubim et Seraphim incessabili voce proclamant.

The triple Sanctus is then recited. It is followed by three more lines that begun with the pronoun in the accusative case. In this series God is praised by select groups of saints in heaven: the apostles from the New Testament, the prophets from the Old, and the martyrs from the life of the Church:

> *Te* gloriosus Apostolorum chorus,
> *Te* prophetarum laudabilis numerus,
> *Te* martyrum candidatus laudat exercitus.

The next line, still using the pronoun in the accusative, leaves the celestial sphere and mentions the confession made by the Church on earth:

> *Te* per orbem terrarum sancta confitetur Ecclesia.

This section reaches its climax with the triumphal phrase *Patrem immensae maiestatis.* The prosody of the prayer emphasizes the first syllable of *Patrem* and the words *immensae maiestatis* bring the prayer almost to a stop as it presents God the Father as the center and origin of all things, even of the Holy

Trinity. These lines are followed by two that mention the Son and the Holy Spirit.

The prayer then addresses Christ in the next five segments, each of which begins with the pronoun in the nominative case, *Tu*. In their meaning they resemble the middle part of the Nicaean Creed. The first two lines speak to Christ in his life in the Trinity:

> *Tu* rex gloriae Christe,
>
> *Tu* Patris sempiternus es Filius.

The next two speak of the Incarnation and the Redemption:

> *Tu*, ad liberandum suscepturus hominem, non horruisti Virginis uterum.
>
> *Tu*, devicto mortis aculeo, aperuisti credentibus regna caelorum.

The final part speaks of Christ's return to the Father and his return to the world as judge:

> *Tu* ad dexteram Dei sedes in gloria Patris.
>
> Iudex crederis esse venturus.

A sixth passage is added as a petition to Christ, beginning with the pronoun in the accusative case, asking him to help the servants he has redeemed and to number them among the saints in eternal glory:

> *Te* ergo quaesumus, tuis famulis subveni, quos pretioso sanguine redemisti.
>
> Aeterna fac cum sanctis tuis in gloria numerari.

Thus, in sequence the prayer uses *Te, Tibi,* and *Te* again, in three triplets in addressing God in his transcendence, and *Tu* five times in addressing the Incarnate Word. The pronouns are used in petition and praise, but they are also used to make an implicit claim to truth about the life of the Holy Trinity and its work of Creation and Redemption.[12]

---

12. I am grateful to Kevin White and Matthias Vorwerk for some expert comments on this postscript.

PART III

THE HUMAN PERSON

SOUL AND THE TRANSCENDENCE
OF THE HUMAN PERSON*

As human beings we are animal and organic, but we also carry out spiritual activities. We are not only animals; there is a spiritual side to us that becomes manifest in what we do. The spiritual activities of human beings stem from our reason and the kind of freedom that reason makes possible.

The difficulty of recognizing spiritual life

What do we mean when we say that human beings have a spiritual dimension? We mean that in some of our activities we go beyond or transcend material conditions. We go beyond the restrictions of space and time and the kind of causality that is proper to material things. We do things that cannot be explained materially. To speak adequately about ourselves, we must use categories different from those used to speak about matter.

It seems intuitively obvious that human beings enjoy such a spiritual dimension in their lives, that we are more than material and animal beings. In our contemporary culture, however, to claim that we have a spiritual dimension is controversial, because much of our culture takes it for granted that we are simply material things. It assumes that anything that seems spiritual will sooner or later be explained away as the working out of material bodies and forces. Nothing spiritual has yet in fact been explained away in that manner,

*Permission to reprint granted by: The National Catholic Bioethics Center, 6399 Drexel Road, Philadelphia, PA 19151, 215–877–2660 (v); 215–877–2688 (f); visit www.ncbcenter.org.

but the culture assumes that it inevitably will be, that everything spiritual will be boiled down to the material.[1]

Such a reduction of the spiritual to the material, such a denial of the spiritual, is carried out in three lines of argument. First, our rational activities, both our knowledge and our willing, are said to be reducible to neurological processes; the mind and the will are to be reduced to the brain and nervous system. The mental and spiritual dimensions of man are reduced to biology. The neuroscientist William H. Calvin says, for example, at the end of one of his analyses of the brain, "None of this explains how the neurons accomplish these functions . . . but I hope that the foregoing explains why brain researchers expect to find the mind in the brain."[2]

Second, our neurological processes and all the rest of our bodily activities are explained as the effect of molecular biology; they all come from the chemical structure of cells and the activity of the DNA working in the cells of our bodies. The biology of our bodies is reduced to the chemistry and physics of our cells. The logic, therefore, is that the spiritual is reduced to the biological, and the biological to the chemical.

The third line of argument against the spiritual dimension of man lies in

---

1. The much discussed book by Edward O. Wilson, *Consilience: The Unity of Knowledge* (New York: Knopf, 1998), attempts to give a comprehensive explanation of the human person and society in terms of the evolution of matter; human beings are said to be "organic machines" (p. 82). A typical passage is the following: "As late as 1970 most scientists thought the concept of mind a topic best left to philosophers. Now the issue has been joined where it belongs, at the juncture of biology and psychology. With the aid of powerful new techniques, researchers have shifted the frame of discourse to a new way of thinking, expressed in the language of nerve cells, neurotransmitters, hormone surges, and recurrent neural networks. The cutting edge of the endeavor is cognitive neuroscience . . ." (p. 99). Three other widely noted books expressing a reductive understanding of man are: Francis Crick, *The Astonishing Hypothesis: The Scientific Search for the Soul* (New York: Charles Scribner's Sons, 1994); Paul M. Churchland, *The Engine of Reason, the Seat of the Soul: A Philosophical Journey into the Brain* (Cambridge, MA: The MIT Press, 1995); and Patricia Smith Churchland, *Neurophilosophy: Toward a Unified Science of the Mind-Brain* (Cambridge, MA: The MIT Press, 1986). There are many works being published now about the brain and human activity. The works of the neuroscientist Antonio Damasio are especially interesting philosophically and less reductive; see *Descartes' Error: Emotion, Reason, and the Human Brain* (New York: G. P. Putnam's Sons, 1994), and *The Feeling of What Happens: Body and Emotion in the Making of Consciousness* (New York: Harcourt, Brace, 1999). For a less deterministic understanding of the function of genes, see Evelyn Fox Keller, *Reconfiguring Life: Metaphors of Twentieth-Century Biology* (New York: Columbia University Press, 1995), and *The Century of the Gene* (Cambridge, MA: Harvard University Press, 2000).

2. William H. Calvin and Derek Bickerton, *Lingua ex Machina: Reconciling Darwin and Chomsky with the Human Brain* (Cambridge, MA: The MIT Press, 2000), p. 72.

the Darwinian theory of evolution, which thinks it can give us the complete story of how we developed from physics to chemistry to biology to psychology. Evolution as an ideology is important in the cultural controversies of our present day because it claims that someday it will be able to show how the specifically human being developed randomly from matter and material forces. It claims it will show that the more complex, the organic, and the spiritual are the resultants of material forces combining with random mutations. They are the resultants of a combination of necessity and chance, with no providential or creative intelligence behind them, and no transcendence of space, time, and material causality. Darwinian evolution is presented as the alternative to the biblical narrative.

The extent to which evolution is related to rejection of divine providence is candidly expressed in the following passage by the linguist Derek Bickerton. He complains that many behavioral scientists want to deny that human beings are different from other animal species. He disagrees with them, and says that their failure to recognize the obvious difference is a case of throwing the baby out with the bathwater. He explains: "The bathwater that such thinkers wish to throw out is the Judeo-Christian belief that humans are different from and superior to other creatures because God created them separately and divinely ordained that they should be so. The baby in this case is the lamentable fact that, cut it how you will, we *are* radically different from other species, and to deny it (while eating a microwaved dinner or riding in a mass-produced auto) is hypocrisy."[3] Bickerton takes it for granted that belief in Creation should be eliminated, but he wants to preserve the difference between man and animals, a difference that was introduced through the clever calculation of evolution: "We are different, not because God specially made us so, not even because it is better so—it is perfectly possible to believe we are different and to wish we were not. We are different because evolution made us that way, because (for perfectly valid evolutionary reasons) it provided us, but no other species, with language."

This reductionist and materialist world picture has not in fact been proved by science, but it is taken for granted as the way things must be. It is a hope, and those who believe in it claim that sooner or later science will

3. See Derek Bickerton, *Language and Human Behavior* (Seattle: University of Washington Press, 1995), p. 113.

substantiate this picture. If Darwinian evolution is taken as a replacement for the biblical narrative, this hope in the ultimate explanatory triumph of science may be taken as the replacement for biblical hope in salvation.

I dare say that many Christians, who believe in a spiritual dimension of man and the world, may themselves be unduly disturbed by this picture of things. They may worry that the materialists might really know something, or may find something out, that will definitively show that what seem to be spiritual activities are really only the outcome of material forces. In this cultural situation, the challenge for Christian philosophy and theology is to bring out the distinctive nature of spiritual activities, to show what they are and how they are present to us. Our challenge is to show that human beings are truly involved in activities that transcend the restrictions of space, time, and matter, that we do accomplish things that are spiritual, and that therefore we are spiritual as well as material beings. It is to show that what we mean by spirit could never be boiled down to matter, that it would be meaningless and incoherent to try to reduce the spiritual in this way.

The difference between spirit and soul

I wish to take some steps in meeting this challenge, and I will begin by making a distinction between spirit and soul. Soul is proper to all material living things: men, animals, insects, and plants have soul, but soul is not something separate from their bodies. Soul is not a separate entity, not a ghost in a machine, and we must try to speak about it in such a way that we do not give the impression that it is a separate thing. A good synonym for the word *soul* is *animation,* and this word has an important advantage: we are much less tempted to think that the animation of a living thing could be found apart from that thing. You cannot have animation all by itself; it has to animate something. Animation or soul makes a living thing to be one thing, one entity. Soul is the unity of a living thing. It is also the source of the activities that thing carries out when it acts as a unified whole. Soul becomes visible not by introspection, but publicly in the conduct of living things, and the kind of soul a living thing has is shown by the kind of activities the living thing can perform.

In animals and plants, soul is exhausted in animating the body. In the case of man, however, there is an aspect of soul that enables him to live a spiritual life. In man the one soul is the source of a spiritual life as well as a bodily, organic one. Spirit and soul are not simply equivalent.[4]

I would like to spell out more fully the distinction between spirit and soul. Consider angels. Angels are spirits, but they are not souls and do not have soul. They live a spiritual life, they think and they decide, but they do not animate a body. By their nature, they are not involved in matter. But let us turn our attention away from the high domain of angelic spirits; let us look at more familiar worldly things, where traces of spirit without soul can also be found, in bodily things that show the effect of human rational activity. Consider something like furniture. Furniture shows the effect of human reason, and therefore it has something spiritual about it; it has a residue of spirit, but it does not have soul, because the life of reason that generates furniture does not dwell in the wood itself; it dwells in the human beings who make the furniture. In man, however, the same principle that generates spiritual activities also enlivens the body.

In both angels and furniture we have spirit but no soul, and in animals and plants we have soul but no spirit. Only in man do we have both soul and spirit; we have the animation that makes a body into one organic, active entity, but we also have the capacity to act in ways that are not limited to the body, ways that transcend the space, time, and causation that are proper to the body. This combination of matter, soul, and spirit makes man a great mystery. We are bodies and animals, and yet we live a spiritual life. It is only because we are both spiritual and ensouled that we form churches and political societies, establish universities and research centers and libraries, perform dramas and watch football games, and come together to talk about what we are.

Before we leave this distinction between spirit and soul, let us say a word about the way soul is related to the body that it animates. In living things, it is not true that all the causation comes from the material elements in the body. It is not true that a living thing is merely the effect of the mechani-

---

4. A very good treatment of the difference between soul and spirit can be found in Dom Anscar Vonier, O.S.B., "The Human Soul," in *The Collected Works of Abbot Vonier*, vol. 3 (Westminster, MD: The Newman Press, 1952), pp. 3–66. Abbot Vonier wrote this work on the soul in 1912. Some of the best contemporary philosophical writing about the human person and the human spirit can be found in the work of Robert Spaemann. See his *Personen. Versuche über den Unterschied zwischen "etwas" und "jemand"* (Stuttgart: Klett-Cotta, 1996).

cal and electromagnetic forces that combine to make it up; rather, in living things the matter itself is shaped and reshaped by the thing as a whole, and hence by the animation of the thing. All forms of soul—plant, animal, and human—change the matter that they enliven. Living things contain chemical molecules that are not found and could not be found except in living things, and matter is formulated into these incredibly complex states by the living whole of which that matter is a part. The whole forms its own specialized matter. Furthermore, such complex matter does not just come to be under the guidance of the whole; it also *acts* in function of the living whole, in function of its animation. The way the parts of a cell function is the effect of the body acting as a whole. There is a downward causality from soul to the matter that it composes as a living whole.

In other words, in a living organism, the whole regulates the parts and their activities. It is not simply the case that one part of the organism regulates another—that one neuron does something to another, or that one part of the brain acts upon another. Rather, the whole regulates all the parts. That is what animation means, that a whole regulates itself and all its parts.

To clarify the manner in which the material components of a living thing are affected by the whole, consider the difference between a living being and an artifact, such as an automobile. The materials in an automobile are not changed by the automobile as a whole. The steel remains steel, the plastic remains plastic, the rubber remains rubber, no matter what happens to the car and no matter what the environment is like. But in a living being, the whole entity changes the matter that it takes into itself: it shapes its own bones, muscles, nerves, blood, and enzymes, and it is constantly reconfiguring and activating the matter in its cells. For an automobile to be like a living thing, it would have to change its own matter depending on its surroundings and its age and what it had to do at the moment. It would have to regulate itself and heal itself. Cars do not adapt in that way because they are not self-regulating, living things. Cars do not heal themselves. Much to our inconvenience, a car cannot repair a flat tire the way our bodies heal a wound. Cars are not animated, they do not have soul, but living things do compose their own matter and guide their own development precisely as animated.

And animation also means that the entity acts and interacts outside of itself as a whole, that it does things that the elements could not do by themselves or in combination. An animal attacks its prey, it nurses its young, it builds a nest, it learns to fly, it is fed by its parents. These activities are not merely the resultants of the elementary forces; they are new kinds of activities that are proper to the entity as a whole. The activities of plants, animals, and human beings are specific to the things in question, each taken as an irreducible whole. And in human beings, we have not only the animation of a body but the life of a spirit, a rational and responsible life.

Spiritual activity in human knowing

I would like to convey in an intuitive way what we mean by spirit and its life. We should not take spiritual activities to be something ghostly. It is not the case that spiritual things are given to us only through introspection or through self-consciousness or feelings. To say this would be to speak in a Cartesian way: everything spiritual would be inside. Rather, spiritual activity is present whenever we do things that escape the confinements of space, time, and matter. We do this all the time, and we do it in a public way.

For example, when we rationally communicate with one another, we carry on a spiritual activity, because we share a meaning or a thought or a truth with other people at other places and times. The same meaning, the same thought, the same intellectual identity, can be shared by many people, and it can continue as the same truth over centuries of time, when, for example, it is written down and read and reread at different times in history. Such a truth transcends both space and time, and it transcends material causality as well, because it is the kind of thing that matter alone does not generate. The same truth can be found in many places and in many minds. Also, a cultural object like a drama is a spiritual thing. Shakespeare's *Macbeth* has been achieved over and over again in many places and times when it is performed, read, and interpreted, and yet it is always the same thing. It transcends its embodiments, even though, being something human, it needs its embodiments to be realized. Mathematical formulas, recipes for food, machines, furniture, clothing, flags, political actions, all are spiritual things at least in part. A crumbling ancient temple and the ruins of a castle also have a spiritual aspect; they show the presence of reason even while they are being reclaimed by space, time, and matter, and the traces of spirit in them are slowly vanishing. There is something bittersweet about such things, as the signatures of reason in them are gradually extinguished. Human beings saturate the world with spiritual accomplishments, and in doing so they transcend their bodily existence.

Human spirituality can be present in the things that people say and do and make, it is made present in words and machines and furniture, but it is also present in a much more intense way in the human body itself. We have seen that all forms of soul transform the body they animate, and in human beings the rational dimension of soul also exercises downward pressure on the matter that it informs. The human body is made to be ingredient in a spiritual life. The human brain, for instance, is considered the most complex nonlinear system in the universe,[5] but we should not think that human rationality and spirituality come simply from material causes in the brain. It is more appropriate to say that human rationality somehow shapes the brain; the brain itself is formed by what a human being is and does.[6] And not only the brain, but also the human face and the hand are shaped by what we are and what we do, as well as by the material we are composed of. Human emotions, desires, and self-awareness are also modified by the fact that they are elevated by reason. The *telos* of all these things is not just mechanically caused. The human body is enlivened and formed by a soul that permits rational life.[7]

5. See Wilson, *Consilience,* p. 97: "Overall, the human brain is the most complex object known in the universe--known, that is, to itself."

6. See Calvin and Bickerton, *Lingua ex machina,* p. 146: "...The newly emerged syntax would itself have acted as a selective process, tilting the balance in favor of any changes in the nervous system that would lead to the construction of more readily parsable sentences."

7. The contrast between living things and artifacts can be used to shed some light on the dualism that some thinkers introduce between body and soul. Plato, for example, claims that the soul can exist apart from its bodily material, and that it can even migrate from one body to another. Aristotle insists on a close unity between animation and the animated body, but even he speaks of a part of reason (and hence of what we have called spirit) as coming from outside. But St. Thomas Aquinas, in his controversy with the Latin Averroists, says that reason belongs to the individual human soul itself, and stresses even more than Aristotle the unity of the human being. In artifacts, however, there is a dualism between the traces of spirit and the matter that embodies them. Of course, the artist or the maker wants as good a fit as possible between the matter and the form and function he puts into it. The carpenter wants the wood to be appropriate for the table, the artist wants the stone to be the right material for the sculpture. Still, the matter is prepared *before* it enters into the fabricated object; the artistic form does not animate and determine the matter the way the living form shapes its own matter. Even if the fabricator makes a special matter for the artistic object, such as corian for countertops or concrete for a building, it is the maker, and not the form, that makes the matter what it is. The form remains somewhat alien to the matter, because the form of the artifact is the work of the spirit of the artist, not immediately of his soul. The artist produces the work through his thinking and choices, not through generation.

Consider, furthermore, the difference between the demolition of a fabricated object and the death of a living thing. Suppose a statue is smashed into small pieces, so that nothing of the statue's form remains. The pieces of marble continue to be marble, because they were not constituted as

The human body is also affected by the rational interactions that human beings enter into. The human brain and nervous system, for example, can function within human language only if such language is learned during a specific period, a window of opportunity in the child's development. If the child is deprived of human linguistic interaction during that critical age, the person will not become able to learn to use human grammar. He will be stuck at the level of what is called protolanguage, not language itself.[8]

In Thomistic philosophy, the rationality of the human person is usually associated with the ability to think about all forms of being and to achieve universal concepts.[9] The universality of human understanding is the central phenomenon used to show the rational and hence spiritual nature of the human soul. Such universal thinking is able to escape the confinements of space, time, and material causality. In it we adopt a standpoint that is not limited in the way sensory experience is limited. This is a good approach to human rationality, but other phenomena can also be introduced to confirm it, such as our ability to use language with its grammar, the ability to intend things in their absence, and phenomena like picturing and quotation, as well as the specifically human form of remembering the past and anticipating the future. All these topics can be developed to show in greater detail the transcendence of the human person.

---

marble by the form of the statue. But when an animal dies, not only does the animal cease to be, but its matter decomposes and ceases to be the kind of matter that it was when the animal was alive. Philosophical dualists interpret living things after the fashion of fabricated things, and take the body as only externally related to its animation. In the case of the human being, they take the soul to be essentially the spirit and see it as present in the body as the artistic form is present in its matter. The matter can go its own way and leave the spirit or soul unaffected. (The problem of dualism, addressed in this note, was introduced by Cardinal Francis George, O.M.I., during the discussion at the conference where this paper was first presented. Cardinal George also raised the issue discussed below in note 13.)

8. On the difference between language and protolanguage, see Derek Bickerton, *Language and Species* (Chicago: University of Chicago Press, 1990). Bickerton claims that protolanguage is an entirely different kind of communication than language; the latter includes syntax and the former does not. Protolanguage occurs in children under two years of age, and people who fail to develop real language may be lodged in protolanguage for their entire lives; see pp. 110–18.

9. See, for example, Kenneth Schmitz, "Purity of Soul and Immortality," *Monist* 69 (1986): 396–415. For a comprehensive study of Thomas's doctrine on the immateriality of the human intellect, see Michael J. Sweeney, "Thomas Aquinas's Commentary on *De Anima* 429a10–429b5 and the Argument for the Immateriality of the Intellect" (Ph.D. Dissertation, The Catholic University of America, 1994). This work includes an extensive bibliography.

Spiritual activity in human willing

I have discussed briefly the way human spirituality expresses itself in cognition and communication. Let us consider the way it appears in volition, in human responsibility and freedom. In normal circumstances, people are held responsible for what they have become, and such accountability is not found in the case of animals or plants. A particular deer, for example, may be the best in the herd or it may be one of the inferior members, but in neither case do we say the deer is morally responsible for being what it is. The deer may have had to fight to assert its status, but the question of moral responsibility does not arise. The animal does not *have* its nature the way a human person has his. But if a mature human being is courageous or cowardly, temperate or intemperate, energetic or lazy, generous or avaricious, we acknowledge that he is that way through choices he has made. He has shaped his own life, and he has done so in a deeper and more personal, more spiritual way than even his soul has shaped him. He is what he is not just because he was born a human being, nor just because he lived in this particular situation, but most of all because he did what he deliberately chose to do in his circumstances. He lived his life, and continues to live it, with responsibility, because he can know what he is doing and can make choices to determine not only the world around him but himself as well. We define ourselves within our humanity because we are rational, because we are spiritual. We may not be famous, we may never be mentioned in the newspapers or on television, but each of us lives his own life and answers for it and in doing so he acts spiritually. Animals and plants do not do this, and hence they lack the dignity as well as the responsibility of persons.

This spiritual responsibility of persons shows up vividly for us in their benevolence and malevolence, in the good or bad things they do to us. If an animal attacks us, we consider ourselves unfortunate, but we do not bear resentment toward the animal; we do not think that we have been treated unjustly or malevolently. But if a human being deliberately injures us, we do bear resentment because we see that the agent acted through knowledge and choice.[10] He understood us as someone to be harmed, and it was through

---

10. See Robert Sokolowski, *Moral Action: A Phenomenological Study* (Bloomington: Indiana University Press, 1985), pp. 56–57. Also "What is Moral Action?" in *Pictures, Quotations, and Distinctions: Fourteen Essays in Phenomenology* (Notre Dame: University of Notre Dame Press, 1992), pp. 261–76.

that understanding that the injury was done. It was a spiritual and not just a natural infliction of harm. Human benevolence and generosity, as well as human friendship, are also expressions of spiritual rationality.

Political life is brought about through man's spiritual nature. People form political societies not just because they herd together like animals, but because they share an understanding of the good, the noble, and the just, and this common understanding is the basis for a life in which people can pursue goods that are common to the entire community, not just individual goods. Consider how complex political life is, and how intricate the decisions that are made in it. Such decisions are public achievements and they are done by many people working together. They could never be reduced to the materiality of the brain or the body alone. As John C. McCarthy writes, "In what way . . . could the known laws of physics even begin to explain Abraham Lincoln's decision on March 12, 1864 to appoint General Ulysses S. Grant commander of the Union armies? What would be the shape of the formula astute enough to recognize McClellan's performance in that office as a failure, to say nothing of a formula powerful enough to predict that failure?"[11] How could Lincoln's decision ever be explained as the resultant of a complex network of purely material forces? The action is public and it can be described and explained only in terms of rational, spiritual categories, not material ones. The action can be explained only as the performance of a whole individual with spiritual powers, the performance of a human person.

It is a curious thing that human beings spend so much energy denying their own spiritual and rational nature. No other being tries with such effort to deny that it is what it is. No dog or horse would every try to show that it is not a dog or horse but only a mixture of matter, force, and accident. Man's attempt to deny his own spirituality is itself a spiritual act, one that transcends space, time, and the limitations of matter. The motivations behind this self-denial are mystifying indeed.

Spirituality in religion and Christian faith

The fullest way in which human spirituality is visible is found in the practice of religion. Religious ceremonies and activities are specific to hu-

---

11. John C. McCarthy, "The Descent of Science," *The Review of Metaphysics* 52 (June 1999): 846. This essay is a review of Wilson's *Consilience*.

man beings; animals do not have processions, rituals, or hymns. Religion is the apex of human rationality, because it deals with the highest truth and the greatest good. It is man's response to what is first and best in the world or beyond the world, and it sheds light on all the other things that man knows and loves. If the exercise of truth is a spiritual activity, then our response to the source of truth is even more spiritual. This religious striving toward the first and the best is found in all human beings, even those who are materialistic reductionists. They too find in evolution a kind of supreme, quasi-providential power that guides the development of the world. We have already mentioned Derek Bickerton's claim that evolution made us what we are and, for good reasons of its own, provided us with language; in a recent report about the role of sleep, the neuroscientist Terrence J. Sejnowski says, "Why do almost all of us need eight hours of downtime each night? Our sensory systems are down, our muscles are paralyzed and we are very vulnerable. Evolution must have had a purpose in mind."[12]

The various religions in human history are different ways of articulating the whole of things and of responding to the divine power or powers that govern the whole. As Christians, we believe our faith is more than one religion among many. We believe that in the events of the Old Testament God intervened providentially in the life and events of the Jewish people, and that in Christ he not only spoke to us but became one of us, and thereby elevated human reason and human spirituality to a level beyond what it could reach by its own efforts. Reason and spirit become deepened in the words and actions of Christ, who told us of a truth that exceeds anything we could naturally attain, revealed a divine love that is stronger than any human friendship, and disclosed an eternal life that is more than we could hope for in our natural condition. Human spirituality, the elevation of the human body into a life of reason and spirit, is so much deepened by the work of Christ that the human body, even as a physical thing, can now share in his Resurrection and in eternal life. The fact that the human body can enter into the spiritual activities of rational thinking and responsible action provides a kind of apologetics for the possibility of the resurrection of the body, in which, through the saving power of God, the body is even more intensely elevated into a spiritual condition.

12. Terrence J. Sejnowski, "Experts Explore Deep Sleep and the Making of Memories," *The New York Times,* November 14, 2000.

Concluding remarks

I wish to close with a practical recommendation. Our modern culture tends to think of human beings as merely material things, and it encourages them to act accordingly. The Church, through her teaching, liturgy, and practice, is a witness to the spiritual nature of man, to his personhood. She is a witness not only to the Word of God but also to the rational nature of man. It is the mission of the Catholic educational system, on all levels, to be involved in this witness, to help students to become more clearly and reflectively aware of human spirituality, to teach them how to think about human beings in a way that respects their personhood, to provide them with categories appropriate to human nature in all its fullness, and to convey to them the true sense of teleology that must become part of our understanding of the world.[13] T. S. Eliot formulates this goal in these words: "The purpose of a Christian education would not be merely to make men and women pious Christians: a system which aimed too rigidly at this end alone would become only obscurantist. *A Christian education would primarily train people to be able to think in Christian categories,* though it could not compel belief and would not impose the necessity for insincere profession of belief."[14]

To help people be able to think in Christian categories is a difficult task, since the categories that our culture provides are very different, especially the ones it offers us for thinking about human beings. It is important

13. Some valuable work on the concept of evolution has been done by Richard F. Hassing. See "Darwinian Natural Right?" *Interpretation* 27 (Winter 1999–2000): 129–60, and "Reply to Arnhart," *Interpretation* 28 (Fall 2000): 35–43. Hassing asks: (1) Must we say that there is one good that all living things seek? Is the good for all living things transspecific, the same for all species? (2) Or must we say that living things develop in such a way that they seek goods that are species-specific, that is, goods that are proper to the species in question, including the human species? In the first option, all apparently "higher" goods would be explainable as strategies for survival, which is the one good common to all living things and the one guide for all evolutionary development. In the second option, the possibility arises that there are goods specific to human beings, such as truth, moral goodness, and nobility. Hassing also develops the important concept of teleology, or the natural ends of things, in a work that he edited under the title *Final Causality in Nature and Human Affairs* (Washington, D.C.: The Catholic University of America Press, 1997). I would call attention especially to the contributions by Hassing and Francis Slade. See also Francis Slade, "On the Ontological Priority of Ends and Its Relevance to the Narrative Arts," in Alice Ramos, ed., *Beauty, Art, and the Polis* (Washington, D.C.: The Catholic University of America Press, 2000), pp. 58–69.

14. T. S. Eliot, "The Idea of a Christian Society," in *Christianity and Culture* (New York: Harcourt, Brace and World, 1940), p. 22. Italics added.

for Christian schools and universities not only to teach but also to develop, through research and writing, a deeper understanding of human spirituality, and to formulate it in terms that are appropriate for our day and age, in which we take into account evolution and neuroscience and molecular biology, as well as artificial intelligence and computer science. I think that many, if not most, Catholic colleges and universities have lost the distinctiveness of their mission in the liberal arts and sciences, and a major reason for this loss is the fact that in the past forty years Thomism ceased to be the unifying focal point, and nothing has taken its place. A revival of what I would like to call "streamlined Thomism" would be very appropriate in Catholic education today, along with a special focus on the human soul, the human spirit, and the human person. Such an effort would be in keeping with the vision expressed by Pope John Paul II in his encyclicals *Fides and Ratio* and *Veritatis Splendor,* as well as his Apostolic Constitution *Ex Corde Ecclesiae.* The effort is called for not only by the needs of the Church, but by the perils to human nature and the human person that are arising in our contemporary world. It would be of great strategic importance in dealing with questions of medical technology, bioethics, the biological and spiritual origins of the human person, and the dignity of human life, from conception to natural death. The Church could perform a great service to all people of good will if she were to offer them a deeper and more spiritual way of thinking about the human person.

LANGUAGE, THE HUMAN PERSON, AND
CHRISTIAN FAITH

I wish to discuss the human person and its relation to language and Christian faith. I will begin with a point that I take from the work of the German philosopher Robert Spaemann.[1] The point deals with the logic of the term *person*.

'Person' is a strange noun

The word *person* functions in an unusual and interesting way. It is not what philosophers call a "sortal" noun. It does not mark off a species or a genus in the way that terms like *tree* or *animal* or *house* or even the term *man* do. Each of these terms—*tree, animal, house, man*—expresses a kind of thing, but the term *person* does not, even though grammatically it might seem to do so. The word *person* does not "sort out" one genus or species of things over against all the others. Furthermore, because terms like *tree* or *animal* or *human being* each name a kind of thing, it also makes sense to speak of an individual in each of these species. We can properly speak of "an animal" or "a man." In fact, we do also speak of "a person," but this grammatical possibility masks an important conceptual difference. We really cannot speak of "a person" as an instance of a species.

To illustrate the strangeness of the word *person,* consider the following

---

1. Robert Spaemann, *Personen. Versuche über den Unterschied zwischen "etwas" und "jemand"* (Stuttgart: Klett-Cotta Verlag, 1996), pp. 14–15.

situation, which Spaemann describes. It would make sense for me to say to you, "Come here, I want to show you a tree," or, "Come here, I want to show you a house." It would also makes sense for me to say, "Come here, I want to show you a human being." The term *human being* or *man* is the name for a biological species and it is a sortal term. It would not make sense for me, however, to say to you, "Come here, I want to show you a person." The term *person* has another kind of logic.

The reason why the word *person* has another kind of logic is that from the beginning it is a radically individualized term. It expresses a singularity. In this regard, it is like the term *this*. I could not say to you, "Come here, I want to show you a this." For that matter, it also makes no sense for me to say to you, "Come here, I want to show you an individual." The terms *this* and *individual* are also essentially formal and particular, and do not mark off a genus or species. The word *person* functions in the same way. Grammatically it may look like a sortal term, but it really is not one. I hope that these initial remarks have induced enough of a perplexity, enough of an *aporia,* to help us begin to see that persons are not like other entities.

Persons lead their lives

Why does the word *person* function in this manner? Why does it not connote a genus or species? The word acts in this odd way not simply because of the peculiarities of the English language, but because of the way persons exist. Persons are subsistent individuals. More precisely, they are individuals that are rational, and their rationality makes them more radically individual than beings that do not possess reason.[2] Beings with reason become individualized in a new way. It is true, of course, that other things are individualized; Fido is an individual and so is the tree by my window; but persons are individuals in a manner that is special to them. Persons are singularities and not just individuals.

To bring this out, consider the difference between the way an animal develops throughout its life and the way a human being develops. An animal grows and reacts to things that happen to it, and the governing role in its development is the animal's soul, its being as an animal. Animals are innocent and blameless of what they have become. We do not say that Fido

---

2. Thomas Aquinas, *Summa Theologiae* I, q. 29, aa. 1–3.

should be proud of the way he has conducted himself throughout his life, and we do not say that an alley cat should be ashamed of itself for what it has become. They have not *led* their lives. Dogs, cats, horses, and trees unfold according to what they are and in response to what happens to them and in regard to the circumstances in which they find themselves. Their nature, their souls, regulate their behavior, and they themselves cannot make their souls better or worse.

Human beings, in contrast, can shape their own souls. The souls of human beings are not the ultimate governing power, the *hēgemonikon,* over their lives. Human beings do not simply unfold in response to occurrences and circumstances. At a certain point in life, human beings become to some degree responsible for the state of their souls. What they are is in part—indeed, in the most crucial part—their own doing. They are not responsible for having being born as human beings, but they are responsible for being the kind of human being that they have become. The state of their souls has been determined in part by themselves, and since their souls are the origin of their subsequent inclinations and actions, human beings themselves determine how they will be inclined to act in the future. To this degree, they "own" themselves. They *have* led their lives. Human beings are more individualized than are other things in the world, because they have dominion over their actions and over their lives as a whole, and in this way each of them shows his singularity.

How can this be? Why is it that human beings have this dominion over themselves? Why are men held responsible for themselves in a way that animals are not? How is it that we *lead* our lives? It is, of course, reason that gives human beings this capacity, but why should this be so? Why should our reason individualize us in such a radical way, and why does it make us responsible for what we are? Let us explore the way in which reason functions.

Person and syntactic speech

So far, we have approached reason through only one perspective. We have spoken about it as that which gives us dominion and responsibility over our actions and over our lives. Obviously, in order to be able to have such a dominion, we must be able to reflect on our actions and on our lives. As human agents, we are not simply absorbed in what we are doing, with only a marginal awareness that we are there doing it. We are, in addition, able to examine what we are doing, compare different courses of action, think about what we wish to pursue, and prefer some things to others. We are able to deliberate, to distinguish between our purposes and the ways we might achieve them, to become aware that *we* are acting and that we can act in different ways. We have to be able to think about our actions and about ourselves as well as the things around us.[3]

Such a reflective dominion over our conduct could not be the first, the only, or the primary exercise of reason. The dominion over our actions is rooted in still another form of reasoning that is more elementary, the ability to think in the medium of speech.[4] It is only because we can speak thoughtfully that we can reflect, deliberate, choose, and act.

What does it mean to think in the medium of speech? It is to present things as articulated into wholes and parts, and to do so for ourselves and for others. Reasoned speech is like a magic wand that we wave over things, which brings out the parts and wholes that can be shown forth in things: their identity, their features, their relationships. When we speak, when we wave this wand, things become articulated and disclosed, for ourselves and for our interlocutors.

However, we do not just articulate the *things* that we present. The process is more complicated than that. While we explicate things, we also explicate the words we speak. The speech that we declare is itself articulated into its own kinds of parts and wholes. We continually assemble and reassemble the wand itself as well as the things we wave it over. We display things and think about them by structuring our speech.

Our articulation of speech is on two levels. First, each word is internally made up of phonemes or parts of sound; each word is made up of vowels and consonants. Second, each statement is made up of lexicon and grammar, of content and syntax. The phonemic structure inside a word establishes each word as such, and these words are then conjoined in grammatical and lexical sequences. When all this happens on the side of speech, some parts of the world come to light. The artful combinatorics in words and sentences

3. This point is clearly brought out by Alasdair MacIntyre, *Dependent Rational Animals: Why Human Beings Need the Virtues,* The Paul Carus Lectures (Chicago: Open Court, 1999), pp. 53–61, 91.

4. "To think in the medium of speech" is a phrase that I have taken from the writings of the Scottish philosopher David Braine. See his book *The Human Person: Animal and Spirit* (Notre Dame: University of Notre Dame Press, 1992), p. 5.

lets the articulation of things take place, whether we speak of such things in their presence or their absence. Human reason can articulate on all these levels; it keeps all of these dimensions in mind, and all of them are significant: it composes words out of phonemes and statements out of words, and simultaneously it displays things in their parts and wholes. We pack so much intelligence into our words that things themselves begin to appear in the light that the words give off. The person who accomplishes this, furthermore, does so for himself and for others. All discourse is in principle a matter of conversational reciprocity. Thinking in the medium of words is inherently public and so is human reason.

The most conspicuous feature of our verbal articulation is the way in which phrases are embedded into one another. This is the work of syntax; it makes it possible for us to segment our speech, and also to segment our displays, into parts that are not just concatenated sequentially one after the other, but are stacked within one another, in the fashion of Chinese boxes or Russian dolls. Speeches of unlimited complexity become possible. It is this embedding, as the American linguist Derek Bickerton has shown, that differentiates human speech from animal cries and sounds.[5] It is specifically the syntactic element in speech that raises our verbalization into rational discourse. Syntax provides the rational form for the more material contents of what we say.

But we should not take syntax just by itself. Syntax has to be related to the phonemic structure within each word, and it is specifically the consonants that function on this level in a manner analogous to syntax.[6] Consonants are like the syntax within words. Consonants clip and trim the words we speak, and we have to be socialized into them, just as we have to be socialized into syntax and judgment. Consonants order the more elementary vowel sounds, the wails and howls and whimpers and glee that do not need to be taught to us. Vowels alone would be an unlettered human voice; it is the consonants that make the voice rational. This phonemic structuring,

5. See Derek Bickerton, "Pidgin and Creole Languages," *Scientific American* 249 (1983): 116–22; *Language and Species* (Chicago: The University of Chicago Press, 1990); *Language and Human Behavior* (Seattle: The University of Washington Press, 1995); Derek Bickerton and William H. Calvin, *Lingua ex Machina: Reconciling Darwin and Chomsky with the Human Brain* (Cambridge, MA: The MIT Press, 2000).

6. Linguists find the distinction between vowels and consonants to be inadequate and replace it with the distinction between what they call sonorants and obstruents.

moreover, does not come to pass in isolation of the higher, syntactic structuring; rather, the consonantal shaping of sound occurs in the context and under the teleology of syntactic patterning. Consonants are introduced under the downward pressure of syntax.

The vowel dimension in words is more associated with emotion, and the consonant structure is more associated with reason. Vowels are especially involved with feeling, with our biological and sensory appreciation of what is going on and what is happening to us. The emotive dimension of vowels is especially affiliated with singing and with music generally, but human singing requires also the clipping and cutting of consonants if it is to become thoughtful melody, if it is to become a song that exhibits intelligence. Consonants introduce the rigor and determination of reason into the melody of vowels.

May I also observe that human laughter, which is another sign of human rationality, is also shaped by consonants. Laughter is made up of vowel sounds segmented into short bursts by simple consonants: ho-ho-ho or ha-ha, for example. A pure long vowel sound is not laughter; it is more like a wail and more like an animal sound. There is little intelligence in it.

We have spent some time looking at the intricacies of speech on the phonemic and the sentential levels, and we have emphasized the active, formal role of consonants and syntax. None of these structures, however, neither the word nor the sentence, are ends in themselves. All of them are achieved in the context and under the teleology of manifesting the way things are. All of them are achieved in the service of truth, the disclosure of things through human judgments and inferences. Phonemic and grammatical structures, with their parts and wholes, are accomplished in order to bring out the parts and wholes of things; they are achieved under the downward pressure of the disclosure and communication of truth. They are all in the service of the logic and human reasoning that are the primary work of human beings as agents of truth, that is, of human beings as persons. Once we are into phonemes and syntax, we are also already into the combinatorics of logic, which is the structural part in the achievement of truth.

But if we wish to examine the accomplishment of truth, it will be very helpful for us to pay attention to phonemic and grammatical structure; this focus will make our treatment of reason and truth more tangible. Our philosophical analysis of logic and truth, as well as our discussion of the human person, can be made much more concrete if it is carried out in relation to the phonemic structure of words and the syntactic structures of sentences.

We have explored some aspects of what it is to think in the medium of speech. We have emphasized the formal aspects of linguistic structure (the syntax and consonants). Another kind of composition occurs in picturing, painting, and sculpture, in which we bring about an artificial, structured, and thoughtful perception. Very briefly, I would like to draw some analogies between painting and speech. In a painting, the role of vowels is played by colors and the role of consonants is played by lines. Colors are the more elemental component and lines the more rational. This point is well brought out by Norbert Lynton in a review of an exhibition at the Royal Academy in London. He writes, "Color is notoriously difficult to engage with intellectually. . . . John Gage, a rare expert on color in art and in history, reminds us in the catalogue that in the nineteenth century color was still regarded with suspicion by 'many critics.' The academic tradition considered color an ornament added to *disegno,* subversive if unconstrained by correct draughtmanship and truth, revealing base animal instincts."[7] Furthermore, something like grammatical syntax occurs in the spatial placement of objects and areas within the painting: things are embedded within other things. In the works of Vermeer, for instance, maps and landscapes are often placed on the wall behind the human figures in the paintings, and their location and their contents are significant.[8] They are like subordinate clauses in the overall statement of the painting or perhaps like steps in an argument. In paintings, however, the embedded parts and wholes are spatial and simultaneous, not temporal and sequential as in speech, and yet the articulation in the painting is also geared toward the truth of a disclosure.

To study such formal structures is to elaborate what the human person is as an agent of truth, as the entity that thinks in speech and in other mediums. The analysis can become very complex: think how the various languages introduce their own specific nuances into human reason, how they introduce variations in structure that serve both elegance and intelligence. It

7. Norbert Lynton, "Shades of the Animal Instinct," *Times Literary Supplement,* September 13, 2002, p. 18.

8. See Elise Goodman, "The Landscape on the Wall in Vermeer," in *The Cambridge Companion to Vermeer,* ed. Wayne E. Franits (New York: Cambridge University Press, 2001), pp. 72–88. For the reason why Vermeer's *The Astronomer* contains a painting of Moses being found among the bulrushes, see Klaas van Berkel, "Vermeer and the Representation of Science," ibid., p. 134.

should be clear that to consider the human as the agent of truth is to offer a new formulation of the classical definition of person as an individual substance of a rational nature.

Syntax in practical agency

I do not want to give the impression that human reason is limited just to theoretic or contemplative things. It also functions within human desires, and here again it does so by introducing something like syntactic structures into them. Human loves, hates, and actions are rational because they too involve articulation into parts and wholes that can be embedded in one another. I would like to spend some time discussing the syntax that shapes human desire.

To clarify the structure of human desire and aversion, consider the differences between needs, wants, and wishes. *Needs* are proper to any living thing, plants as well as animals and human beings. Such things must draw parts of the world into themselves in order to maintain their own identity, that is, in order to stay alive. They need certain things from outside themselves in order to remain what they are. *Wants,* however, are proper to sentient beings, to animals. A plant has needs but it does not have wants. Wants are the needs that are felt by certain living things, and the entities in question have to act in certain ways in order to satisfy their wants; they have to go somewhere or chase something in order to do what they feel needs to be done. Human beings have needs and wants, but they also have *wishes.* Wishes are the form of wanting that is proper to rational beings, to agents of truth.

Wishing ranges over very great distances. At its greatest extreme, we can and do wish for impossible things, things that cannot be done by anyone. This shows the great range of human reason. Secondly, however, we can wish for things that we ourselves cannot accomplish but that other people can. We must depend on others to satisfy these wishes. And finally we can wish for things that we ourselves can bring about. Even here, however, wishing involves a certain distance, because we do not wish for things we can do directly; we wish for things that we can achieve only by taking steps, by doing other things that lead to what we want. When such wishes kick into action, when they become effective and begin guiding our thinking and our conduct, they become intentions. We begin to deliberate under their aegis, we sort out the various ways we could bring about what we wish for. We begin to see the ends *in* the means. The means become embedded into the ends. This is where practical syntax comes into play, as we distinguish various ways of acting in view of the purposes we have in mind. The distinction between purposes and means is a thoughtful shaking out of parts and wholes in regard to action.

But there are also other forms of syntactic articulation that come into play in regard to the way we wish for things and conduct ourselves. The structure of a middle between the extremes of emotion and action is a syntactic, rational pattern and marks off the good action and emotion as opposed to the wicked one. The structures of justice, whether distributive or corrective, are also forms of syntax; in fact, they are almost mathematical in their complexity. Still another form of practical syntax can be found in the more intimate but equally precise calibrations of friendship, in which we wish for the good of the friend as our own good. We should notice that Aristotle places the treatment of friendship at the culminating point in his *Nicomachean Ethics.* I would claim that the structures of friendship mark the highest form of moral activity and reasoning, and that other forms of ethical conduct participate in friendship.[9] And the singularities of persons come to the fore in the best kinds of friendship, in which each friend is irreplaceable for the other.

In all these activities and forms of wishing, the rational activity of articulating wholes and parts comes into play. There is moral syntax in human action, and it engages the issue of truth. Because action is syntactic it can be truthful or false. We do not just introduce fascinating patterns into our conduct when we act as moral agents. Rather, we act in keeping or not in keeping with what we are, with what others are, and with what the thing we are doing is. There is a truth or a falsity to what we do, and even in our actions we remain agents of truth. Every articulation is a manifestation and hence an act of truthfulness, even in the order of action. Another way of making this point is to say that the formal structures of moral conduct must be measured by our nature and its teleologies, by what we are as human beings. Our personhood has as its task the care of our human substance and its life. Just as consonants need vowels and syntax needs lexical contents, so the

9. On the moral dimension of friendship, see Robert Sokolowski, "Friendship and Moral Action in Aristotle," *Journal of Value Inquiry* 35 (2001): 355–69, and "Phenomenology of Friendship," *Review of Metaphysics* 55 (2002): 501–20.

structuralism of moral action needs the material goods that are brought to perfection in human conduct.

Singularity of the person in action and speech

I would now like to turn back to the radical individuality of each person, and specifically of each human person, to show how the exercises of reason that we have described, in both the theoretic and the practical order, can account for such singularity. Before doing so, may I mention a paradox about human beings: it is our soul that defines us as human beings, as members of a species, as individuals in a kind, and yet one of the powers of our soul, the rational power, endows us with an indexicality or singularity that makes us responsible for the life we live as human beings. Part of our soul allows us to exercise a government over the whole of our soul and makes us irreducible to the species that defines us. Through part of our soul we can determine how the soul will be concretely shaped. We enjoy, paradoxically, both spirit and soul, both reason and organic life. Human beings are both spirit and animal, and it is not easy to bring these two dimensions together. Let us then try to clarify the singularity each of us enjoys as a human person. We shall do so by playing two human relationships off against one another: the relationships we have within a family, and the relationships we have in a conversation.

Robert Spaemann observes that human familial relationships are different from animal relationships because they remain with us throughout our lives; among human beings, "the mother remains the mother. This does not hold in animals. When [among animals] the biological function is extinguished, the relationship comes to an end and the animal falls back into the conduct it would have towards any other member of its species."[10] Thus, in contrast with what occurs in the animal world, a human being's father and mother continue to be recognized as such even if both the children and the parents have grown old. Each individual retains his or her special position within the family: as grandfather, uncle, grandmother, aunt, first cousin, son and daughter, and so on. We each maintain our place on the chessboard of familial relations. In the animal kingdom, these singular positions and their loyalties are not sustained. It is the species that counts, not the individual, and

10. Spaemann, *Personen*, p. 79.

relationships established at birth give way to anonymity as time goes on. The individuals get absorbed into the herd. Even if some animals can recognize others as belonging to their species or their pack, they recognize them as members of the clan, not as these individuals with their history and specified location within the network of familial relationships. Animal species do not engender a history. We would not, for example, write the history of the generations of beavers that have lived in a particular lake, because the beavers don't *do* anything, not in the sense of human transactions, but we could write the history of what happened to a human settlement there and what its members have done.

In fact, Spaemann observes that each human being has a special place not only within his immediate family but also within the whole human family. He says that persons compose a system of relations "that bestows a place that comes just once [einen einmaligen Platz] for each person in relation to every other."[11] In our familial and community relationships we are singular and not just individual. This placement of ours, furthermore, is involved in the role we have in the human conversation, the second theme I wish to investigate.

Each human being is positioned in the human conversation, and this role that we have, this persona that we take on, is verbally expressed in the personal pronouns of our languages: the first person expresses the one who speaks, the second person expresses the one who is addressed, and the third person expresses the one who is spoken about but is not engaged in the conversation. We use these pronouns to identify ourselves as ordinary things in the world, but we also use them, especially in the first and second person, in a more dramatic way: we use them to appropriate or attribute an act of reason to ourselves or to others, as when we say, "I know that it is raining," or "I suspect that he will come," or "You want to return home." Let us call this a "declarative" use of these pronouns. The declarative use of personal pronouns quintessentially designates us as agents of truth, as persons.

Through our acts of reason, we stand out as entities that have an opinion about the world, and we also stand out as entities that intend to do certain things. We take a position as datives of manifestation. We enter into conversational reciprocity. We learn to speak and we become able to make judg-

11. Ibid., p. 196.

ments by being initiated into conversation by others. In such conversing, such turning toward others in speech, we can be quoted by other speakers. We stand out as agents of truth, as persons who represent a certain "take" on the world. The "take" that we have, the opinion we possess, the way the world seems to us, is, furthermore, the matrix for our actions and hence for the history that we have in common with others. It is the matrix for what we and others have done. The way the world shows up for us opens the space within which we lead our lives. As datives of manifestation and as origins of action we are irreplaceable, and hence we hold our distinctive place in our familial relationships and in human conversation and history. To be quotable is to be singular. Our reason establishes us as persons, with the ontology and logic that persons enjoy.

Notice how a materialist reductionism destroys this anthropology and the human dignity that comes from it. If our minds were reducible to our brains, our reason would be a mere development of our bodies, and our claims to be truthful would be only our bodies in motion. We would lose the singularity and the responsibility we have as persons. We would be explained by physics and biology. *We* would not be there to respond to the truth of things, and, in theological terms, there would be no need for a special creation of each human soul. But this is not the case; our reason is not the outcome of merely biological development. Our reason and our dignity as rational beings, furthermore, are not just the outcome of cultural reciprocities. We are persons not because we are given that dignity by others, but because we come into the world endowed with it. *We* come into the world to lead our lives; we are not commissioned by others to do so. Other people must recognize us as agents of truth; they do not give us that dignity.

The human person and Christian faith

In the final section of my paper, I will speak briefly about Christian faith. All of my remarks so far might have seemed rather humanistic or philosophical; what is the relation of all this to Christian faith? We know that historically the concept of person was deeply influenced by Christian theological controversies dealing with the Incarnation and the Holy Trinity. The classical definition of the person was formulated by Boethius in a theological treatise. It is also the case that Christian faith has stimulated a tremendous expansion of culture: in music, painting, literature, and science, all of which are emblems of human reason.

I would like to claim that Christian faith intensifies the various exercises of reason that we have been discussing. Christian faith is not an alternative to reason but an enhancement of it. In sharpening human intelligence, Christian faith confirms the personhood that is made possible by reason. It has this effect on human reason primarily because in Christian faith we come to a new "understanding" of who and what God is, to a new appreciation of divinity, but I do not wish to discuss this fundamental issue now.[12] Let us examine two other topics.

Consider the intensification of *friendship* that occurs in Christian belief. We have claimed that in the natural order, friendship is the highest form of moral action and other forms of moral action participate in it. But the highest form of friendship that Aristotle and Plato describe is the kind that occurs among human beings; Aristotle explicitly says that there could be no friendship between a human being and god.[13] In human friendships, each person is recognized in his singularity. Such relations among human beings become placed into a new register when the relationship between men and God is described in terms of friendship: at the Last Supper, Christ says to his disciples, "You are my friends if you do what I command you" (John 15:14) and he goes on to contrast friendship with servitude: "I no longer call you slaves, because a slave does not know what his master is doing. I have called you friends, because I have told you everything I have heard from my Father" (John 15:15). The new friendship is made possible by what Christ has told us, by the truth he reveals and by the expansion of reason that he affords. This friendship is also made possible, correlatively, by the faith that is our response to what Christ tells us. Certain kinds of friendship and generosity, certain kinds of moral syntax, now come into play because of the truth revealed by Christ.

This new kind of friendship is called charity and it is made possible by

12. For a discussion of the Christian understanding of the divine, see Robert Sokolowski, *The God of Faith and Reason: Foundations of Christian Theology* (Washington, D.C.: The Catholic University of America Press, 1995).

13. Aristotle, *Nicomachean Ethics* VIII, 7, 1159a4–5: "For much can be taken away and friendship remain, but when one party is removed to a great distance, as god is, the possibility of friendship ceases."

the grace of God, who loved us before we loved him. Our natural friendships and natural virtues are developed as the truth of our human nature,
but friendship with God and the corresponding friendship we should have
with one another are developed as the truth of our relationship with God.
Not just nature but grace is the source of such virtue. This enhancement of
friendship is based not only on the words of Christ but also on the revealed
truth that the life of God himself is carried on in friendship, in the mutual
and highly specified generosity among the Divine Persons. Their personhood consists not in cultivating their nature, as it is with us, but in donating
and receiving it, in being thus related to one another. In Christian faith, the
Divine Trinity of Persons in one Nature, one Being, becomes the paradigm
of what it means to be a person. Our way of being persons, distributed as it
is singularly among individuals, is now seen to be only a derivative form.

Finally, Christian faith involves revealed *truth*. This means that the declarative use of personal pronouns comes into play in such faith. The Christian says, "I believe," in response to the word of God, whether that word was
uttered through the psalmist, the prophets, and the law of the Old Testament,
or by the Incarnate Word in the New Covenant, the Divine Person who
became a human being and took on the history of a human life, which is
the actualization of a human substance. Christ began to use the word "I" to
declare himself both to us and to the Father.[14] Christ is an agent of truth, a
person, in a manner much deeper than any of us could be on our own, and
he permits us to incorporate ourselves with him; we can join with him in
addressing the Father and in donating ourselves to the Father, in an act of
human dedication that differs from any other commitment we can make. In
Christ, the full truth of the psalms, the prophets, and the law is disclosed to
us, and so is the full truth of human nature and the human person. Both language and the human person come to perfection in Christian faith.

14. See Robert Sokolowski, "Revelation of the Holy Trinity: A Study in Personal Pronouns,"
chapter 9 above.

THE HUMAN PERSON AND
POLITICAL LIFE

I wish to discuss the relationship between the human person and political life, with some reference to the way this relationship has been understood by Catholic thinkers. My remarks will be a venture into political philosophy, but it would be appropriate to begin with a few comments about our present historical situation.

Political philosophy in recent Catholic thought

Political philosophy has been short-changed in Catholic thought in the past century, during the Thomistic revival following the encyclical *Aeterni Patris* of Pope Leo XIII in 1879. In the departmental structure and the philosophical curricula that prevailed in many Catholic colleges and universities during the first two thirds of the twentieth century, political philosophy would usually be located not in philosophy departments but in political science. In seminary programs, there was effectively no political philosophy whatsoever. The philosophy manuals of the early and middle part of the century covered political philosophy, if they treated it at all, as a division of ethics. In the great manual written by Joseph Gredt, O.S.B., for example, which was entitled *Elementa Philosophiae Aristotelico-Thomisticae,*[1] one finds extensive treatments of logic, epistemology, philosophy of nature, philosophical psychology, metaphysics, theodicy, and ethics, but in the nearly one thousand pages of the two volumes, there are only some twenty pages, at the very end

---

1. Joseph Gredt, O.S.B., *Elementa Philosophiae Aristotelico-Thomisticae,* 2 vols. (Freiburg: Herder, 1953).

of the second volume, devoted to "civil society," and this brief section terminates with a two-page treatment *de bello,* on war. This long philosophical work, therefore, does not end peacefully, and it clearly does not offer a solution to the political problem.

It is true that some of the most important twentieth-century Catholic philosophers devoted much of their work to political philosophy: Jacques Maritain wrote such books as *Man and the State, The Person and the Common Good, Things That Are Not Caesar's, Integral Humanism, Freedom in the Modern World* (the French title was *Du régime temporel et de la liberté*), and *Scholasticism and Politics (Principes d'une politique humaniste),* all of which deal with politics, and Yves R. Simon wrote *The Philosophy of Democratic Government,* among other titles in political thought, but these two authors were the exception rather than the rule. At Louvain's Higher Institute for Philosophy, for example, there was no representation of political philosophy. Jacques LeClercq wrote in social ethics and social philosophy, but not political thought as such. What was done in political philosophy added up to a relatively small achievement in this field, compared, say, with the work that was done in metaphysics, philosophy of science, ethics, and the philosophy of man. This lack of interest is rather strange, since political life originally provided the context for philosophy, in the life of Socrates and in the writings of both Plato and Aristotle. The lack of concern with political philosophy should provoke our curiosity and perhaps even our wonder.

Recently, at the end of the twentieth century and the beginning of the twenty-first, a number of important Catholic thinkers in Paris have addressed issues in political philosophy. Pierre Manent is the most conspicuous of these, but one must also mention Rémi Brague, Alain Besançon, and Terence Marshall. Their work has been influenced by Raymond Aron and Leo Strauss. We should also call to mind the work, in the United States, of Ernest Fortin, A.A. (Boston College), James Schall, S.J. (Georgetown), Francis Canavan, S.J. (Fordham), and Charles N. R. McCoy (Catholic University), but it is interesting to note that all these persons were or are academically "housed" not in philosophy but in departments of politics, or, in the case of Fortin, in theology. There were other thinkers who approached social and political problems, such as John Courtney Murray, S.J., and John A. Ryan in the United States and Denis Fahey and Edward Cahill in Ireland, but again they tended to discuss these issues in terms of Church-State relations and moral theology, and did so in a somewhat more deductive manner than would be appropriate for political philosophy.[2]

I should add that Pope John Paul II, in his philosophical writings on the human person, does address the phenomenon of community in his article "The Person: Subject and Community,"[3] and in the last chapter of his book *The Acting Person*.[4] That chapter is entitled "Intersubjectivity by Participation" and is found under the more general heading of "Participation." This general discussion of community, however, does not develop a specifically political philosophy, although it certainly points the way to it. The Holy Father's work in inspiring and promoting the Solidarity movement in Poland, and the great contribution he made in bringing down one of the worst tyrannies in the history of humanity, are further reasons why philosophical and theological reflection on political life should occur in a cultural center dedicated to his name.[5] I would also like to commemorate the work of Jude P. Dougherty, who is being honored by this conference, and to note the keen interest he has had in political life and political thought, an interest that has been expressed in his activities and many of his writings.

The human person and politics in Aristotle

The classical and unsurpassable definition of the person was given by Boethius early in the sixth century: a person is an individual substance of a rational nature. This definition highlights rationality as the specifying feature of persons; a person is an individual being that is endowed with reason.[6] According to this definition, there may be persons—divine or angelic—who

2. Political philosophy is treated in a more deductive way when it is approached through theology and revelation because it is placed in and derived from a moral context that is more comprehensive than its own. In Socrates, Plato, and Aristotle, political philosophy moves toward its first principles from political life itself.

3. Karol Wojtyla, "The Person: Subject and Community," *The Review of Metaphysics* 33 (1979): 273–308.

4. Karol Wojtyla, *The Acting Person,* trans. Andrzej Potocki (Dordrecht: Reidel, 1979).

5. An earlier version of this paper was given at a conference honoring Jude P. Dougherty. It was held jointly at The Catholic University of America and the John Paul II Cultural Center in Washington, D.C.

6. Boethius's definition does not involve a genus and specific difference, because *individual substance* could not express a genus except in a purely verbal or logical sense. The term expresses a particular right from the start, not something common. Persons are essentially indexical. See Robert Spaemann, *Personen. Versuche über den Unterschied zwischen "etwas" und "jemand"* (Stuttgart: Klett-Cotta, 1996), pp. 32–44. Spaemann shows that the term *person* is not a sortal expression.

are not human beings; they too could be individual entities invested with a rational nature, but of course such persons would not enter into politics. Political life requires body and soul as well as personhood.

Persons, in Boethius's definition, are individual entities that possess reason. It is the power of reason, with all that it implies, that makes us to be persons. Even when we use the word *person* in a less technical way, simply to highlight the fact that the individual in question is a human being and should be treated as such, we imply that the dignity he has and the respect he deserves follow from his rationality and not his feelings. It is because he is rational, an agent of truth, that he must be "treated as a person and not a thing."

Now, human reason and hence human personality are exercised in speech, in science and the search for wisdom, in ethical conduct, in friendship, and in religion, and they are also exercised in a distinctive manner in political life. Political societies are communities specifically made up of human persons. If we are to speak about the human person, our discussion would be sorely deficient if we did not treat the domain of human political conduct and if we did not specify how human reason, in thought and in action, is at work in it.

It is not just that human beings live together; men live together in families and the kind of extended families we could call villages or tribes. Such communities come about by natural inclination and do not need founders. They are not the outcome of deliberation, reasoning, and argument, as political societies are. They do not have to be conceived in thought before they come into being. Political societies need to be established by acts of reason, and people who succeed in this enterprise bring about a great good for others: Aristotle says that "the one who first established [such a community] is the cause of the greatest goods,"[7] because founders make possible for man a civilized and virtuous life, a life lived in view of the noble, the good, and the just, a life in which human excellence can be achieved and the worst in man can be controlled: "For man, when perfected, is the best of all animals, but when separated from law and justice, he is the worst of all."[8] Think of the

7. *Politics* I, 2, 1253a30–31. I have used the Jowett translation of the *Politics*, which is found in McKeon's *The Basic Works of Aristotle* (New York: Random House, 1941), as well as the translation by Carnes Lord (Aristotle, *The Politics* [Chicago: The University of Chicago Press, 1984]), but have made many revisions of my own.

8. *Politics* I, 2, 1253a31–33.

benefits that millions of people have enjoyed because of the acts of reason that achieved the founding of the United States of America, most conspicuously, the acts of thinking that took place during the Constitutional Convention in 1787, in the debates during the years that followed, in the ratification of the Constitution by individual states from 1787 to 1789, and at the inauguration of George Washington as the first president in 1789. All these events were exercises of reason, and they in turn followed upon the American Revolution itself, as well as the colonial period that preceded it, when the habits of free political life were established among the people.

It is an act of reason, and therefore an eminently personal action, to establish a political society. To underline this point, consider the fact that animals also live together, but their association is not the outcome of an exercise of reason on their part. There are no founders in animal societies; Richard Hassing has asked, ironically, "Would Aristotle say that the first founder of chimpanzee society was responsible for the greatest of chimpanzee goods?"[9] The question simply does not apply. There are no founders of animal societies. Also, there are no Washington Monuments or Jefferson Monuments in ape or elephant society, because there are among apes and elephants no founders who exercise their reason to establish a society in which reason flourishes. One of the things that reason does when it prospers in a civilization is to acknowledge, by the building of monuments, the founding acts of reason that established the space within which the monuments could be built. This is not to demean ape or chimpanzee or elephant or dolphin society, but to highlight the human difference and the rational character, hence the specifically personal character, of human political association. Political society is established by a determination of the noble, the good, and the just, which is expressed and then desired by reason.

It is important to note, furthermore, that although political life needs to be established by an act of reasoning, it is not therefore a purely conventional thing. It still remains part of human nature, but of human nature in its teleological understanding, when human life is seen at its best; it is not part of human nature in the genetic, biological sense.[10] I doubt that researchers in

---

9. Richard Hassing, "Darwinian Natural Right?" *Interpretation* 27 (Winter 1999–2000): 148.

10. When the causality of the *telos* is denied or abandoned, the mind recoils into simply mechanical and genetic explanations.

biology will find a gene that programs for political constitutions or a cluster
of neurons that generates them.

Political life is not only founded by an act of reason; it is also sustained
and justified by reason. It is carried on by public discussion, in which reason
itself is elevated into a higher kind of life than it can reach in familial and
tribal community. In the *Politics,* Aristotle describes political society as the
culmination of human communities. In cities, he says, there are two irreducible parts, the wealthy and the poor, and the shape that political life takes on
results from the perennial struggle between these two groups to rule over
the whole.[11] The tension between the richer and the poorer parts of a society makes up the *perpetuum mobile* for politics. When the wealthy rule for
their own benefit, the city is an oligarchy; when the poor rule for their own
benefit, the city is literally a democracy, a rule by the people or the many,
since there normally are more poorer than wealthier members of society.
Aristotle says that the best outcome for most people in most places at most
times, the practically best form of the city generally, is the republic, the *politeia,* which is intermediate between oligarchy and democracy. In a republic, a
large middle class—middle in both an economic and an ethical sense—is established between the rich and the poor, and the laws and not men rule, and
they do so for the benefit of the whole city, not for any particular part.[12] To
live this way is a great human accomplishment. It is a truly exalted exercise

11. The "political triangle" of oligarchy, democracy, and republic is treated in book 4 of the
Politics. The determination of the rich and poor as the irreducible segments of the city is done in
chapters 3 and 4. Democracy and oligarchy, the most common forms of political life and the expressions of these two parts of the city, are treated in chapters 4 and 5. Chapter 6 is devoted to the
various modifications of oligarchy and democracy. The republic is discussed in chapters 7 and 8.
The fact that it is the practically best form of rule is shown in chapter 9. Chapter 11 gives advice
on how to strengthen the middle class. One reason why a republic is a good form for political
life is the fact that it allows many people to participate in ruling, to be citizens, but without being
partisan in their rule. There is more talent, judgment, and virtue in many than in one or a few;
see *Politics* III, 11, 1281a39–b21. Aristotle also notes that democracies are particularly vulnerable to
demagogues, the "leaders of the people"; see *Politics* IV, 4, 1292a4–38, and V, 5, 1304b19–1305a36.

12. It should be noted that in his discussion of the republic in *Politics* IV, 7–9, Aristotle does
not claim that the republic as such promotes virtue or nobility; he presents it rather as a resolution
of the parallelogram of political forces, in which the interests of both the poor and the rich are
best reconciled. The two groups are blended into a middle class that will rule through the laws for
the advantage of the whole. Virtue as the overriding end of the republican city will arise through
that city's participation in aristocracy; see below, note 13. This "value-free" understanding of the
republic is expressed in the brief description given in IV, 8, 1293b33–34: "For the republic is, to
state it simply, a mixture of oligarchy and democracy." See also the same chapter, 1294a22–25: "It

of reason for citizens to allow the laws to rule, to have the strength of reason and character to subordinate themselves to the laws, which they allow to rule for the benefit of the whole. Not all people have the civic habits and public vision to let the laws and not their own partisan interests rule over the whole; not all people are immediately capable of being citizens.

This triad of oligarchy, democracy, and republic is the core of Aristotle's *Politics;* the entire work pivots around this triangle. I would also make the stronger claim that what Aristotle is describing here is the truth of human political life, and not just his opinion or a description proper to his time and place. He is presenting the "mobilities" of political life, and the various solutions and deviations that are proper to it. What he describes goes on even now, so long as we continue to have a political life. Aristotle is describing politics as a human thing, as a human possibility, not just as a historical fact. If we fail to see this, it is because we ourselves have become incapable of recognizing human nature and have fallen into historical story-telling instead.

Aristotle also discusses monarchy and aristocracy, in which one man or a few virtuous men rule for the good of the whole, and these two forms serve as a kind of norm for what all cities can be.[13] Because they admit only a few people to rule, however, they may not be possible once societies become very large (Aristotle admits this limitation),[14] but they must be kept in mind as part of how we design and live our politics: when the laws are made to govern, they should rule as virtuous agents would rule. Also, there is an important qualification in his definition of aristocracy. Aristotle says that aristocracy can be defined in two ways. You have an aristocracy, first, when the virtuous rule because of their virtue (the virtuous become the establishment, the *politeuma*), or second, when whoever is ruling exercises his or their

---

is evident that a mixture of the two--of the wealthy and the poor--is to be called a republic, while a mixture of the three [wealthy, poor, and virtuous] should more particularly be called an aristocracy (in addition to the genuine and first form)."

13. Kingship is treated and its problems discussed in *Politics* III, 14–17. In chapter 18 Aristotle says that the virtue of a good king and of true aristocrats would be the same as the virtue of a good man. Book VII in its entirety seems to be a more extended treatment of the best regime, along with remarks about the material conditions under which it could be realized.

14. At III, 15, 1286b8–10, Aristotle says, "And it is probably for this reason that people were originally ruled by kings, because it was rare to find men who were very much distinguished by their virtue, especially since the cities they inhabited then were so small." See also III, 17, where Aristotle says that there may be some populations in which it is best if one individual or one family should rule.

rule for the sake of what is best for the city and its members.[15] Because of this second definition of aristocracy, there can be an aristocratic component to every form of constitution, including a republic.

On the margin of all these forms of political life stands tyranny, the catastrophic disaster that is always there lurking as the threat to political life. It is the ever-present sinkhole on the margin of politics. It will always be there; nothing we can do can definitively exclude it as a possibility. In tyranny there is no longer any political life, but only servile subjection to a ruler or rulers who rule for their benefit alone, without any virtuous guidance or purpose. To be ruled tyrannically is incompatible with human nature.[16]

In Aristotle's view, the best kind of political community will be made up of elements from all the good regimes: there will be monarchic, aristocratic, and popular elements in the various parts of the government. This variety will provide a kind of tensile strength for the city. Each type of city has its own proper political virtue: even the deviant regimes, such as the oligarchic and the democratic, try to shape the people in the city to fit the constitution, and for this reason every city is concerned not only with economic matters, public safety, and defense, but also with the virtue of its people.[17] This conformity of the upbringing with the constitution will happen as a matter of course in every political society, but all the regimes have to be measured by the standard of the virtuous man, and the more closely the virtue of the city approximates that of the good man, the agent of moral truth, the better the city will be as a human achievement.

And what is common to all cities in which there is a political life—in opposition, for example, to tyranny, where there is none—is the fact that people do argue about who should rule, that is, they argue about what kind of virtue will set the tone for the city. People who claim that they should rule are trying to do more than just get themselves into the public offices; first and foremost they are also trying to establish a certain way of life, one that they embody, in the community that they want to rule. There always

---

15. *Politics* III, 7, 1279a35–37.

16. *Politics* III, 17, 1287b37–41; Aristotle says there is no people that is *tyrannikon* by nature, nor is any fit for the other deviant regimes.

17. Each city has to habituate and educate its people to fit the constitution of the city: *Politics* V, 9, 1310a12–38. Even oligarchic and democratic cities must do this. If the habits of the people do not fit the laws of the city, Aristotle says, the city will be like the *akratic* man, whose reason and passions are at odds with one another.

are "culture wars" in political life. Oligarchs, for example, want to live according to the principle that if we are different in one respect, that is, in regard to wealth, we are different absolutely and should be treated as such. The "virtue" in oligarchy is measured by the possession of wealth. Democrats, on the other hand, want to live by the principle that if we are equal in one respect, that is, in regard to liberty, we should be considered equal absolutely, and "virtue" for the extreme democrats is the ability to do whatever you wish, the liberty to satisfy any impulse; that is the kind of life they promote.[18] When people argue that they should rule, they are exercising their reason; this particular exercise of it is higher than the exercise one finds within the family or the village, where such argument about rule does not take place, just as foundings do not take place. Because it is reason that makes us persons, the people engaged in political life are acting more fully as persons than they are able to do in their families and villages. They strive to project and embody a form of human life; they do not just deal with the necessities of life.

It is also the case that there is no one form of the city that is the best absolutely everywhere. Much depends on the population, the circumstances, the lay of the land, the history of the people, and other things. Aristotle distinguishes four senses of the best in politics: first, the best "as we might pray for it," when all the circumstances are favorable (we may not be able to implement this best form, but we must keep it in mind); second, the best in particular circumstances; third, the best that we can achieve when are faced with a city that is already established; and fourth, the best for most people in most circumstances (effectively, this is the republic).[19] Political excellence for Aristotle is therefore flexible, adaptable, and analogous, not univocal. It is the outcome of prudential, not mathematical, reason.

Aristotle's description of political life is not relativized by history. It ex-

18. For the understanding of justice proper, respectively, to oligarchs and democrats, see *Politics* III, 9, and V, 1, 1301a25–b4.

19. The four senses of "best" are found in *Politics* IV, 1, 1288b21–39. It is important to note that the very best form of the city does not signify an "ideal" city, one that would demand preternatural circumstances or a transformation of human nature. Rather, it is the city one could bring about if all the circumstances and conditions were the best one could possibly hope for. Such a city may be practically unrealizable, but not unrealizable in principle. The wonders of modern technology tempt us to think that preternatural circumstances may in fact be attainable, and that a utopia may no longer be as distant as once was thought.

presses the political possibilities of human nature, and it is as true now as it always was. Aristotle's *Politics* formulates the substance, the *ousia* of political life better than any other work that has ever been written.[20]

The modern situation

I wish to claim that in our contemporary exercise of political life, in our practice, we *do* conform to Aristotle's analysis, *to the extent that we still have a political life.* For example, in the United States the richer and the poorer are clearly appealed to, respectively, by the Republicans and the Democrats, at least as these parties were defined for most of the twentieth century, and the problem is to fashion a republic, with an inclusive middle class. There are monarchic and aristocratic elements in our political life, and there is always the danger of tyranny. The major difficulty in our modern situation, of course, is the scale of society and the technology that makes such a scale possible. How can anyone survey the common good? How can any political form be embodied in tens or hundreds of millions of people? This is the great challenge to political prudence in our time.

But although we conform in practice with Aristotle, the *idea* we have of political life in our present day is quite different from what we find in his teachings. In our public discussion of political life, we tend to think that there is one form of government that ought to be installed everywhere. We call it democracy, and we are impatient if we find places in which it has not been realized; we call such places undeveloped countries, implying that they are politically either childish or stunted.

When we speak this way, our speech is, I believe, caught up in an ambiguity. I think we confuse two things: the republic and the modern state. The republic is the political form in which laws, not partial, one-sided, self-interested men rule; it is Aristotle's *politeia,* the constitution that is generally the best that can be attained by most people in most places. The modern state, on the other hand, is something that arose through modern political philosophy. It claims to be something radically new and radically diff-

---

20. For recent commentaries on the *Politics,* see Mary P. Nichols, *Citizens and Statesmen: A Study of Aristotle's* Politics (Lanham, MD: Rowman and Littlefield, 1992); Michael Davis, *The Politics of Philosophy: A Commentary on Aristotle's* Politics (Lanham, MD: Rowman and Littlefield, 1996); Peter Simpson, *A Philosophical Commentary on the* Politics *of Aristotle* (Chapel Hill: University of North Carolina Press, 1996).

erent from earlier forms of government. It is meant to be a definitive solution to the human political problem, not a solution for this time and place. It was initially visualized by Machiavelli and baptized by Jean Bodin with the name *sovereignty*.[21] It was comprehensively described by Hobbes, and worked out and adjusted by subsequent thinkers like Locke, Rousseau, Kant, and Hegel.[22]

When we speak of democracy, we tend more or less to think that we are speaking of a community in which the laws rule, not men, but usually we are really speaking about a modern state, the one informed by sovereignty, not a society informed by one of the political constitutions described by Aristotle. We also tend to think that the modern state, modern democracy, has arisen as a perfect, culminating development in human history. It is not seen as one of the forms of political life among many, the form that we may be able to achieve if we are lucky and intelligent enough.

Let me express my own value judgment at this point. To the extent that the word *democracy* means a republic, it presents a good thing, a form of political life to which one can properly dedicate oneself, one that can be in conformity with human nature and human virtue. The political problem is to determine, by practical wisdom, how the rule of laws ordered toward human excellence can be implemented in our day and age, in whatever part of the world we inhabit. To the extent, however, that the word *democracy* means the modern state, the one described by Hobbes and glorified by Hegel, it presents a great human problem and an ominous threat to the human person. It is a formula for organizing deracinated human beings.

The modern Hobbesian state was nurtured in absolute monarchies in the early modern period, it showed its face in the French Revolution, and it came into full view in the National Socialist and the Marxist-Leninist-

---

21. Bodin expressed his concept of sovereignty in his *Les six livres de la république* (1576). See the selections in *On Sovereignty*, edited by Julian H. Franklin, Cambridge Texts in the History of Political Thought (New York: Cambridge University Press, 1992). On p. 1 Bodin says, "Sovereignty is the absolute and perpetual power of a commonwealth. . . ." He models the sovereign after God (pp. 46, 50). He also admits that the concept of sovereignty is not present in Aristotle (pp. 47, 50). As Julian Franklin observes, for Bodin "citizenship does not necessarily imply political participation as in Aristotle" (p. 1, footnote).

22. On the concept of sovereignty see Francis X. Slade, "Rule as Sovereignty: The Universal and Homogeneous State," in John J. Drummond and James G. Hart, eds., *The Truthful and the Good: Essays in Honor of Robert Sokolowski* (Boston: Kluwer Academic Publishers, 1996), pp. 159–80.

Stalinist totalitarian regimes in the twentieth century. In this conference, we commemorate the work of Pope John Paul II, a man who experienced both these horrors, the Nazi and the Stalinist. He reacted to them, in his actions and words, with a courageous defense of the human person in its dignity before God. His defense of the human person, furthermore, is based essentially on truth, on the human person's ability to hear and discover the truth about the world, about himself, and about God. Pope John Paul II reminds us that human beings are individual substances of a rational nature, and that through their reason they can respond to the splendor of truth, even in the face of powers that do their best to extinguish the truth and annihilate the human dignity that flows from it. They truly are powers of darkness, for whom will triumphs over intelligence, power over reason, and choice over life. The problem of the modern state, furthermore, was not resolved by victory in the Second World War and the end of the Cold War. It continues in the development of the therapeutic and managerial state, and much of the human drama in regard to the modern state is going on in this very city and its suburbs. What will we have: a genuine republic or a Leviathan masquerading as a republic? The question is still open, and human success, in the short term at least, is by no means assured, but it is possible. As this struggle continues into the future, it is quite appropriate that there be in this city an embodied presence of John Paul II, shepherd and stubborn reminder of the dignity of man.[23]

Contrasts between republics and the modern state

Let us speak further about the choice between a republic and Leviathan. I would like to bring out three ways in which these two forms of political life differ. To be more accurate, I should not call them two forms of political life, but the form of political life and the form of mass subjection and individualism.

First of all, in the republic, and in all good political constitutions, reason can be exercised. Men can think and express themselves. The republic is not possible without active human reason. Such reason is exercised in the founding of the city, in the deliberations that go on to determine courses of ac-

---

23. As mentioned above in note 5, the conference at which this paper was originally given was held, in part, at the John Paul II Cultural Center in Washington, D.C.

tion, and in specifying the laws of the city and adjudicating the application of the laws. All those who are citizens are able to enter into such exercises of reason; that is what it means to be a citizen, to be able to enter into political reasoning. But besides these political or prudential exercises of reason, there is also in the republic the recognition of the power of theoretical reason, of understanding for its own sake. Besides the ethical and political life of reason, there is a life of simple understanding. Aristotle recognizes this in book 10 of the *Nicomachean Ethics,* where he says that the highest human happiness is found in the theoretic life, but he also acknowledges it in a very dramatic way in book 7 of the *Politics,* chapters 2 and 3.[24] He says that the life of thinking is higher than the political, and he implies that if one does not acknowledge the excellence of the life of thinking, one will try to satisfy one's thirst for the infinite by ruling over others, and one will therefore try to magnify this domination over as many people as possible, at home and abroad, even over one's neighbors and parents and children and friends.[25] In other words, the life of ruling is not the simply highest life; we have to take our bearings from something higher. This also means that there is something in us that transcends political life, and only when political life acknowledges such transcendence can it find its proper place in human affairs. Only then will there be limited government. What this means is that a true republic, a city limited by laws, will have respect for the person as an agent of truth, both in the practical and in the theoretical order. The reason of the human person has its own directedness and its own appetite for truth; it is not just a tool in the service of subrational desires.

The modern state, in contrast, as described by Hobbes and embodied in totalitarian forms of rule, denies the domain of truth. For it, reason is a tool. The modern state is constituted as a new reality, as the sovereign, by an act of sheer will by men in the state of nature, and it exercises its own power simply for its survival and to prevent the state of nature from returning. The sovereign state is separate from the people and it lords over them. For Hobbes, the metaphysical reality of the state is made up of its own power and its own decisions. There is no truth of human nature by which it must be measured and to which it must be subordinated. The state determines even the kind of

---

24. Aristotle's argument is developed in *Politics* VII, 2–3, especially in 1325a31–b32.
25. *Politics* VII, 3, 1325a34–41.

religion—the grasp of transcendence—that it will tolerate. The citizens or subjects are not agents of truth in any way; when they express their opinions, they are, according to Hobbes, engaged in vain posturing, not true deliberation: "For there is no reason why every man should not naturally mind his own private, than the public business, but that here he sees a means to declare his eloquence, whereby he may gain the reputation of being ingenious and wise, and returning home to his friends, to his parents, to his wife and children, rejoice and triumph in the applause of his dexterous behavior."[26] For Hobbes, the sovereign's will alone should determine public affairs, and even the religious opinions of people have to be segregated into privacy. Such religious beliefs have no public standing as possible truths and cannot be presented as such.[27] George Orwell was not wrong when in *1984* he has the totalitarian O'Brien controlling not only what you should do, but also how and what you should think, even what you should think in mathematics.[28] There is nothing to transcend the sovereign; as Hobbes's predecessor and guide, Niccolò Machiavelli, put it, any ideal or best kingdoms, whether Christian or Greek, are figments of the imagination, imaginary kingdoms, that bring about ruin rather than preservation.[29]

In this political viewpoint, intelligence becomes merely calculation and pragmatic coping with the material needs of life. Even the social contract is just the work of calculating reason. Reason is not insight into truth, because there are no natures or forms of things to be understood. There is only

---

26. Thomas Hobbes, *De Cive* 10, §15. See also chapter 1, §2: "All free congress ariseth either from mutual poverty or from vain glory." I have used the 1650 English translation of this work, which was written and published by Hobbes in Latin; see *De Cive: The English Version*, ed. J. H. Warrender (New York: Oxford University Press, 1983). The translation was long considered to have been done by Hobbes himself, but recent scholarship claims otherwise. See Noel Malcolm, "Charles Cotton, Translator of Hobbes's *De Cive*," in *Aspects of Hobbes* (New York: Oxford University Press, 2000), pp. 234–58.

27. On the essentially public character of Christian belief, see Francis X. Slade, "Was Ist Aufklärung? Notes on Maritain, Rorty, and Bloom, With Thanks but No Apologies to Immanuel Kant," in Daniel McInerny, ed., *The Common Things: Essays on Thomism and Education* (Washington, D.C.: The Catholic University of America Press, 1999), pp. 48–68.

28. On Orwell's insight into the reality of the Soviet system, see Alain Besançon, *La falsification du bien. Soloviev et Orwell* (Paris: Julliard, 1985). The second part of this book is entitled "Orwell ou la justification du mal." Besançon's work abounds in striking phrases. In describing the radical falsity of modern totalitarian rule, he speaks of "ce mensonge universel" (p. 176), and he says, "Un homme sans mémoire est d'une plasticité absolue. Il est recrée à chaque instant" (p. 183).

29. Machiavelli makes this claim, of course, in the famous chapter 15 of *The Prince*.

the calculation of consequences. The epistemological skepticism of modernity is not unrelated to its metaphysics and political philosophy. Indeed, Hobbes's understanding of men as machines and thinking as mechanical motion, which is presented at the beginning of *Leviathan*,[30] is also not unrelated to his political philosophy: this is how human beings must understand themselves if they are to subject themselves to Leviathan. It is how the philosophical spokesman for Leviathan wants them to understand themselves. The mechanistic interpretation of human beings offered to us by reductive forms of cognitive science, in which mind is replaced by brain and human beings are not seen as agents of truth, is teleologically ordered toward the modern state in its pure form.

This then is the first contrast I wish to draw between classical and modern political philosophy: modern thought subtracts the issue of truth from the domain of politics, but a republic acknowledges both practical and theoretical truth and the human person's ability to attain it. We might ask ourselves which of these two options is characteristic of our own political culture.

The second point I wish to make is that modern political thought considers the state to be an inevitable development in the history of humanity. For Aristotle, the various constitutions come and go as events move along and people respond to them. There is no necessary destiny driving them on and nothing is definitive; circumstances and choices permit now this form, now that to prevail, and sometimes the political society falls into tyranny. Aristotle encourages us to do the best we can in the situations in which we find ourselves. Political life is an exercise of prudence.

In the modern understanding, and especially in the twist that German idealism and Hegel have given it, the modern state is a definitive achievement. No further prudential and philosophical reflection is necessary concerning political society, because the final answer has been reached in the evolution of world history. This is why we take it for granted that what we call democracy should be installed everywhere, and why we call countries in which it does not exist "undeveloped" countries, or, more hopefully, countries "on the way to development." This belief in the historical necessity of the modern state might also explain why political philosophy has been stud-

---

30. See the Introduction and first six chapters of *Leviathan*.

ied in departments of political science, not in departments of philosophy, in Catholic and non-Catholic institutions alike. The political question is not open any longer. The state is a necessary thing—generated by historical if not cosmic necessity—and hence it is an object of social science, not of fundamental philosophical reflection. Nature has been overcome by history, and the unsettled arguments about who should rule and what form of government should prevail, the disputes among parties, can now be put to rest. The declarations of the end of history proposed by Alexandre Kojève and Francis Fukuyama are related to this understanding of the modern state.

In contrast with this view of modern politics, I would claim that human nature has not changed, and that political life is the same now as it always has been, and that what is truly civic and political in modern states is precisely what is still functioning as a republic, as a rule of laws, in which people are citizens and not subjects, in which it is still possible to deliberate and voice opinions about how we should live, where we can still express ourselves about the noble and the just, and can ask whether the laws we live under are or are not in conformity with the ends of human nature and the truth about man.

In order to foster true political life, it is necessary for us to change our understanding of the history of philosophy. It is necessary for us to overcome the segmentation of philosophy into ancient, medieval, and modern. We must avoid thinking that we can only understand philosophers as the products of their historical circumstances, the products of their epoch. We must recover the idea that philosophy is a perennial thing, that there are philosophical truths that persist throughout all the periods and ages, and that there is a truth about human nature and about political life that has been there all along. Human nature does not change, and the nature of political life does not change either. The only thing we have to relativize historically is the modern state, not the political life that we find described in Aristotle. The modern state can be explained by its historical circumstances and it can be transcended. Aristotle has brought to light the nature of political life, while Machiavelli, Hobbes, and their followers have described and fabricated a construct, one that is not in keeping with human nature, human reason, or the human person, one that can be explained by the historical circumstances of its emergence.

We have contrasted the republic and the modern state in regard to the issue of truth and in regard to the issue of historical inevitability. The third contrast I wish to draw between the republic and the modern state concerns the relationship each of these forms of rule has toward other social authorities and other communities, such as the family, the Church, private associations, unions, businesses, educational institutions, and the like. The republic presupposes prepolitical societies. It does not claim to fabricate men or to make men human. It assumes that families and neighborhoods, churches and private associations, can all do their irreplaceable work in forming human beings, and it facilitates and crowns their work by its own, by establishing the city under laws, the city that both presupposes such prepolitical societies and brings them to their own perfection. This assumption of prepolitical societies is expressed in Aristotle's *Politics* by the fact that the household is treated in book 1 as a presupposition of political life, and in that book Aristotle says, "For the political art does not make men."[31] The city makes citizens, but it does not make human beings.

The sovereign state, in contrast, the Leviathan, levels all prepolitical communities and authorities. It makes a clean sweep. The only private societies that it tolerates are those that it permits to exist for its own purposes. Instead of assuming prepolitical societies and bringing them to a higher perfection, the modern state is related to individuals, which it takes out of the state of nature and transforms into a human condition. This change is vividly expressed by Rousseau, who in *On The Social Contract,* describes the legislator or the founder as follows: "The man who makes bold to undertake the founding of a people should feel within himself the capacity to—if I may put it so—change human nature: to transform each individual . . . into a part of a larger whole, from which he in a sense draws his life and being. . . ."[32] We have seen attempts in twentieth-century regimes to displace and replace the family itself, as well as neighborhoods, educational institutions, and charitable entities such as hospitals, by massive governmental bureaucracies and mobilizations. The *homo sovieticus* was only the most extreme form of this titanic totalitarian effort, and we can see what it did to people who lived under it and were its targets. Human cloning and the artificial conception of human life may be a Western scientific version of the same thing. But a coherent

31. *Politics* I, 10, 1258a21–22.
32. Jean Jacques Rousseau, *The Social Contract,* translated by Willmoore Kendall (New York: Henry Regnery Co., 1954), book 2, chapter 7, pp. 57–58.

society is not possible in a Hobbesian state, because such a state is not in keeping with the nature of man.

Concluding practical remarks

I have discussed both classical political philosophy—which I would characterize not as classical but as perennial—and the modern state, and I have tried to draw some contrasts between them. We have discussed them in regard to three issues; first, whether or not they acknowledge truth and human reason; second, whether they are the outcome of prudential achievement or historical inevitability; and third, whether or not they acknowledge prepolitical human beings, societies, and authorities. It should be obvious that the issues we are discussing are of great human importance. Human life can be terribly tortured by forms of association that destroy political life, and political life can be destroyed by rampant individualism no less than by totalitarian regimes. Modern individualism—what is called liberal individualism—harms the person slowly and silently through a notion of freedom as absence of any and all constraints on the individual's choice; liberal individualism thus undermines its own moral preconditions of self-control, self-governance, and internal, moral freedom. At the other extreme, the collectivism of communism and fascism harms the person suddenly and directly and loudly, through a violent abuse of power that destroys freedom, both external and internal. Thus the two seemingly different modern regimes both destroy the person, although in different ways.

The central question of the last part of my paper is, In what way can the human person be protected, preserved, and enhanced in our modern political context? Can we draw up some agenda items for academic life, for the Catholic Church, and for ourselves?

The practical task is for the Church to continue to be active in her defense of the human person. She has in fact done so in things like the Solidarity movement, pro-life causes both in particular countries and internationally, in her educational system, and in her health-care institutions. In other words, the Church herself should continue to act in the public domain. Precisely by defending and exercising her own right to be independent, she creates a wider space for political life for others as well. Political liberty can be preserved only by being exercised.

In a more theoretical domain, the Church can pay greater attention to issues of political philosophy in her academic institution and even in her seminaries and centers that train people for ministry. It is important to educate people for citizenship, and this does not just mean informing them about the procedures of voting and the mechanisms of government. If men and women are to be citizens, they must be educated about what is at stake in political life, and they must be made better aware of how civic life can be lost. They need a vocabulary for political matters, and the Church can help them acquire it. The clergy and religious should also be helped to understand the nature of political life, lest they become unwitting collaborators in the triumph of the modern sovereign state.[33]

In particular, the Church should insist on the role of truth in human life and the relevance of truth to political society. In this domain there are a whole cluster of issues of great personal and political significance. It is important to teach both students and parishioners about them, but it is also important to deepen our theoretical understanding of these concepts, and to make room for them in the contemporary cultural and theological conversation. To be more specific about these theoretical issues, it would be important, first, to validate the fact that truth is obtainable, to show that the human mind is able to discover truth, and to spell out the various kinds of truth and the force and extent of each. To do this is not a mere exercise in epistemology, but a defense of the human person as an agent of truth. To defend the possibility of truth is to defend human dignity. The encyclicals *Fides et Ratio* and *Veritatis Splendor,* as well as the apostolic constitution *Ex Corde Ecclesiae,* are a marvelous charter for this effort. Second, it would be essential to clarify what is meant by human nature and to show how we can speak about human nature. One of the central concepts that needs to be clarified and defended in this respect is the concept of teleology, not only in regard to human nature but in regard to things like life, politics, and religion. Things have ends built into them, and natural ends, the natural perfections of things, are not overridden by the purposes we might have, purposes that we might impose on things. We cannot understand anything unless we know what its end is, that is, unless we know what it is when it is acting at its best.[34]

---

33. See Alain Besançon, *La confusion des langues: La crise idéologique de l'Église* (Paris: Calmann-Levy, 1978). An earlier but less forceful version of this work appeared as an essay, "The Confusion of Tongues," *Daedalus* 108 (Spring 1979): 21–44.

34. For an excellent philosophical treatment of teleology, see two papers by Francis X. Slade:

These issues of truth, human nature, and teleology lie very deeply hidden within contemporary political life. They are at the heart of many current controversies. If the Church were able to formulate them well, and use her educational institutions to develop and teach them, she would be engaged in politics in the best and most appropriate way: not in particular, partisan political activity, but in what we could call the higher politics, the understanding of human life in its principles and in its excellence, the definition of the good human life. The Church in her teaching and in her educational institutions should not measure herself simply by the norms set by the secular world. She should set her own agenda, drawing on her own tradition and inspiration. Through her tradition of natural law, the Church has the resources to redefine the contemporary political conversation in terms of the ends of human nature. By witnessing to the truth the Church would be defending the human person, and would thus make a unique contribution to our contemporary culture and civic life. She would also continue the spirit and teaching of one of her greatest figures, Pope John Paul II.

"On the Ontological Priority of Ends and Its Relevance to the Narrative Arts," in Alice Ramos, ed., *Beauty, Art, and the Polis* (Washington, D.C.: The Catholic University of America Press, 2000), 58–69; and "Ends and Purposes," in Richard Hassing, ed., *Final Causality in Nature and Human Affairs* (Washington, DC: The Catholic University of America Press, 1997), pp. 83–85.

THE CHRISTIAN DIFFERENCE IN PERSONAL RELATIONSHIPS

We wish to discuss the difference that Christian faith makes in the relationships that occur among persons. In order to develop this issue, we first should explore the understanding we have of persons. There are, of course, persons in God—the three persons of the Most Holy Trinity—and angels are persons too, but we wish to discuss the human person. In exploring this topic, I will especially draw on the work of Robert Spaemann, a German Catholic philosopher who is now emeritus professor at the University of Munich. I would especially like to use his book, *Personen,* which has the marvelous subtitle, *Versuche über den Unterschied zwischen "etwas" und "jemand"*[1] [Essays on the Distinction between "Something" and "Someone"]. The first point I wish to examine deals with an unusual feature that belongs to the "logic" of the word *person.*

The logic of personal terms

The strategic distinction that we need to make in order to bring out what is meant by *the human person* is the distinction between a human being and a human person. Every human being is a human person, but the meanings of these terms—the terms *human being* and *person*—are different, and if we can tease out this difference we will have made an important step in

---

1. Robert Spaemann, *Personen. Versuche über den Unterschied zwischen "etwas" und "jemand"* (Stuttgart: Klett-Cotta, 1996).

determining what the person is. Here is the way that Spaemann works out this difference.[2] He observes that the term *human being* or *man* is the name of a species or a genus of living things. These names are what philosophers of language call "sortal" terms, words that mark off a kind of entity, just as the terms *elephant* or *oak tree* or *spider* do. Such terms pick out or "sort out" one of the many species of things in the world: besides elephants, oak trees, spiders, and hydrogen atoms, there also are men or human beings. Such words name a universal. This universal, in turn, can have individuals that fall under it. We can speak about the genus *man* and we can also speak about individual men or human beings, just as we can use the word *tiger* to speak about both the species tiger as well as this or that tiger.

We might be surprised to hear this, but the word *person* is not such a sortal term. It does not name a genus or species or kind of entity. It does not name a universal that encompasses a multitude of individuals. Rather, the term *person* is radically individualistic from the start. The term *person* is, in this respect, like the demonstrative pronoun *this*. The term *this* cannot be used to mark off a genus or species; it too is not a sortal term. The term *this* is individualized every time we use it. It is formal and does not have a de-limited content that is marked off from other kinds of things.

Spaemann illustrates this difference between sortal and nonsortal terms in the following way. In regard to sortal terms, it makes sense for me to say to you, "Come here, I want to show you an oak tree," or "Come here, I want to show you a man (or a human being)." In such cases, I would be trying to show you an individual in a species. But it does not make sense for me to say to you, "Come here, I want to show you a person," no more than it would make sense for me to say, "Come here, I want to show you a this." Neither a person nor a this is an individual within a species. The logic of the term *person* is very tricky, much more puzzling than it might appear at first sight.

One might ask, "Why get into these logical conundrums? We want to hear about the person, about his dignity and originality and rights. Why should we care about sortal and nonsortal terms?" In reply to this objection, I would note that the logical peculiarity of the term *person* brings out the fact that each and every person is radically individualized. To express this feature of persons, I would like to introduce the term *singularity*. Each

2. Spaemann, *Personen,* pp. 14–19, 25.

person is a singularity. Each human person is not just a member of the species *homo sapiens,* but a singularity as well. Furthermore, each human being is more than an individual; Fido the dog and Leo the lion are individuals in their respective species, but they are not singularities, not persons. A human being, John or Jane, is both an individual in a species and also a singularity or a person. A human being is more radically individualized than is a dog or a lion. This difference is important in dealing with things like evolution or the physiological basis for human existence, or even for things like cloning and issues related to the right to life. I would also claim that the Catholic belief that each human soul is individually created by God is related to the singularity of the human person.[3] In things like psychological counseling, it is important to realize that the therapist is not just dealing with an entity that needs to be made organically whole but also with a person who has a certain status and dignity as such. Finally, in the Middle Ages many thinkers who spoke about personhood stressed the incommunicability of the person, and my use of singularity is just a contemporary, phenomenological way of naming the same distinction.

So we have the human being and we have the person. The philosophical problem is, How do we reconcile these two things? How do we reconcile the fact that a human being is a member of a species, the species *man,* and also a singular person? The danger that lurks in this question is that we may say that there are two things in us: there is the human being and there is the person, as two entities with one somehow dwelling in the other. This would be a false and harmful approach. Somehow we have to show that there is only one thing, one entity, which is both an individualized nature and also a person. Animals and plants do not present this dilemma; they just are individuals in their species. They are subordinate to their species; even in the practical order, their existence is governed and exhausted by the well-being of the species. Human beings are also governed to some degree by their species and the inclinations that are natural to it, but in addition they exercise a government over themselves, and they do so because they are persons as well as individuals. They are not reducible to their species or their inclinations.

However, we must be careful not to go to the other extreme; we must

---

3. The singularity of persons is also reflected in the traditional belief that each angel is a species unto itself. One might just as well have said that each angel is a singularity. Angels do not share a nature in common; they are not individuals in a species.

not push this self-government into an existentialist excess. A Sartrean self-creation would detach the person from the human being and make him capable not only of governing his human nature but of creating it as he sees fit. Both extremes, the reductionist and the existentialist, must be avoided. Human beings have a human nature and also govern themselves, but they must govern themselves in accordance with the truth of their human nature. How can both these dimensions be harmoniously thought together? We need to work out a distinction between the human being and the person, but we must avoid a separation between them.[4]

Reason as that which makes us persons

Why do human beings have this complexity, this duality of being both human beings and persons? It is our reason that makes the difference. One of the powers of human nature is reason or intelligence, and this power, which stems from our human being, makes us transcend our human being; it makes us to be persons and not just individuals. Our reason singularizes us and makes us subjects as well as members of a species. Because of our reason we share in the form of personal being that is proper to angels and even to God.

To refine our terminology, let us draw the distinction between soul and spirit. Soul is the animation of a body. Every living thing has a soul: animals and plants are organic, animated beings, and so are men.[5] But besides having souls, human beings also have spirit, which involves the power of reason. Many thinkers, of course, have understood human beings as radically divided into two parts, the body and the spirit, and some have even thought that the rational part of the soul preexists its life in the body. But in the Christian understanding, the spirit is the culminating part of the soul, and man is one being, not two. Man is both a human being and a person, and to formulate how these two dimensions come together is one of the perennial challenges for Christian thinking.

I would like to develop two ways in which human reason is manifested.

4. On the centrality of distinctions in philosophical thinking, see Robert Sokolowski, "Making Distinctions," in *Pictures, Quotations, and Distinctions: Fourteen Essays in Phenomenology* (Notre Dame: University of Notre Dame Press, 1992), pp. 55–91, and "The Method of Philosophy: Making Distinctions," *Review of Metaphysics* 51 (1998): 515–32.

5. On the difference between soul and spirit, see chapter 5 above.

These two themes will bring out more fully how reason establishes the singularity of persons. One way deals with cognition and the other with action.

First, the cognitional approach. When we thoughtfully articulate an object or a situation, we express it in speech; we make judgments. We say things like "The weather is improving," or "He has shown himself to be a liar," or "No one can take this from me." We exercise our reason when we articulate such things. Even if we are dealing with human emotions, there is an element of judgment and of reason in what we experience and express. If I am angry at you, it is because I think that you deserve this anger, that you have done something insulting or unjust to me or one of my own. Human emotion involves an opinion and hence it involves reason. The basic use of reason is to articulate a state of affairs and to express it in a judgment or statement or opinion. But then we can go one step further beyond this rational articulation; we can say things like, "*I know* that the weather is improving," or "*I think* he is a liar," or "*I am* very angry with you." In expressions like these, the use of the first-person pronoun, the use of the word *I,* is special; I would like to call it the declarative use of the first person, as opposed to the merely informational use. What we do in such declarative usage is to confirm or ratify a certain statement or opinion. We explicitly appropriate the judgment we have made, and we mention ourselves as the ones who take responsibility for what we are saying. We do more than make an assertion; we put ourselves manifestly on the spot, we engage our responsibility in an explicit way, we declare ourselves. In doing so, our personhood comes to the fore. Our singularity as cognitive agents is mentioned. I think that the declarative use of the first-person singular is a distinct and important phenomenological presentation of the human person.

Second, the domain of action. Here, our rationality and personhood come to the fore in the fact that we gradually become responsible, and are held to be responsible, for what we have become in our lives. We are not responsible for having been born as human beings, with all the emotions and inclinations that belong to our nature, but we do gradually make our own choices and appropriate our actions and thereby determine how we will be as human beings. Our choices do not only change things in the world; they also change us into being the way our choices are. We gradually specify the manner in which we will be inclined to act in the future. We are not responsible for being the kind of entity that can become angry, but we are in part responsible for the way in which our anger tends to be exercised. We are responsible, in large part, for our second nature, our character, for the shape that our natural inclinations and emotions have taken on.[6] We do not praise or blame an animal for being ferocious or submissive, but we do praise or blame human beings for becoming courageous, cowardly, or rash, for having become dissolute or frugal, prudent or frivolous. We may have been born with inclinations that tend toward one or other of these conditions, but in the end we have made the many choices that fixed our character along one line or another.

With these two points behind us, I think we can now say something a bit more precise about how our rational powers fit in with our human nature, how our personhood and our human being are related to one another. Once again, I wish to make use of Spaemann's thought.

Through our reason, we shepherd or cultivate our own concrete human being. Our human being, our concrete human nature, the nature we are born with, *will* develop in one way or another. It is something that is not complete when we are born; it will unfold, and how it unfolds depends on us. The ultimate responsibility for how this human being develops lies within that human nature itself, in its rational power. We as persons cultivate *how* we exist as human beings. Animals and plants develop according to their nature and in response to circumstances, but they do not govern themselves nor are they applauded or condemned for what they have done with their lives. There may be a statue for Man o'War in Lexington, Kentucky, but not, strictly speaking, because of what that horse did with his life; still less, incidentally, would we find a statue being put up for him by other horses. Animals and plants do not *lead* their lives, but we do lead our lives. The statue of Man o'War is different from a statue of Robert E. Lee or Stonewall Jackson. To put it in another way, as human beings we *have* our nature; we are not simply identical with it. We can take a certain distance to our concrete human being; as Spaemann puts it, "[Man] *has* a nature. Nature does not have him."[7] As persons we shepherd ourselves, and we must cultivate ourselves in accordance with the nature that we have.

These remarks will suffice, at present, for our discussion of the concept

6. See Aristotle, *Nicomachean Ethics* III, 5.

7. Spaemann, *Personen,* p. 105.

of person. Now we must turn to another theme, to the fact that we cannot cultivate ourselves in solitude. We cannot actualize our own human being without the presence and assistance of other human beings, that is, without being engaged in personal relationships.

Intersubjectivity

A human person cannot actualize and cultivate his human nature without the involvement of other people, other persons. It is not the case that our cognition or our action can take place within us simply as individuals. Our cognition and our actions are not merely natural processes.

Consider, for example, the judgments that we make. Judgments or opinions do not arise in us simply as a result of an internal natural process. It is not the case that a judgment occurs when a sensory impact is elevated into intellectual cognition by some sort of activity in the brain or by the intervention of cognitive faculties such as the agent intellect. A judgment is not a solitary thing that just takes place within us, any more than a vote or a complaint is a solitary thing. *We* as cognitive agents have to achieve our judgments, and we do so in relation with others. What happens when we engage in a judgment is that one person draws the attention of another person toward some object, and then says something about that object. In its original form, a judgment occurs between people. Only subsequently, and only after we become quite sophisticated, do we become capable of making judgments for ourselves alone, of thinking simply in solitude. Our cognitive abilities become actualized among people, and they also depend on emotional forces: we need security, confidence, and patience to be able to refer to things and truthfully say something about them. Even the imposition of names on things takes place among people; for a child to learn that a certain sound is the name of some object, the child must realize that someone else is using this word to refer to that thing.[8] If an object and a sound merely come together, the child may associate the sound with the object but will not take the sound to be the name of the thing. The person becomes activated as an agent of truth in reciprocity with other people. The mind or the reason of the person becomes activated intersubjectively.

8. See Paul Bloom, *How Children Learn the Meaning of Words* (Cambridge: The MIT Press, 2000), pp. 55–87. See also the excellent book by Kyra Karmiloff and Annette Karmiloff-Smith, *Pathways to Language: From Fetus to Adolescent,* (Cambridge: Harvard University Press, 2001).

It should be even more evident that human moral conduct develops only in interaction with others. The virtues of justice and friendship obviously can occur only when we act with and toward other people, but even the more subjective virtues of temperance and courage can be developed only under the guidance of others. Temperance and courage require a rational form, the structure of a middle between extremes; they are thoughtful virtues, not just impulses. Other people share their virtue and their moral assessments, their prudence, with us as they open up for us the possibility of living a life in accordance with virtue. It is true that some people may be able on their own to transcend a debased and hopeless moral environment, that their goodness may seem to come almost from nowhere or almost entirely from within them; I believe that such a person is what Aristotle calls the "godlike" man.[9] But even such people require other persons as foils to stimulate their own entrance into moral excellence.

I would like to add one more point in regard to the intersubjective character of moral action. It deals with the role of friendship in human conduct. Traditionally, friendship is not listed among the moral virtues. The classical "cardinal virtues" are courage, temperance, prudence, and justice. However, I have tried to argue that in Aristotle's *Nicomachean Ethics* friendship plays a much more central role in the discussion of the moral virtues. Several virtues, including courage and temperance, are treated in books 3 and 4, and justice is discussed in book 5, but friendship is treated in two books, 8 and 9, toward the end of the work. I think that friendship, and specifically noble friendship, is the culmination of moral virtue; the ability to be a friend in the highest and best way is the moral perfection of human nature, according to Aristotle. Justice is not the highest virtue after all; friendship is. Friendship is beyond justice. In perfect and noble friendship, the friends wish well toward each other specifically in their respective individualities, and their friendship makes it possible for them to accomplish things they never could have done apart from the friendship. I would also like to claim that all the other virtues, even those of courage and temperance, participate in friendship; in courage and temperance we become friends with ourselves as we attain harmony between our reason on the one hand and our desires and aversions on the

---

9. On the godlike, see Aristotle, *Nicomachean Ethics* VII, 1, and also the important cryptic remark at X, 9, 1179b22–23.

other. It should also be clear, I think, that justice can be seen as a participation in friendship.[10]

If friendship does have this exalted role in human moral excellence, then it is all the more clear that we become virtuous only through our activity with other people and toward other people, just as we actualize our reason only with other people and toward other people. Our personhood is actualized intersubjectively, even in the natural order. Such perfection occurs first in familial relationships, of course, as the child learns to speak and interact in response to his mother's initiatives and reactions, but such a familial achievement could not be the highest form of human personal existence. As important and as fundamental as it may be, it would become stifling if it were made into the largest context. The human person has to expand beyond the family into the village and then into the city, or at least into whatever approximation to the city he is fortunate or unfortunate enough to live in. Political life, with its virtues of justice and civic friendship, perfects the human being and it even brings prepolitical societies to their own perfection. A family that is deprived of a political context is less excellent as a family. The intersubjectivity that allows human beings to be actualized as persons extends as far as the political domain.

There is a passage in Henry James's *The Ambassadors* that brings out the difference between the human being and the person. It also shows the connection between personhood and human relations. At one point in the story, Lambert Strether looks back on his life and the many disappointments in it. He faces "the fact that he had failed, as he considered, in everything, in each relation and in half a dozen trades."[11] The narrator then says, about Strether's life: ". . . Though there had been people enough all round it there had been but three or four persons *in* it."[12] Only a handful of other human beings were fully engaged in his life, as rational and moral agents, hence as persons. All the others simply "stood around" his life; they were there as individuals, as human beings or "people," generic but uninvolved.

---

10. On the place of the virtue of friendship in moral philosophy, see Robert Sokolowski, "Friendship and Moral Action in Aristotle," *Journal of Value Inquiry* 35 (2001): 355–69, and "Phenomenology of Friendship," *Review of Metaphysics* 55 (2002): 451–70.

11. Henry James, *The Ambassadors* (New York: W. W. Norton and Co., 1964), p. 61.

12. Ibid.

The Christian dimension

In the rest of my paper, I will discuss how Christian faith and under-standing modify the personal relations we have been examining. It was nec-essary for me to spend a lot of time on the person and on intersubjectiv-ity, in order to provide the context within which the Christian difference comes into play.

In our spontaneous, natural understanding, the understanding that we find expressed, for example, in Plato and Aristotle or in pagan religious writ-ers, we take the world as the ultimate whole of things, the ultimate con-text. The divine principle is the highest, best, and most powerful element in this whole, in this world or cosmos. The divine is the governing and sacred element. But Christianity radically adjusts this understanding. It takes the whole of things, the cosmos or the sum of all entities, not as the unquestion-able background against which all things, including the divine, are deter-mined; rather, it takes the whole of things as being there because of a choice made by the Creator. And God is understood as not having needed to create, as being so perfect and subsistent that no perfection could be added to him. The world is seen as created out of a freedom and generosity that satisfies no need on the part of the Creator.

Christian faith, obedient to divine revelation in the Old and New Cov-enants, also believes that God, who created the world out of sheer generos-ity, became part of the world in the Incarnation; in the person of the Word, the divine nature became joined with a human nature. The Incarnation also reveals to us the inner life of God, the truth that God is not a solitary being but a Trinity of Persons even while remaining one God. What do these ar-ticles of Christian faith—Creation, Incarnation, and the Holy Trinity—im-ply for the human person and for interpersonal relationships? I would like to discuss two major topics.

The first topic is the difference that occurs in regard to human moral conduct. We have seen that it is possible to consider friendship as the high-est virtuous activity in the moral domain. However, for pagan thinking, the highest friendships we are capable of are, quite naturally, those that occur among human beings. According to Aristotle, friendship with god or the gods is impossible, because the difference between mortal and immortal be-ings is too great: "When one party is removed to a great distance, as god is, the possibility of friendship ceases."[13] But in Christian faith, we believe that God became man and invited us to friendship with him. In chapter 15 of St. John's gospel, during the discourse at the Last Supper, Jesus says to his disciples, "You are my friends if you do what I command you." He calls them friends, *philoi,* and he goes on to draw a contrast: "I no longer call you slaves, because a slave does not know what his master is doing." A slave does what the master commands, but he does so blindly; he does not understand the thinking of the master. Christ does not want that kind of obedience from those who follow him; rather, he continues, "I have called you friends, because I have told you everything I have heard from my Father." The reason why the disciples are his friends is that they have been introduced into the truth of the relationship between Christ and the Father; they now are capable of understanding in faith, and so they are friends and not slaves.

We should not underestimate the startling originality of such statements. To say that human beings can be friends of God, and that they have received the truth of God's own life, is truly overwhelming. The idea that we could be friends with the first principle of the universe is something that would sound like utter foolishness to pagan thinkers; they would see it as totally lacking in sobriety and realism. This friendship with God is made possible by the incarnate presence of the Son of God; we can become friends of Christ and hence share in his Sonship. Furthermore, the focus of this new truth and this new status is on God himself. What this new truth reveals is not how wonderful *we* are—we did not and could not have earned this friendship by anything we might have done—but how all-powerful God is; God could humiliate himself in the Incarnation and in Christ's atoning death, and still remain the eternally omnipotent and glorious Creator of everything that is. No human being could have imagined a God like this. We know of this God, this divinity, only because Christ has told us everything he heard from the Father, and we must respond by doing what he has commanded us. Without Christ we would not have dared to think such things. We have to be called to faith and must respond in obedience.

Furthermore, because Christ draws us into this form of friendship with God, it becomes possible for us to declare ourselves, to use the first-person singular pronoun in our relationship to God himself. We can say "I believe,"

13. Aristotle, *Nicomachean Ethics* VIII, 7, 1159a4–5.

or "I love," or "I beseech," not only before other people but also before and toward God. Through the words of Christ we know that God hears us; we come to know that such declarations are not just imaginary exercises or empty self-deceptions. We speak and declare ourselves not only before other men but also before God; we therefore act as agents of truth before God; we exercise our rational cognition and our rational action, which now are elevated by grace into a set of exchanges that would not be possible or conceivable as part of our natural endowment. This life with God, in which we act as friends of Christ and adopted sons of the Father, is based on truth, not on blind obedience, and hence it elevates our rational personhood, our agency in truth. I think that this theme of the enhancement of truth that faith brings has been developed in a moving way by the writings of Pope John Paul II, especially in his encyclicals *Veritatis Splendor* and *Fides et Ratio.*

I should also like to mention that this new friendship with God, in grace and in charity, is anticipated in the Old Covenant. Consider the psalms, where the psalmist, and the believer who prays the psalms, repeatedly addresses God and glorifies and thanks him, expresses sorrow for sins, and petitions him for his help. In the psalms as well as in the prayers of Abraham, Moses, and the prophets, human beings begin to declare themselves before Jahweh. God's radical transcendence is not compromised by this intervention in the world, through which he chooses a people and guides them in providence, and in which he allows them to address him. But this providential presence of God in the world reaches a greater intensity when God not only intervenes in the world but also becomes part of it and allows us to address him in friendship in his incarnate presence. Through grace we become able to act as agents of truth before the Father.

The second major topic I wish to examine is the interpersonal relationships that exist within the Most Holy Trinity. Here I wish to discuss how the divine nature is related to the three persons of the Trinity. When we spoke about the human person, we tried to show how the person is distinguished from the human being, from the man, from the concrete instance of human nature. We showed that the concrete human nature needs to be developed, to be shepherded throughout its life. We are not born in a perfect condition; as human beings our lives and inclinations need to be brought to a finished state by the choices we make. As we lead our lives, it is our rationality, both theoretic and practical, that enables us to cultivate our nature and bring it to its state of happiness or frustration. We have dominion over our acts and we lead our lives. In this human condition, each of us is one human being and one person: we have one life and one governing power within that life. Human rationality is distributed among individual substances and singular persons.

In God, however, there is one divine nature but three persons, Father, Son, and Holy Spirit. And obviously the divine nature is not something that needs to be cultivated and brought to completion; it is not like our natures, which are born imperfect. The divine nature is eternally the perfection of existence. How are the persons in the Holy Trinity related to this divine nature? They do not strive to perfect it, but they are distinguished by the way in which they bestow and receive it. The Father is distinguished from the Son through the action of generation.[14] In this action, the Father expresses himself totally in the Word that is generated; as Jesus says in St. John's gospel, "Everything that the Father has is mine" (John 16:15). In the same gospel, Jesus addresses the Father and says, "Everything of mine is yours and everything of yours is mine" (John 17:10). Christ does not say these things only as a man; he also expresses his divine life and being as having been given to him by the Father. The divine nature, everything that the Father is or has, is given over to the Son, who receives it from the Father. The Holy Spirit, the third person of the Trinity, is distinguished by the action of spiration, in which the Spirit proceeds from the Father and the Son together. These actions and receptions—generation and filiation, spiration and procession, as St. Thomas Aquinas names them[15]—are all internal to the Holy Trinity, and they permit there to be a community in the one true God. As Aquinas says, "If there were not a plurality of persons in the divinity, it would follow that God would be alone or solitary."[16]

These three persons are distinguished by the way the divine nature is given and received. It might be misleading to say that the Father *gives* the divine nature to the Son, because that would seem to imply that this donation was a matter of choice, the way Creation is. Within the Holy Trinity, the Father essentially expresses himself in his internal Word; this expression is called a generation, and so the Word is also the Son. As St. Thomas says,

14. *Summa Theologiae* I, q. 28, a. 4.   15. Ibid., I, q. 28, a. 4.
16. Ibid., I, q. 31, a. 3 ad 1.

"The Father does not generate the Son by an act of will *(voluntate),* but by nature."[17] According to St. Thomas, the generation of the Son is done by way of intelligence, and the generation of the Holy Spirit is done by way of the will. The two spiritual powers in the divine nature, intelligence and will, issue in the Son and the Holy Spirit. In the appropriate sense of giving, however, we could say that the Father gives the divine nature to the Son, who receives it from him, and the Father and the Son give the divine nature to the Holy Spirit, who receives it from them. As St. Thomas says, "The Holy Spirit . . . accepts the nature of the Father, just as the Son does."[18]

We could not say, therefore, that the divine persons perfect the divine nature, but it could be said that they give and receive it. It is in the nature of God that he gives and receives, so charity or generosity makes up the life of the Holy Trinity. As St. John says in his first letter, "God is love" (I John 4:8, 4:16). The Father does not just give some of what he is, or some of what he has; he gives everything, the entire divine nature, to the Son. This total giving within the Trinity is reflected in the death of Jesus. Through the dominion he had over his actions, he handed over his incarnate life and being, his entire human nature, for our salvation. Christ did not just give something that he had; he gave himself in an offering for us. As the Letter to the Hebrews says, "he entered once for all into the sanctuary, not with the blood of goats and calves but with his own blood . . ." (Hebrews 9:12). Such a donation could have been done only once because it was so complete, and it reflects in a created way the kind of generosity that occurs within the Holy Trinity. The crucifixion is therefore an icon of the charity within the interpersonal life of God, and the Resurrection bears witness that this charity and life are not overcome by either sin or death.

Through Christ's action and through grace, we are enabled to become friends of the incarnate Son of God. We also learn, if we are attentive to the words of Christ and the inspiration of the Holy Spirit, that the life within God is trinitarian and generous, a kind of friendship beyond human measure. It is only logical, then, that our own human relationships should reflect these truths. St. John's first letter tells us, "Let us love one another, because love is from God" (I John 4:7). There would be something grotesque in accepting the truth about the divine nature and then acting in a way that con-

17. Ibid., I, q. 42, a. 2. See also q. 41, a. 2.
18. Ibid., I, q. 35, a 2.

tradicts it. As Christians, our actions and our lives are profiled against the background of the Holy Trinity and the Incarnation. The charity we are called to, however, does not override the demands of the natural human virtues, such as temperance and courage, justice and prudence, and also human friendship. These things have their own logic and their own necessity, but they are now understood as participating in the goodness of the God who created them out of sheer generosity.

Christian revelation, therefore, confirms human personal relationships even as it takes us beyond them. It does so because it confirms human reason, the reason that makes us persons, even as it raises us beyond reason into belief in the Word of God.

WHAT IS NATURAL LAW?

Human Purposes and Natural Ends

Ethics in general, and medical ethics in particular, are obviously related to human self-understanding, to what we could call philosophical and theological anthropology. Our understanding of what is ethical and unethical is connected to what we take ourselves to be. The relationship, however, is not one-sided. It is not the case that we could work out a comprehensive description or definition of human nature as a purely theoretic enterprise and then apply this knowledge to practical issues, the way we might work out some ideas in mathematics and then apply them to problems in engineering and physics.[1] Rather, the working out of the definition and description of human nature is at the same time the formulation of what we *ought* to be as human beings, because the good or perfected state of man, which is the issue for ethics, is what defines human being. The normative is also the definitional. We cannot describe what man is without specifying the human good, without showing what it is to be a good (and consequently "happy") man. To want one of these dimensions without the other would be like wanting to study physiology, whether human or simply animal, without mentioning health and its various contraries, such as illness, injury, and impairment.

But human nature is more complicated than physiology. There are few

---

1. Even in mathematics, the relationship of theory and practice is not one-sided. Many innovations in mathematics arise from real problems of computation, not from abstract mathematics. The stimulus to mathematical thinking often lies in real-world questions.

disagreements about what constitutes health and sickness, but there are many opinions about what constitutes human excellence. As Aristotle says, we all agree on a *name* for human happiness, but we disagree very much on what makes it up.[2] Still, the fact that we have at least a name in common is important; it shows that we start with some common ground in this domain. We may differ about the *what* of happiness, but not about the *that,* nor do we differ on the fact that we want and need to be happy. The reason we can argue about these differences is that they all pertain to one and the same quest and target. The just man and the hedonist might act very differently, but in some sense they are aiming at the same thing. We are all concerned not just about living but about living well, not just about life but about the good life, and this little difference, between living and living well, greatly complicates the human condition. In fact, it makes it to be the *human* condition. When we say that man is a rational animal, we do not just mean that he is an animal that calculates and draws inferences; we mean, more substantially, that he is an animal that is concerned about living well and not just living.

The distinction between ends and purposes

To explore this complexity of human beings, I wish to discuss the difference between ends and purposes. The distinction has been formulated by Francis Slade, in a striking modern recapitulation of classical philosophical ideas.[3]

An end, a telos, belongs to a thing in itself, while a purpose arises only when there are human beings. Purposes are intentions, something we wish for and are deliberating about or acting to achieve. Ends, in contrast, are there apart from any human wishes and deliberations. They are what the thing is when it has reached its best state, its perfection and completion in and for itself. Ends and purposes are both goods, but goods of different ontological orders.

Purposes come into existence when human beings set out thoughtfully

2. Aristotle, *Nicomachean Ethics* I, 4.

3. See Francis Slade, "On the Ontological Priority of Ends and Its Relevance to the Narrative Arts," in *Beauty, Art, and the Polis,* edited by Alice Ramos (Washington, DC: The Catholic University of America Press, 2000), pp. 58–69; and "Ends and Purposes," in *Final Causality in Nature and Human Affairs,* edited by Richard Hassing (Washington, DC: The Catholic University of America Press, 1997), pp. 83–85.

to do something. Purposes are wished-for satisfactions in view of which an agent deliberates and acts. A man might set various purposes for himself, such as becoming a lawyer, supporting his family, going on vacation, or giving someone a gift, and he will do various things toward achieving this purpose: he will apply to law schools, get a job, buy tickets, or go shopping. Once a man has a purpose, he articulates the various ways in which the purpose can be achieved (this "shaking out" of means toward the goal is called deliberation); he then performs the action that, as far as he can see, is the best option in the present circumstances (this selection is called choice).[4] Thus, purposes exist "in the mind" and not in things, and they exist only because there are human beings. It would be correct but somewhat misleading to say that purposes are psychological entities, because they are more conceptual and logical than, say, moods or emotions, but it would be true to say that they are part of *our* thinking and that they are different from the ends found in things, which are there independently of our wishes and actions.

Ends, in contrast, do not spring into being through human foresight. They do not spring into being at all; they come about concomitantly with the things they belong to. Things might spring into being when they are generated or made or occur by accident, but ends do not arise without the thing. An end is the finished, perfected state of a thing, the thing when it is acting well as what it is. To clarify this point, we must distinguish three kinds of ends.

First, some ends are, in principle, entirely unrelated to human beings. The end of a tree is to grow, sprout leaves, nourish itself, and reproduce: to be active and successful as a tree, as an entity of this kind. The end of a zebra is to grow to maturity, nourish itself, reproduce, and live with other zebras. Trees and zebras function well *as* trees and zebras when they act this way, and we know what a tree and a zebra are when we can say what it means to act well as a thing of this kind. A zebra might break its leg and or be eaten by a lion, but possibilities like these do not define what a zebra is. They are not part of what it is, its essence, which is displayed most fully not when the zebra merely exists but when the zebra is acting well.

Second, some ends belong to things that have come into being through human agency. Artifacts and institutions, things brought about by human

4. Aristotle's analysis of wishing, deliberation, choice, and ends is found in *Nicomachean Ethics* III, 1–5.

making and agreements, have essences and ends. It is not the case that only natural substances have a telos. Consider an institution such as an art museum. Its telos is to make works of art available for public viewing, and part of this activity will be the acquisition and preservation of such works. The end of a bicycle is the transportation of individuals, and the end of a ballpoint pen is to be used in writing or drawing. In each case, the end defines what the thing is. It is interesting and important to note that even though artifacts and institutions are brought about by human beings to serve our purposes and our ends, we cannot change what they are. We might suppose that because we have made them, we could turn them into anything we wish, but they resist such manipulation; even as instrumental beings, they have their own nature or essence and ends. They inhabit a niche in the possibilities laid open in the world. We may have brought them into being, but they do not become our purposes. They retain their own ends and we have to subordinate ourselves to them.

To claim that institutions and artifacts had no definition, and that they could be changed by us at will, would mean that they could not be ruined or destroyed by us. Any change would just be a redefinition, carried out by us, who would have freely defined the thing in question in the first place. We could not really "spoil" anything, but experience shows that we can and often do.

I would like to illustrate this understanding of ends by quoting from a book review. The reviewer, Josie Appleton, describes a book based on a series of lectures given by five directors of major museums in the United States and Great Britain.[5] The lectures were given at Harvard in 2001–2002. Many of the speakers complained about the tendency of museums to engage in all sorts of activities unrelated to what we could call their proper end, such as "inviting you to try on period costumes or make your own ceramic pots." In describing the "key insight" of the book, the reviewer says, "Each public institution has an essence, a reason for its existence, be it making sick people well, improving general welfare, or, in the case of museums, collecting and exhibiting art."[6] She adds that an institution will keep the public's

5. Josie Appleton, "One at a Time," review of *Whose Muse? Art Museums and the Public Trust*, edited by James Cuno (Princeton: Princeton University Press, 2003), in the *Times Literary Supplement*, March 26, 2004.

6. I particularly like the remark that a thing's "essence" is a "reason for its existence." A classical metaphysician could not have said it better.

trust only if "it remains true to its essence." These remarks are an excellent expression of what ends are and the obligations they impose on people who deal with the things in question.

We have listed two kinds of things that have ends: first, nonhuman things like zebras, trees, and spiders, and, second, human institutions and artifacts, such as museums and ballpoint pens. There is a third kind that must be added to the list. Human beings themselves have ends. They have an overall end, which we could call happiness, and which is easy to name but difficult to define; but there also are ends for the various powers that human beings enjoy. There is a telos for human sociability, for example, for human thinking, for human sexuality, for bodily nourishment, for dealing with dangerous and painful things. There is also a telos for human bodily and psychological health. It is especially this third category, the ends of human nature, that gives rise to moral problems. In this category it is most difficult for us to discover what the ends truly are, because here our purposes and our ends become most entangled with one another. Our inclinations and desires give rise to purposes, and sooner or later a conflict arises between what we want and what we truly are. It is quite easy to see what the ends of nonhuman things are; it is more difficult to unravel ends and purposes in regard to institutions and artifacts; but it is extremely hard to distinguish ends and purposes in regard to our own nature and its powers. To explore this problem, we must examine more carefully how ends and purposes come to light. This essay will essentially be a study of the kind of truth associated with ends.

How ends are differentiated from purposes

It is not the case that ends are presented to us all by themselves, separate from purposes. It is not the case that we first get a clear, vivid idea of the ends of things, and then only subsequently attach our purposes to them. Moral issues would be much simpler if this were so; indeed, if it were so, there would not be any moral problems. Our moral measures would be easily accessible. The human problem arises precisely because we have to *distinguish* ends and purposes in our activity, and it is often difficult to do so. Ends and purposes come to light in contrast with one another. For example, the end of medicine is the restoration and preservation of health, but a man might have many different purposes in practicing medicine. He may intend to heal people and keep them healthy, he may intend to earn money, he may intend to become famous, he may intend to become a politician, or, if he is a vicious agent, he may want to become adept at torturing people. At first, medicine comes to us soaked through with such purposes, often with many of them, and it takes moral intelligence to make the distinction between what belongs to medicine as such and what purposes we have in practicing it. Obviously, the people who teach the medical student will talk about the distinction, but ultimately the student and later the doctor has to make the distinction for himself; the teacher cannot make it for him. No one can make a distinction for anyone else; a distinction is someone's mind at work. The telos and the essence of the thing come to light for us precisely in contrast with our purposes, and our purposes also come to light in contrast with what belongs to the things themselves.

It is even misleading to say that ends and purposes come to us entangled with one another. This way of putting it suggests that we already have differentiated the two but that they have at this moment become enmeshed. Rather, what occurs is that the very contrast between ends and purposes has not yet arisen, that the very categories are not yet available. What we begin with precedes the distinction, and the distinction needs to be made. It has to be made, furthermore, not in placid contemplation of a neutral scene, but in the tumult of desires, emotions, and interests, in the thick of things.

Many of our purposes are compatible with the ends of the things we are involved with. Earning income by being a doctor is not incongruent with the end of medicine, but it can become so, just as it can enter into collision with being a lawyer or a statesman. This conflict happens when the purpose overrides the end and works against it, when, for example, an estate lawyer delays the execution of a will in order to increase his fee, or when a doctor performs unneeded surgeries in order to be able to charge the insurance company. Using a ballpoint pen as a bookmark does not conflict with the end of the writing instrument, but using it to pry things open may well do so. Distinguishing the ends of things against the pressure of our own purposes is analogous to distinguishing the just against the pressure of our own interests. In both cases, we let the objectivity of things come into our consciousness, but the objectivity enters there not as a solitary visitor, all by itself; it enters by being differentiated from what we want.

Is it possible that someone's purpose can coincide with the end of the thing? Certainly, it can; a doctor can have as his purpose here and now the restoration of this sick person's health. The end of the medical art is in this case the purpose the physician has in mind as he practices his art, and one hopes that a physician would in general have as one of his purposes the end of the art of medicine, that he would respect the end of his art and not let his other purposes override it. But even when purpose and end overlap, there remains a difference between them, and the distinction still comes into play. One and the same good presents itself under two guises, as the end of the art and as the purpose of the agent. A formal distinction arises in the way the good appears even though the good, healing this sick person, remains materially the same; the end does not turn into a purpose, and the purpose does not become an end. The fact that the material good remains the same might conceal from us the fact that there are two ways in which it can appear, two faces that it can present.

Let us suppose that a given doctor does have healing as his purpose in practicing medicine; his purpose is the same as the end of the art. Even this would not be enough. Such a doctor would still not think clearly if he assumed that healing is *only* his purpose, or that it is only the purpose of his associates in the art, and that no defining constraints came into play from the art itself, apart from the purposes of the practitioners. If he thought this way, he would not see or admit that healing, besides being his purpose, is also the end of the art, and that he and his colleagues could not define it in any other way; he would not see that he and his colleagues *should* have as their central and non-negotiable purpose the restoration and preservation of health. Medicine is so defined not because society wants to determine it this way, but because that is what it is.

Barriers to the distinction

Not everyone is able to distinguish the end from the purpose. There are at least four types of people who are impeded from distinguishing them: the impulsive, the obtuse, the immature, and the vicious.

First of all, it takes a certain development just to be able to have *purposes*. Children and childish people do not yet have purposes. They want things, and they might want things in the future, but they do not distinguish between what they want and what they are doing now, that is, they do not "shake out" the difference between purposes and the steps to attain them. Children are, quite naturally, impulsive. They have not yet developed the ability to think clearly about what they wish for, nor can they distinguish between what they wish for and what they can do now, nor can they discover optional ways of getting to what they want, nor can they determine which is the best and most feasible way to get what they wish, nor can they, finally, take the first step, as well as all the succeeding steps, to get what they want. To articulate a situation and a desire in this way is practical thinking. It is the introduction of moral syntax into our consciousness. Impulsive people have not developed this power of reason, this power of practical categoriality. Their future collapses into their present. Children are naturally impulsive, but some people remain childish even as they get older. Thus, Aristotle says that a young man, because of his impulsiveness and lack of experience, is not an appropriate hearer of lectures on political matters, and then he adds, "It makes no difference whether he is young in years or youthful in character; the defect does not depend on time, but on his living, and pursuing each successive object, as passion directs."[7]

Second, we may have become adult enough to establish distinct purposes and to determine the steps that lead to them, but we may still be unable to appreciate the presence of other people with their purposes. We permit entry into our awareness only of what *we* want. We remain unable to see that other people have their viewpoints and needs, that we are not the only agents involved in our situations. To fail to be "objective" in this way is to be what I would like to call "morally obtuse" as opposed to being vicious. Someone who double-parks his car and blocks traffic may not be malicious—he doesn't *want* to injure other people—but he is morally obtuse. He is simply and happily oblivious to the fact that there are other people in the situation who are being seriously inconvenienced. His consciousness does not expand enough to include the perspectives of others, even though he is able to distinguish means and purposes in his own case. A patient in a hospital room may keep the television playing all night long "so that he can sleep," oblivious to the other patients in the room. Such obtuseness is a failure in practical thinking, but it is different from vice and also different from the childishness in which one cannot distinguish a purpose from the means of attaining it.

Third, immaturity is the state of mind in which we are unable to dis-

7. Aristotle, *Nicomachean Ethics* I, 3.

tinguish what we (and others) want from the demands and obligations of the world itself; that is, we fail to distinguish our purposes from the ends of things. To be able to make this distinction is to be "objective" in a new way, one different from simply recognizing the presence of other agents. If we merely recognize other people and acknowledge that they too have purposes, all we would have is a world of cross-purposes and ultimate violence, which would amount to a war of all against all.[8] This is where the apotheosis of autonomy and choice leads. Recognizing the ends of things and the ends of our own nature, however, would help pacify this conflict. The only alternative to such peace through the truth of things is the establishment of a will that is overwhelmingly powerful, the sovereign or Leviathan, who pacifies by decree and not by evidence, and for whom there are no ends or natures in things. Let us use the term "moral maturity" to name the ability to see that things themselves have their own excellences that need to be respected if the things are not to be destroyed. This virtue enables us to take up a viewpoint that goes beyond our own desires and the desires of others.

Fourth and last, there is vice. We may acknowledge the ends of things and the viewpoints of other persons, but we deliberately and maliciously let our purposes override them. We fail in regard to justice not because we are impulsive, obtuse, or immature, but because we are unjust. We *want* to de-

---

8. See Slade, "On the Ontological Priority of Ends," pp. 67–68: "What happens when end is reduced to purpose and consequence becomes visible in the films of Quentin Tarentino, which picture a 'world' in which there are only purposes of human beings, a 'world without ends.' In such a world there cannot be any congruity or incongruity of purposes with ends. There being no ends by which purposes can be measured, all purposes are in themselves incommensurate and incongruous with one another. This is a world in which everything is violent, because there is no natural way for anything to move. But a world in which everything is violent means that violence becomes ordinary, the usual, the way things are. The violent displaces and becomes 'the natural.' . . . The violence shocks [us] because we are not nihilists, because we are still measuring what people do in these films by a world in which there are not ends, not just human purposes. . . . A world of purposes only is a world of cross-purposes, the definition of fiasco."

Slade goes on to say that if the world had nothing but purposes the narrative arts could not exhibit the forms of things and the forms of human life; it could only show off the style of the artist who composes the work of art. Every life then becomes "a tale told by an idiot, full of sound and fury, signifying nothing," with the difference that Shakespeare knows the distinction between an idiot's tale and a human life, while Tarentino does not. Slade compares Tarentino with Kafka, who also describes a world without ends, but who knows how terrifying it is; Tarentino, in contrast, finds it funny. Slade says, "A world of fiasco is a world in which guilt is impossible, because guilt requires responsibility for actions, and there are actions only if purposes are measured by ends." One should notice the idea that true human action, true *praxis,* can occur only when the distinction between ends and purposes is at least glimpsed by the agent.

stroy the thing in question—the educational institution, the work of art, the church—and we want to injure others. We don't simply do unjust things; we are unjust; we do not, say, simply commit a murder; we are murderers. We have gotten to be this way because of the choices we have made in the past. The inclination to destroy the thing is always associated with some malice toward others; we destroy the thing because it could be a good for others.[9]

These, then, are four ways in which the truth of ends can be occluded: impulsiveness, moral obtuseness, immaturity, and vice. In any given case, the lack of moral insight into the ends of things might be explained by some combination of these four, just as an agent's deficiency might be caused by something intermediate between weakness and malice. What we are discussing is the way that the difference between ends and purposes comes to light, which amounts to the way in which the truth of things is disclosed. If we are to show how truth occurs, it is necessary to show what impedes such an occurrence, what hides the truth. We can appreciate a disclosure only in contrast with the forms of concealment that are proper to the thing in question.

How ends are distinguished from conventions

There is one more distinction that needs to be made in discussing how the ends of things come to light. We have examined how they are played off against purposes, but they should also be contrasted with conventions, which are different from the institutions and artifacts that we discussed earlier. Institutions and artifacts exist independently once they are made, but conventions—manners and morals—are ways in which we act as human beings. They are more proximately related to our human nature and its ends, because they indicate how we should conduct ourselves, how we should become actualized.

We normally encounter the good and the bad, the noble and the ugly, the obligatory and the prohibited, in our society's laws, customs, manners, and morals. The challenge we initially encounter in life is to make our inclinations, purposes, and choices conform to the injunctions of our community. In most cases it is right and good to conform to social norms, because they are usually reasonable expressions of the natural good. Social conven-

---

9. On the role of malice and friendship in morals, see Robert Sokolowski, "Phenomenology of Friendship," *Review of Metaphysics* 55 (2002): 451–70.

tions and moral traditions, based on long and localized human experience, are normally an embodiment of what is good or bad in itself, the good or bad by nature. Our initial moral challenge is to become "law-abiding citizens," people whose purposes are in harmony with the laws and moral traditions of their community.[10]

Still, conventions cannot be the final word, just as our purposes cannot be the final word. Sometimes conflicts arise in regard to the moral traditions themselves and criticism is necessary. The way things are done needs to be more adequately adjusted; but adjusted to what? What else, but to the way things are? When this sort of "crisis" occurs, we appeal at least implicitly to the ends of the things in question; this appeal is made even by people who may deny that things have ends. What else could one invoke?

Suppose, for example, that in a given community the art of medicine routinely involved abortion, infanticide, and euthanasia, and that it trained its apprentices in these procedures. P. D. James's novel *The Children of Men* presents a chilling fictional picture of a situation in which the sick and elderly are granted a "quietus" (which they are not pleased to undergo). It is, first of all, questionable whether under these conditions the medical art could survive, because people would hesitate to go to doctors and hospitals if killing were to be one of the available "treatments."[11] Acting against the end of the art will tend to destroy the art. But suppose the art were being practiced in this manner; some people would argue against using medicine to kill, and their argument would be based both on human dignity and on the fact that this aspect of "medicine" is opposed to medicine; it is opposed to the essence and the end of the art. Their argument would be based on the nature of the art as well as on the dignity of human nature, that is, on the telos of each of the entities involved in the practice. As another example, suppose that

---

10. Thus, for Aristotle, the first meaning of justice is the lawful: *Nicomachean Ethics* V, 1.

11. At one point in P. D. James's novel, the protagonist, Theo, is in a museum in Oxford and passes by the custodian, whom he recognizes as "a retired classics don from Merton." He asks him how he is, and the custodian replies nervously, "Oh, very well, yes, very well, thank you. . . . I'm managing all right. I do for myself, you know. I live in lodgings off the Iffley Road but I manage very well. I do everything for myself. The landlady isn't an easy woman . . . but I'm no trouble to her. I'm no trouble to anyone." Theo wonders what he is afraid of: "The whispered call to the SSP that here was another citizen who had become a burden on others?" *The Children of Men* (New York: Warner Books, 1992), pp. 120–21. The passage is a fine expression of the radical individualism in the modern state: "I do everything for myself."

polygamy were accepted in a certain community.[12] To argue that the practice should be changed, one would appeal to one of the ends of marriage, and the argument would be specific and concrete, showing that this way of being married conflicts with the kind of friendship and commitment that marriage "in itself" implies. Such conflicts between an established convention and the way things ought to be show that conventions do not cage people. Conventions can be questioned and changed, and they are questioned when one thinks that they do not properly express the reality they deal with (in these instances, with the art of medicine and the institution of marriage). The ancient practice of suttee in India would be another example; the British abolished the practice not because they simply preferred other customs, but because it was contrary to human nature and the nature of marriage.

This does not mean that the critic of a law or a practice has a full, independent vision of the nature and end of the thing in question and that he compares the convention with it; rather, faced with the law or custom, he knows and says that "this is not the right way to do things" (an observation that might well put him into some tension with his fellows). He knows the end at first more by negation than by positive insight. It is a contrastive knowledge, not an independent vision, but it is still a grasp of the thing itself over against its distortion. The true comes to light against the established delusion. Thus, one of the ways that ends are manifest is in contrast with custom and convention.[13]

It is not the case, however, that we get a view of the thing's telos only when there is a conflict between the convention and the end. It is also possible for someone to have the insight that this convention or this practice, this way of doing things, does indeed reflect the end of the thing in question. It takes intellectual strength to make this distinction, because we have

---

12. Here is an interesting passage in which a writer fails to distinguish between customs and the ends of things: ". . . Monogamy, albeit in various different forms, was the norm in classical antiquity, and it is still the norm in most Western civilizations (except in Utah). It is all too tempting to see those features of our culture which we have retained since antiquity as somehow natural for any human society, but of course there is no reason to make this assumption." Emily Wilson, "Why Exactly Do We Look Back?" *Times Literary Supplement* (25 June 2004), p. 6 (a review of Simon Goldhill, *Love, Sex and Tragedy* [Chicago: University of Chicago Press, 2004]).

13. I have developed this theme in an earlier essay. See "Knowing Natural Law," in Robert Sokolowski, *Pictures, Quotations, and Distinctions: Fourteen Essays in Phenomenology* (Notre Dame: University of Notre Dame Press, 1992), pp. 277–91.

to see one and the same thing in two guises, as good by convention and also as good in itself. Most of the time we simply accept the conventional good on its face; it is the way everybody does things, and so it must be right; it is the way things ought to be. To be able to give arguments based not just on convention but on the way things are is a more sophisticated achievement. It involves the recognition, not attainable by everyone, that there are two kinds of "ought." It is analogous to the physician's ability to see healing as both his purpose and the end of his art.

In either case, whether we are distinguishing the ends of things from conventions or from our purposes, we need to have a certain intellectual flexibility. It is more than the power to distinguish one thing from another. We need the ability to distinguish two dimensions, two ways in which something can be good: as an end or a convention, or as an end or a purpose. Distinguishing dimensions is more difficult than distinguishing things. When people deny that there are natural ends to things, they do not merely fail to distinguish one thing from another; they fail to appreciate that there are two ways in which goods can present themselves to us. The ability to make this distinction belongs to practical as well as theoretic reason.

In the previous two sections we showed how ends are differentiated from purposes, and we examined four obstacles to that differentiation. In this section we have spoken about the distinction between ends and convention. I now wish to make what might seem to be a rather sudden leap in my argument; I wish to introduce the notion of natural law. This topic might seem different from what we have been discussing, but it really is not.

Natural law

I wish to use an important and illuminating observation by Francis Slade, a way of defining natural law that has, I think, considerable intuitive force. To the question "What is natural law?" one can answer very simply: "Natural law is the ontological priority of ends over purposes."[14] Natural law is shown to us when we recognize that there are ends in things and that our purposes and choices must respect their priority. This understanding of natural law would imply that our discussion of ends and purposes in this es-

---

14. Slade formulated this concept of natural law in conversation. I am grateful for his permission to use it in this essay. The formulation is implied in the title of his essay, "On the Ontological Priority of Ends and Its Relevance to the Narrative Arts," cited above in note 3.

say has all along been a treatment of natural law and the way it is manifested to us. The precedence of ends over purposes occurs especially in regard to the ends that are proper to human nature and its various powers. For example, the ends built into human nourishment must be seen to govern the way we eat, and the ends built into human sexuality must be seen to govern the way we live with our sexuality. In both of these powers, we ought not be governed by what we simply want and the purposes we set for ourselves; we must differentiate between what we want and the reality and the telos of the thing we are dealing with. We must have a sense that our purposes must be measured by the way things are, which means that they must be measured by the way things should be. The distinction between purpose and end has to dawn on us, and when it does dawn on us, we experience the pressure and the attraction of the way things have to be; we encounter "the natural law."

We might be tempted to think of natural law as a kind of codex, a set of imperatives that could be formulated in a purely theoretic, systematic exercise, identifiable and arguable apart from any particular moral tradition.[15] The use of the term *law* to name what is good by nature reinforces this tendency. But if we think of natural law in this way, we could easily be led into skepticism: If the precepts of natural law are so lucid and rational, why is there so much disagreement and so much obscurity about them? The fact of moral controversy would, in this viewpoint, show that natural law cannot be a codex, and if that is the only concept we have of it, we might conclude that there is no such thing. If, on the other hand, we recognize that not everyone will have a good sense of the true ends of things (the impulsive, obtuse, immature, and vicious are far less able to recognize them), and if we see such ends not as grasped beforehand but as differentiating themselves from our purposes and our conventions, we will be the more ready to admit that *this* kind of natural law does play a role in our moral thinking, in the way we evaluate situations and agents. This picture of natural law is more realistic and more persuasive precisely because it accounts for the obscurities associated with moral judgments.

It would also be obvious, furthermore, that we are obliged by the ends that come to light in this way. The very fact that they arise formally in con-

---

15. Writers trained as lawyers may be more prone to understand natural law as such a system of imperatives or values.

trast with our purposes shows that our purposes have to be adjusted in view of them; that is what an obligation means. The ends become manifest as what we should respect. Only ends can make us accountable; our purposes have nothing obligatory about them. Ends are not just an aesthetic alternative to our purposes but a "law" in the nature of things. If we are dealing with the thing in question (with medicine and health, with nourishment or sexuality, with goods that we have to share with other people), we dare not let our desires and purposes be the only measure. The thing we are dealing with makes its own demands on us, and it would be unworthy of us not to recognize the excellence that belongs to it. If we genuinely are agents of truth, we cannot let our wishes be the last word. There is a kind of ontological, cosmic justice in being in harmony with the way things are. This sense of obligation may not appear to the impulsive, the obtuse, the immature, and the vicious, but would we want to be the kind of agent that does not acknowledge it? An end should show up for us first and foremost as that which it would be unworthy of us to violate.

This sense of the noble should be the primary and the core sense of moral "obligation." It is not that a law is imposed on us, that we are fettered by an imperative, but that we would be ashamed to act otherwise. Nobility obliges us in a way different from commands. The nobility of what is good by nature shows up most forcefully to the virtuous agent, who experiences it not as an imposed duty but as the way he wants to be. It shows up also to what Aristotle has described as the self-controlled person and to the weak person, the enkratic and the akratic agents, but they experience it more as an imperative and a command arising, to some extent, from "outside" themselves, because their passions are not in harmony with right reason.[16] But the paradigm, the case that provides the focus for orientation, is found in the way the virtuous agent encounters the noble: not as an imperative but as the way he would want to be. In dealing with eating and drinking, for example, a self-controlled or a weak person might find it burdensome to eat and drink moderately, but a temperate person would find it not a burden but the way things should be. It would not be a matter of natural "law" as much as a matter of natural decency.

---

16. Aristotle develops these important moral distinctions, between virtue, self-control, weakness, and vice, in *Nicomachean Ethics* VII, 1–10.

The sense of obligation that ends bring with them is reinforced by the Christian doctrine of Creation, and it is easier to think of the ends of things as being part of a natural law when we understand the world to exist through God's creative wisdom. We then discover not only a law in the nature of things but also a Lawgiver who is responsible for the way things are. This reinforcement of natural ends, however, also introduces a considerable danger. It may tempt us to think of ends as really being the purposes of the divine intelligence and will. This in turn might tempt us to delete or dilute the notion of ends in themselves; we might think that what look to us like natural ends are really, at their core, purposes and not ends, because they are willed by God, and hence the distinction between ends and purposes might be dissolved when we move into the final and ultimately true context. We might also tend to look to revelation for the more definitive communication of the true ends of things; we might, for example, think that the wrongness of certain practices is shown by their being condemned by the Law of Moses and by St. Paul, not by their showing up to human reason as incongruent with the ends of the things in question. Such an appeal to Creation and revelation might make us more inclined to think of natural law as a codex rather than as an experienced obligation. It is true, of course, that revelation will often declare certain natural human practices to be good and others to be bad, but these things also have their natural visibility, and one can argue more persuasively about them if one brings out their intrinsic nobility or unworthiness, their intrinsic rightness or wrongness, as well as the confirmation they receive from revelation.

St. Thomas says that the natural law is promulgated by being written in the human heart. As he writes, "The law written in the hearts of men is the natural law; *lex scripta in cordibus hominum est lex naturalis.*"[17] Aquinas also quotes a passage from St. Augustine's *Confessions,* where Augustine also speaks about God's law as written in the hearts of men, and of course both authors harken back to St. Paul who, in his Letter to the Romans (2:14–15), says, "For when the Gentiles who do not have the law observe the prescriptions of the law, they are a law for themselves even though they do not have the law. They show that the demands of the law are written in their hearts. . . ." We should understand the full meaning of the words used for the heart

---

17. *Summa Theologiae* I–II, q. 94, a. 6, sed contra.

in such passages, *cor* and *kardia*. They do not connote the separation of heart and head that we take for granted in a world marked by Descartes. We tend to think that the head or the brain is the seat of cognitive processes and the heart is the seat of emotion and feeling, but when Aquinas appeals to the heart, he is not saying that the natural law is somehow given to our feelings or impulses instead of our minds. Rather, he claims that we are able to acknowledge, rationally, what the good is.

Premodern thought had not undergone the dissociation of sensibility and rational thinking. In Greek poetry the heart, the chest, and even the lungs were generally taken as the place where thinking occurred.[18] There is something wholesome in this ancient understanding; it is really the entire man, the person, who thinks and knows, not the brain. The carpenter thinks with his hands, the quarterback thinks with his legs and arms, and the speaker thinks with the lungs, mouth, and tongue. We do have to distinguish thinking from other human activities, but we should not take thinking to be only isolated cogitation, only sheer consciousness. Furthermore, Robert Spaemann claims that in the New Testament the word *heart* takes on an especially important meaning.[19] He says the heart is taken to be a deeper recipient of truth than the mind or intellect in Greek philosophy; it deals with our willingness to accept the truth. It is an expression of our veracity, our openness to the truth of things. Spaemann says that the concept of "heart" in the New Testament "means something like the discovery of the person."[20] Still more specifically, in the New Testament it is related to people's willingness to hear and accept the Word of God in Christ.

I would suggest that when Aquinas says that the natural law is written in the hearts of men, he is referring to the capacity for truth that we have been describing when we said that the natural ends of things must be distinguished from our own purposes and from convention. This elementary differentiation, this recognition that my purposes are not all there is, and that the way we do things is not all there is, is a way of being truthful that is achieved

18. See the classic study, Richard Broxton Onians, *The Origins of European Thought about the Body, the Mind, the Soul, the World, Time, and Fate: New Interpretations of Greek, Roman and Kindred Evidence, also of Some Basic Jewish and Christian Beliefs*, second edition (Cambridge: Cambridge University Press, 1954), chapter 2, "The Organs of Consciousness."

19. Robert Spaemann, *Personen. Versuche über den Unterschied zwischen "etwas" und "jemand"* (Stuttgart: Klett-Cotta, 1996), pp. 29–30.

20. Ibid., p. 30.

by the heart, which if it is sound can cut through the impediments of being impulsive, obtuse, immature, and vicious. I hope that my study can serve as a phenomenological complement to Aquinas's ontological analysis, in which he distinguishes between the various kinds of law and shows that natural law is a participation in eternal law. My descriptions have tried to shed light on how natural law is "promulgated" in human experience.[21]

Philosophical and theological anthropology

I would now like to pull together some conclusions concerning the relationship between ethics and philosophical and theological anthropology. Our understanding of ourselves as human beings is related to our understanding of the good and virtuous human life. This end or telos of human being is disclosed by virtuous action, by human beings existing and acting well as human beings. The primary manifestation of such being and acting is carried out by good agents. It is revealed by reason, but by the practical reason of good agents, who show what is possible, not primarily by the theoretical reason of philosophers, theologians, or scientists. Once the good life is manifested in action, philosophy can clarify and consolidate what has been accomplished. It can distinguish the various human lives, the various ways in which people seek happiness, and it can bring out which of these is intrinsically better than the others.[22] For example, one of the forms of hap-

---

21. Aquinas's treatise on law is found in *Summa Theologiae* I-II, qq. 90–108. I have tried to show how the ends of things come to light. My analysis does not claim that we intuit ends; they are disclosed through a distinction, which is more rationally articulated than an intuition. We do not have something simply present by itself to the mind; rather, we have something presented over against something else, and one can discuss such a presentation in a way that one could not argue about an intuition. A distinction, however, is not the conclusion of a syllogism. It can be argued about and clarified, but it cannot be proved. Any attempt to prove a distinction begs the question.

But making a distinction is not the only rational procedure associated with ends. It is also possible to confirm something as naturally good. This is done by showing that the opponent really cannot deny that the thing in question is good; he has to affirm it either in his actions or in other things that he admits to be true, or at least in the way he presents himself and tries to justify his actions in public. This procedure "proves" by refutation, and it is analogous to the way Aristotle argues against those who deny the principle of noncontradiction and other fundamental principles in logic and metaphysics (*Metaphysics* IV, 3–8). The argument by refutation is very important in philosophy generally and in ethics in particular; it is tied to the making of distinctions and to the principle of noncontradiction, that is, to the establishment of a rational speaker. It does not, however, bring out the first and original manifestation of moral goods.

22. Philosophy also introduces its own perfection, but it is theoretic and not practical.

piness that decent people seek is that of honor, of being recognized by others as being good. People are motivated to good actions by the promise of being honored for what they have done. But, as Aristotle points out, honor cannot be the final telos, because it is dependent in two ways: first, it depends on other people, on those who bestow it, and, second, it depends on that for which we are being honored (we want to be honored because we are good, and so the goodness is more excellent than the honor).[23] The "logic" of honor implies dependency; it is at best penultimate. This philosophical clarification points us beyond honor to virtue, and even virtue is not ultimate, because it is only a disposition; it has to be exercised in order to make us truly excellent and happy.

This little philosophical critique is an example of what philosophy can do, but it presupposes that there have been good agents and that people have sought happiness. Practical reason has already been at work; honor and virtue have already come into play. Philosophy does not install the search or even the achievement of the ethical life. Philosophy can show the intricacies of human action and choice, the relations among the virtues of courage and temperance, and justice and friendship, and other dimensions of the moral life, but it always assumes that these things have been achieved by practical reasoning, which is where human excellence and human failure first come to light, where we first come to see what it is to be human. These achievements are then capsulated, polished, and trimmed in moral traditions, in poetry and narratives, in exemplars, maxims, and customs, where practical and theoretic reason join forces with literary skill to present a picture of how we can be. We measure our lives and actions, we understand ourselves and our human situations, in the light and the frame of such paradigms, and occasionally we may need to distinguish between the way things are and the way they are said to be.

Christians believe that God has revealed a deeper sense of goodness and virtue (as well as a deeper sense of evil and vice). Faith, hope, and charity, as gifts of God, dispose us to act in a new context, in which we are elevated into God's own life, through the redemptive actions of the incarnate Son of God. In this domain, we do have a kind of "theoretical" priority of knowledge over practical reason; we have to accept certain truths about ourselves

---

23. Aristotle, *Nicomachean Ethics* I, 5.

before we know we are able and obliged to act in certain ways. However, this new dimension does not override the evidences of natural practical reason. What seemed noble and decent in the natural order remains so, and it is confirmed in its goodness by being involved in this new context of grace. In fact, grace intensifies the appeal of natural virtue, which now shows up not only as admirable, but also as a reflection of divine goodness. Grace heals and elevates nature. For example, the nobility of human friendship, which is a kind of pinnacle of natural human virtue, is enhanced by becoming involved in charity, which is the friendship that God extends to human beings.[24] As another example, the excellence of human marriage is enhanced and its meaning deepened when it is understood not only in the natural order, where it has two ends, the procreation and upbringing of children and the mutual devotion of the spouses, but when it is understood theologically to signify the relation between Christ and the Church.[25] From its earliest times, Christianity differentiated itself from its surrounding world by its attitudes toward abortion, infanticide, and matrimonial infidelity. It worked toward the elimination of slavery and gladiatorial combat, it tried to limit warfare, and it changed the meaning of wealth; as Evelyn Waugh has Lady Marchmain say in *Brideshead Revisited,* "Wealth in pagan Rome was necessarily something cruel; it's not any more."[26] In all such instances, what Christianity offers is not a set of new, unheard-of precepts, but a deepening of what is already appreciated as good. The natural visibility remains. Grace elevates and also heals wounded nature, revelation expands and clarifies human reason. I would suggest that one of the strongest arguments in Christian apologetics is the fact that faith refurbishes what is naturally good. Such clarification of goods is not only a moral theology but also a theological anthropology, because it shows more clearly what human beings are and what they can and should be, that is, what their ends truly are.

24. On friendship as the highest moral virtue, see my essays, "Phenomenology of Friendship," and "Friendship and Moral Action in Aristotle," *Journal of Value Inquiry* 35 (2001): 355–69.

25. St. Thomas Aquinas discusses bigamy and polygamy in *Scriptum super Sententias* IV, d. 33, a. 1; see also *Summa Theologiae* III Supplementum, q. 65, a. 1. He lists three ends of marriage: procreation and education of children, mutual devotion, and expression of the relation between Christ and the Church. He says that a multiplicity of wives would neither necessarily destroy nor impede the first end, it would not destroy the second but it would seriously impede it, and it would totally destroy the third.

26. Evelyn Waugh, *Brideshead Revisited* (Boston: Little, Brown and Company, 1979), p. 127.

PART IV

FAITH AND PRACTICAL REASONING

THE ART AND SCIENCE OF MEDICINE

Just as a mathematician is most fully himself when he is calculating, so a physician is most fully himself, as physician, when he is engaged in medical activity. Medical activity is the actuality of medicine, and both the art and the science are to be defined and understood in relation to it. The art and the science both are as potential activity. It would be a distortion to regard medicine as, say, essentially a science, essentially an understanding of certain natures and relationships, something to which applications were accidental; or to consider it as an art that could be itself without ever coming out of hiding, without becoming active. Both the science and the art would be out of focus without the activity.

But although medical activity is the climax of medicine, it is only a part of medicine. No medical activity activates the whole of the art and science. Knowing what to disregard and what not to do, and being able to do other things in other circumstances, are necessary as a background for acting here and now as a physician. A physician is always more than what he does at any moment. Indeed, the partiality of the practice extends even farther, for the single physician is himself never the embodiment of the entire art and science of medicine. He knows that there are other doctors who know and can do things that he does not know and cannot do. Medical science and the medical art, medical reason and medical ability are essentially distributed and only partially realized in any agent and in any transaction. They remain largely latent even when they are activated in the climax of an action. They are always largely a background and a disposition.

Consequently, the concern of the physician is not only to carry out properly the transaction he is engaged in, but also to preserve the being of his art and science, as the dispositions out of which his actions as a physician emerge. He is obliged not only to his patient, but also to his art and science.

Medicine engages both physician and patient

Let us consider medical activity more closely. A medical action is a transaction between physician and patient. The term *patient* is something of a misnomer. It connotes total passivity and suggests that the target of the action is not thoughtfully involved in the exchange. On rare occasions this may occur; someone may be brought unconscious and with a broken leg to a physician, who may simply proceed to set the broken bone. But this is obviously not normal. The normal situation is that the medical reason and medical ability of the physician are shared to some extent with the patient. The patient has to comprehend to some degree what is going on, and he also has to share in the medical activity. He has to take the medicine, perform the exercises, change his diet, and do many other things that could be called medical care. He has to take care of his health. But his understanding and his activity are under the sway of those of the physician.

Because the reason of both physician and patient are engaged in medical activity, their activity has some of the features of a conversation or dialogue. Some years ago, a psychiatrist named Stanley A. Leavy published a book called *The Psychoanalytic Dialogue*.[1] In it he contrasts psychoanalysis with other forms of medicine. He tries to show that psychoanalytic treatment is like a human exchange; it is not, he says, like the relationship between a patient who is suffering a disorder and the physician who, as a scientific observer, discloses or diagnoses "the objectively present infection or tumor."[2] Leavy is correct in stressing the interpretative and conversational character of psychoanalysis, but the understanding of the medical relationship he uses as a foil is not adequate to medical activity. The physician does more than reveal a disorder. From the beginning, since the patient comes to the physician

---

1. Stanley A. Leavy, *The Psychoanalytic Dialogue* (New Haven, Connecticut: Yale University Press, 1980).
2. Ibid., p. 16.

and explains how he understands his own condition, the medical exchange is one in which the patient also thinks and acts.

But of course the patient and the doctor do not think and act in same way. Because of his art and science, because of the background behind what he is actually doing now, the physician has an authority in this relationship that the patient does not enjoy. His authority is analogous to that of a teacher toward his students. His assessment of the situation and of what is to be performed is the governing assessment as long as the medical relationship lasts. The patient's reason and ability only participate in those of the physician, but they do indeed participate. Because he too is a rational being, the patient is not like an animal that is brought—that does not bring itself—to the veterinarian. It is the presence of reason in *both* patient and physician that makes the medical relationship a human transaction and not merely the exercise of a technical skill.

But what makes it into a specifically medical exchange? How is the physician different from the electrician who comes to wire my house, the mechanic to whom I bring my car, or the barber who cuts my hair? The difference is that in the medical exchange *I myself* am at issue in a way in which I am not in the other cases. Sometimes the medical is defined by reference to the body and its health and disorders, but we should begin with something more basic. The medical is special not because my *body* is at issue, but because *I* am at issue. The medical is so prominent in life because it is engaged in my concern for my very self: not for my house or my car, nor my looks simply, but for my own being. We are human not just because we can calculate, but also and more originally because we are an issue for ourselves, and the medical exchange strikes at this concern. To take the most dramatic case, when we are waiting for the results of a critical test, one, let us say, that is to disclose whether or not we have a serious illness, we find ourselves to be at stake not just in what we have but in what we are. Whether I will continue to have a future, whether what I have done and undergone in the past will still remain as a springboard for further action, how my being in the world will be modulated, all this changes from being a silent undercurrent in life to being the issue I am directly concerned with. The medical exchange is an echo of our anticipation of death, and the prominence that death gives to my very self and what is my own also arises, in a muted form, when a serious medical issue must be faced. And even in the less urgent medical cases, even when we are trying simply to improve our health or to treat some ill-ness that is merely inconvenient, we are acting in relation to ourselves and not merely our possessions.

Of course my concern for my health is not the summit of my concern for my self. It would be hypochondria or neurotic obsession to gear my life primarily to health. I am much more an issue for myself when, say, I am about to act loyally toward my friend or gratefully toward my benefactor or generously toward someone in need; or perhaps when I am about to betray my friend, steal something, or destroy someone's career. When I act mor-ally I will not only affect someone else, but determine myself as well. I will be as these actions are. Whenever any particular issue surfaces for me, I also surface as an issue for myself. These actions will be mine and will be me in a more intimate way than my bodily well-being will be mine and me. And yet, nevertheless, my bodily illness or health will also be me in another way. I am concerned with myself and not just with my body when my bodily wholeness is an issue.

To observe that we as human beings are essentially an issue for ourselves is not to say that we are somehow selfish or self-centered in a morally rep-rehensible way. To speak about our self-concern is not a moralistic observa-tion but a remark about the formal structure of a human person, the struc-ture that underlies our ability to say "I" and "mine" and "my own."[3] Even the most generous act of self-sacrifice and self-forgetfulness is "mine" for the agent. It is owned and is considered his very own. That is why it can be noble and admirable, not just a characteristic of the species but an accom-plishment of this person.

The good involved in medicine

This highlighting, in the medical context, of my concern for myself, this drawing of that concern into the foreground occurs not in solitude but with the involvement of the physician. I do not just worry by myself that I might be getting sick. I become an issue for myself in this explicit way in the com-pany and the presence of the doctor. The doctor is there not formally as a friend, but as a professional. He is there as the embodiment of the medical

3. On the human being and the priority of "one's own," see Martin Heidegger, *Being and Time*, translated by John Macquarrie and Edward Robinson (New York: Harper and Row, 1962), § 41.

art and science, not primarily as, say, my brother or sister or colleague. This does not mean that he becomes malevolent or indifferent, but it does mean that his benevolence is not the same as that of a friend. He recognizes my being as a person, but, as a representative of the art and science of medicine, as one who professes that art and science, he would treat anyone else in my situation as he is treating me. His art lifts him out of a personal involvement: he is there not as John Smith but as the doctor, and I am there not as Aloysius but as the patient.

But the doctor is also John Smith and the patient is also Aloysius. We cannot separate these aspects of being, but we must distinguish them, and we must acknowledge how each accompanies the other and how we can shift from one to the other.

The physician is the embodiment of the medical art. To possess the art of medicine is not merely to know a lot of functional relationships and to know how to operate with them. An art is not merely a technique. An art is the ability to accomplish a good. An appreciation of the good to be done is programmed into the art, programmed not as one more step in its procedures but as saturating every step from beginning to end. Medicine as technique is what is left over when the medical art is drained of its sense of the good. Techniques are the finger exercises of medicine. Technique is cleverness or dexterity, the kind of thing in which computerized expert systems can help us; it is exemplified by, say, accuracy in correlating infections with combinations of antibiotics, or by precision and quickness in surgery. Such techniques can be rehearsed and they can be admired as techniques, but they are abstractions. They are not done in and for themselves; they belong to a larger and different kind of whole. The art itself is not the sum of techniques, and the doctor does not present himself as the embodiment of many techniques. As one who professes the art, as a professional, he presents himself as someone who will both know and be able to bring about the medical good that is possible in the situations that are brought to him. We expect the doctor to be benevolent not as a friend, but as an embodiment of the art, as someone who seeks the good of the art.

But what is the good of the medical art? It is the health of an individual or community; more specifically, it is the preservation or the restoration of the health of an individual or community. And this good exists in a complex way.

Health is there before there is a medical art. The good of medicine is not like the good of football or music, a good that comes into being as the sport or skill comes into being. Health is first of all a condition of a living thing, and it is first and foremost a good for living things, even before there is medicine. Furthermore, health is not only sought by things that are alive, it is also restored by them through the self-healing that living things achieve even without art. The medical art comes on the scene when something can be done about health, when health appears not only as a desirable condition nor just as the outcome of the natural process of healing but as a good that can be brought about through deliberate action. The art becomes developed as we become able to do more and more about health. Such growth takes centuries of experience, insight, and practice, and the art then becomes so enlarged that only specialists can learn it. Health becomes the object of a profession. However, health as a good to be achieved by medical practice, health as the good of the medical art, is also the same health that was sought as a good before there was medicine. The one good becomes targeted or wanted as good from two directions, from the point of view of the living organism that wants to be healthy, and from the point of view of the medical art; in this criss-cross, the perspective of the medical art is secondary and derivative. The physician heals because health already is a good for the living being. The good of the healing art is always already a good for the one who wants to be healthy.

Because health, while remaining the same good, is a good from two different perspectives, there can be interesting oscillations between the two ways in which it can be taken. An innocent example of this oscillation occurs when, say, a patient who has undergone a successful operation is exhibited to a troop of medical students, who are to admire and learn from the skill that was exercised by the surgeon. The good of the art becomes paramount for the moment, and for the moment the art becomes appreciated almost as technique. The patient as such, and his view of the good that was achieved, fade into the background; he may even be a bit embarrassed by all this attention. No harm is done, of course, but the shift in perspective is illuminating. It shows that the good can be seen from two angles and that in a small way the priority of the patient's view of the good can be muted.

In a much more radical conflict of goods, the doctor may use his skill to

torture or to take revenge on someone. He wants not the good of his "patient," but the bad or the harm of his target; the harm to the person's health
becomes formally the doctor's good. In such a case the doctor exercises his
medical technique but not his art; indeed he violates his art, contradicting
and acting against the good that is programmed into it. Strictly speaking, he
does not act as a physician when he does such things; he struggles explicitly
against his art and practice.

And in still another possibility, the physician may become, say, avaricious
or ambitious, and he may perform his actions primarily in order to enrich
or advance himself. In this case the art keeps insisting in his actions; the
good of the art is not directly violated, and it may indeed be promoted if the
practitioner is to achieve the purposes he has set. He will make less money
if he fails to cure his patients. Still, the good of the art has become a means
rather than an end. It is still a good for him, but good primarily as a means to
wealth or power, no longer an end in itself. In such a case there are not two
but three perspectives on the medical good: that of the patient who wants
to be healthy, that of the art, and that of being a means to the doctor's ad-
vancement. The doctor's medical activity becomes subject to alien pressures,
to a field of force generated by a purpose that is only accidentally blended
with the medical good, and it becomes possible that the medical good itself will not be sought in a particular action but will be distorted in view
of the purpose it is made to serve. The doctor will not explicitly want the
bad of the patient, as, say, the torturer does, nor will he fail through careless-
ness, as a poor practitioner might, but he can allow the harmony between
the good as wanted by the patient and the good as sought by the art to be
disharmonized by the purposes he introduces into his assessment of what is
to be done.

In the best and normative case, however, there is no distortion, and in
acting according to his art the physician also seeks the good of the patient.
Because the art of medicine aims at something that is a good for the patient,
the doctor, in the exercise of his art, seeks the medical good of the patient as
his own good. He pursues, professionally, what is good for another. He does
this as a practitioner of his art. The nature of his art, with the perspectives it
provides on the medical good, gives the physician this harmony, and it makes
him, in the good exercise of his art, not only a good doctor but also essen-

tially a good moral agent, one who seeks the good of another formally as his own.[4] The doctor's profession essentially makes him a good man, provided he is true to his art and follows its insistence.

It is important to realize that by being faithful to his art and to the good that is programmed into it, the physician is helped to become a good man. In the philosophical analysis of virtue, a distinction is usually drawn between being good in the various arts and being good as a human being. In the dialogues of Plato, for example, we are often reminded that someone can excel as a craftsman but fail in the art of living. This is a legitimate distinction, but we must not turn it into a necessary separation. Rather, in the important arts, and specifically in the art of medicine, the goodness of the art will help shape the character of the person who practices it, because it will form him into someone who seeks the good of another as his own good. It will help the physician to be excellent not just as a doctor but as a human being. The physician can therefore be grateful to his art not only for the skills he learns from it, but also for the character that it bestows on him.

In addition to his professional benevolence, the physician may also wish his patient well as a friend or as a colleague, but this is not the first relationship between them. Their friendship does not establish them as doctor and patient, and another person who is not a friend or a colleague would not be somehow deprived in entering into a medical relationship with the doctor. The art, with its network of perspectives on the good in question, establishes the way the doctor and patient are to be related in the medical transaction.

The full definition of medical science

We have discussed the medical good as seen by the patient and as seen by the doctor representing his art. But the good is not simply what people desire; sometimes we desire what only seems to be good but really is not. We must ask about the truth of the good in question, and in asking about truth we approach medicine as a science and not just as an art. We approach medicine as an understanding.

Just as the medical art cannot be fragmented into a sum of techniques, so medical science cannot be broken down into information about functional

---

4. On the form of moral transactions, see Robert Sokolowski, *Moral Action: A Phenomenological Study* (Bloomington: Indiana University Press, 1985).

relationships. It cannot be broken down into knowledge about the workings of the various elements, powers, and processes that are relevant to human health. We in our time and culture are inclined to break it down into such particles, because the science that was introduced by Francis Bacon, Descartes, and Galileo does tend to see the world as a network of relationships and laws. The science we inherit from these authors looks away from the forms of things to the elements and forces out of which the things are made. But if this is all our science is supposed to know, then the art associated with it will be mere technique. If we know only a lot of "if-thens," all we will be able to do is to manipulate these relationships, to pull *these* levers and let *that* happen. If we are to go beyond this, we must understand what health is, and since health is an excellence of the human being, we must understand what a human being is and how the excellence of health is related to his complete human excellence.

In fact, every physician knows that he is seeking a good in his practice of the medical art, and he has some sense of how it is related to the over-all human good. But given the modern understanding of science, the physician will not be comfortable in considering this knowledge to be part of his science of medicine. He will say he knows it rather through common sense or through his religious belief or his cultural values. But surely this reflects a deficiency in the science of medicine. The modern science of medicine has been enormously successful in the treatment of diseases and in understanding the mechanisms of the body. Perhaps it could not have achieved its successes had it not limited its focus to the study of structures and functional relationships, had it not abstracted from the definition of larger wholes and forms. Perhaps the controversies and the imprecisions that arise when these issues are faced would have impeded the progress that was made within the more constricted horizon. But although this restriction can be understood and may need to be tolerated, it certainly is not something with which we should be satisfied.

Medicine as science still has more to accomplish along the paths it has been following in the past few centuries. There are diseases still to be understood and treated, there are bodily structures and functions still to be explained. But a more complete natural science would involve not just more of what has been done, but also an understanding of a different kind: the definition of health and disease, the clarification of how the medical good can be related to the political, economic, and personal good, the understanding of the relationship between health and human agency (an issue that is especially urgent in the psychological branches of medicine). To give a more specific instance, medical neurophysiology is incomplete so long as we are not able to say, scientifically, what it means for certain neurological activities to be not just chemical or electrical processes, but also the act of seeing a tree or hearing a song; or what it means for another neurological phenomenon to be identifiable with an immune response. The full scientific truth of neuroanatomy is not achieved until the sense and excellence, the form, of the neurophysiological is understood, until we can state the sense and excellence of what the neurophysiological does; and since medicine aims at preserving or restoring a healthy state, it too is incomplete as a science, as an understanding of the good it is to accomplish, until these dimensions have been introduced. The more complete medical science must reintroduce an appreciation of form, but it must do so in a way that is commensurate with the great advances made in medicine and biology during the era in which science was silent about form.

Medicine and religion

Let us now turn to the religious aspect of medicine. The medical practitioner knows that he is not the origin and controller of everything that goes on through his art. He knows that he only assists processes and forces that occur on their own initiative, that healing originally takes place quite apart from the mind and agency of the physician. The medical art itself is mysterious: its discoveries, its exercise, its successes, are never mastered by any one person, and they depend on forces that will never be fully comprehended and ruled. There is much to revere in medicine.

In the Hippocratic Oath this reverence is expressed in the invocation of Apollo under the name of Apollo Physician—reason and art in the medical form—and in the invocation of Asclepius, the founder of medicine who became a god, and of his daughters Hygieia and Panacea, and finally of all the gods and goddesses. The Hippocratic physician acknowledged his obligations to the powers to which he and his art were subject.[5]

5. On the Hippocratic Oath, see Leon Kass, *Toward a More Natural Science* (New York: Free Press, 1985), chapter 9.

But for Christians, the world has been purged of such divinities and powers. The world is understood as created by the one God, who would be all that he is, in undiminished perfection, even if he had not created. For the pagans the world appears as the necessary, unquestionable background for all the natures and events that come to be within it; the world is a context even for the gods, who take their place within it; but for Christians the world itself is no longer the final setting. The world itself is profiled against a deeper horizon, one in which there could possibly be only the divine and nothing else. The world, with everything in it, does exist, but it exists out of the possibility of not being; and its being is not through inexorable necessity but through the unforced generosity and choice of the creator.[6] And within the created world, human beings are understood not only as created but also as redeemed by God and allowed by grace to share in the divine life. Human being, furthermore, is elevated within the world because it becomes the place where, in the Incarnation, God becomes united with a part of the world and presents himself as part of the world. The divine nature and the person of the Logos become united with the human nature in Christ.

Are the medical science, art, and activity affected by being placed in this new context? How are they affected? It would not be appropriate to define the changes primarily as new or different moral obligations introduced by Christian belief. Rather, any new moral emphases are themselves the outcome of a new understanding of what is involved in medicine. Christian faith reveals further the truth of medicine and what medicine does.

But what further truth is there to be stated? We have already described the nobility of the medical art, its capacity to make its practitioner good not only as a doctor but also as a man. What else is there to say?

The Christian understanding of the world is in some tension with modern science, including modern medical science, in regard to the recognition of the forms or natures of things. Christian belief would emphasize the reality of form as against the scientific tendency to stress the elements and forces out of which things are made. In regard to human being, it would emphasize human nature and the virtues and obligations inscribed in human nature. Of course one need not be Christian to acknowledge form; one need not

6. On Creation and its role in Christian theology, see Robert Sokolowski, *The God of Faith and Reason: Foundations of Christian Theology* (Washington, D.C.: The Catholic University of America Press, 1995).

be Christian to appreciate that things have their specific excellences and internal ends, and to appreciate that the human good and the human end are indicated by human nature. But this sense of a human end is heightened in Christian belief, because living according to virtue becomes not only noble and proper to man, but also in accordance with the creative will of God. The light shed by Creation does not change our human goods, but it gives them a deeper sense. But when Christian theology deals with the new context of Creation, it must be careful not to turn the noble into the obligatory; it must introduce its new context in such a way that the noble remains intrinsically excellent and does not become simply a duty placed on us by a commandment.

In regard specifically to the medical art, it is not the case that Christian belief would have a special access to the virtues and obligations associated with medicine, that it would be able somehow to derive medical goods from new moral principles that are not available to those who are not Christian. It does not have a short cut to the ethics of medicine. Rather, theology must first work with the excellence of the medical art as it shows up to those who practice it well; it must recognize and elaborate the internal good of medicine; then it must place this good in the context of Creation and Redemption and show how the integrity of the good is sustained and how it is heightened and highlighted by Christian belief. It is a question of an identity that is maintained within a new and distinctive set of differences, an instance of the preservation and perfection of nature within the context of grace.

One thing that is appreciated differently in Christian belief is the place of personality in the world. In a strictly evolutionary understanding of the world, the human person is taken as emerging out of the impersonal, subhuman forces of nature; the personal is a kind of excrescence, a fortuitous appearance in nature. In a more classical pagan understanding, the personal may be taken as a permanent part of the world: besides the material elements of the world, there were gods, spirits of various sorts, and even, for some thinkers, the human species as eternal. The world was not conceived to be without mind and life. But in the understanding presented by Christianity, the personal is exalted to a much higher dignity. The personal does not evolve out of the impersonal, nor does it contend with the impersonal, but it could, in God, be all that there is. The very existence of the world is the effect of a personal action. The personal is therefore seen in a new perspective, and even the human person is elevated to a new condition. The existence of the human person is seen as the effect of a personal act, and the destiny of the human person, as redeemed by Christ, takes on a cosmic significance.

And what is at issue in medical activity is not just a living organism, but we ourselves in our bodily and psychological being. If we understand ourselves as created and redeemed, then the issue in medicine is also understood differently: not that the natural good of health is changed, but that its sense and emphasis are modified. Human life and the transmission of human life, for example, are appreciated as a mystery even in the course of nature, but they are more deeply reverenced when life is seen as given by the Creator and redeemed in Christ.

The healing of human life was one of the ways in which the Incarnation of the Son of God manifested itself and one of the ways in which the presence of the Holy Spirit was shown in the early Church. The bodily and psychological cures in the Gospels and the Acts of the Apostles may well serve as an indication that the act of healing is one of the first of the human activities that can be informed by grace. Medicine can then not only express the knowledge of science, the skill of art, and the benevolence of human action; it can be an expression of charity as well.

THE FIDUCIARY RELATIONSHIP AND
THE NATURE OF PROFESSIONS

It has not proved easy to determine what a profession is. There is no problem about the existence and definition of skills and arts: clearly, some people know how to repair refrigerators, treat sick animals, cut hair, and the like. They have cultivated these skills and hence are obviously different from people who cannot do such things well. If the people who have the skills also understand what they are doing, if they have knowledge as well as skill, if they can teach and explain as well as perform, they can be said to possess not only a skill but an art, a *technē*.[1] When people who possessed certain arts formed associations to protect, promote, and teach their art, they were said to form guilds. Arts and guilds are not controversial; they are easy to identify. What more is needed? Is it truly necessary to introduce professions? Why not stay with the arts of medicine and law, and the guilds of doctors and lawyers? Is the distinction between a *technē* and a profession a genuine distinction, or does one term of the distinction, the profession, get absorbed into the other, the art, when we think precisely about the issue? How is a profession different from an art, and how is a profession different from a guild?

Formal knowledge as the distinguishing feature of professions

Bernard Barber lists four features that an occupation must have if it is to be considered a profession: general and systematic knowledge, orientation

---

1. Aristotle, *Nicomachean Ethics* VI, 4, 1140a6–23, and *Metaphysics* I, 1, 981a24–b10.

to community interest, self-monitoring through internalized codes of ethics, and rewards that symbolize accomplishments in work and that are sought as ends in themselves.[2] G. Harries-Jenkins[3] supplies a list of six elements of professionalization, then goes on to subdivide these elements into no fewer than twenty-one subelements. These two authors claim that professions have a definition of their own.

John Kultgen, in contrast, concludes his book *Ethics and Professionalism*[4] with the claim that the distinction between professions and other occupations is, in fact, not a genuine distinction. In a chapter entitled "Professionalism without Professions," he claims that professionalism is a way of being and acting that can be achieved in any occupation. He says that "the ideal of a professional is that of a person dedicated to providing proficient service to those who need it."[5] He describes the various virtues, both moral and intellectual, that a dedicated professional must have; he observes that such virtues can be "deliberately pursued and cultivated";[6] and he claims that all these virtues "are relevant to features of work as such, not just features of particular kinds of work."[7] Since practically everyone provides some sort of specialized labor, each person, he says, contributes something to society and ought to shape his contribution according to professional ideals. Even apparently menial and routine tasks involve some specialization, and if there are forms of work for which the professional virtues seem hardly to be required, societies should organize these occupations in such a way that greater professionalization can be realized in them: "The challenge is to alter the conditions of other kinds of work so as to foster greater self-development and self-expression and to provide conditions in which workers will know and approve the products of their labor."[8] Kultgen maintains that professionalism must be universalized and observes that the term *profession* has suffered extensive "semantic hemorrhage"[9] as more and more occupations have laid

---

2. Bernard Barber, "Some Problems in the Sociology of Professions," *Daedalus* 92 (1963): 672.

3. G. Harries-Jenkins, "Professionals in Organizations," in *Professions and Professionalization*, edited by J. A. Jackson (Cambridge: Cambridge University Press, 1970), pp. 58–59.

4. John Kultgen, *Ethics and Professionalism* (Philadelphia: University of Pennsylvania Press, 1988).

5. Ibid., p. 347.   6. Ibid., p. 360.
7. Ibid.   8. Ibid., p. 361.
9. Ibid., p. 369.

claim to it. Thus, in the terms we used to introduce our question, Kultgen's position would imply that professions do not differ in principle from skills and arts.

Kultgen's proposals have much in common with the encyclical *Laborem Exercens* of Pope John Paul II.[10] In his encyclical, the Holy Father does not discuss professions as such, but he does extend the concept of work to cover many different kinds of human performances: "Work means any activity of man, whether manual or intellectual, whatever its nature or circumstances; it means any human activity that can and must be recognized as work, in the midst of all the many activities of which man is capable and to which he is predisposed by his very nature. . . ."[11] The Pope unifies the concept of work not in terms of the activity that is done but in terms of the one who accomplishes it, the human subject whose dignity, rights, and duties must everywhere be respected.

The book by Eliot Freidson, *Professional Powers,*[12] may be taken as a counterpoint to Kultgen's work. Freidson distinguishes where Kultgen identifies. Freidson's aim is to "emphasize analytical description over abstract theorizing."[13] He provides a highly differentiated view of the professions, distinguishing not only the variety of professions themselves but also the variety of roles found within each profession: the roles of practitioners, administrators, teachers, and researchers. He comments in detail on the various ways professionals exercise power but also stresses the limits of such power, and he criticizes large-scale generalizations, such as the claim that professionals constitute a single new class in our social order or that professionals who are self-employed enjoy greater autonomy and success than those who work for others. He takes the concept "profession" as a historical concept, "an American social category for distinguishing a group of occupations,"[14] but he acknowledges that the concept can apply, with adjustments, to groups of people in other modern countries. Although Freidson stresses detail and variety, he does claim that the professions can be distinguished from other oc-

10. John Paul II, *Laborem Exercens (On Human Work)* (Washington, D.C.: U.S. Catholic Conference, 1981).

11. Ibid., p. 1.

12. Eliot Freidson, *Professional Powers: A Study of the Institutionalization of Formal Knowledge* (Chicago: University of Chicago Press, 1986).

13. Ibid., p. xiv.

14. Ibid., p. xii.

cupations. They are so distinguished, he says, by virtue of the "formal knowledge" they possess, apply, protect, and develop.[15] Members of the professions are the "agents of formal knowledge."[16]

The formal knowledge that is at the core of professions is, Freidson says, specialized knowledge, which is different from what most people know; it requires extensive education and training. It is the knowledge "shared by particular groups of people who perform activities on a regular basis that other people do not."[17] However, it is not just specialized knowledge, which has been found in all civilizations and can be found in the arts; it is specialized knowledge that, in the modern West, has taken on a distinctive character or structure, one that Freidson calls "formal." It has been shaped into systematic theories that explain facts and justify actions. It involves hypotheses, axioms, deductions, and models. Freidson says it is knowledge characterized by rationalization, a term that he takes from Max Weber and defines as "the pervasive use of reason, sustained where possible by measurement, to gain the end of functional efficiency."[18] He observes that "rational" knowledge and action are realized in or associated with contemporary natural science, technology, economic and institutional management, and social organization. He also states that such knowledge does not apply itself; it exists in and is developed by "human agents or carriers."[19] We might say that the formal knowledge is both embodied and applied in and through the professional.

Prudence and the distinction between art and profession

Let us assume that Freidson is correct in isolating the possession of a certain kind of knowledge as the distinguishing feature of a professional. The knowledge in question, furthermore, is useful knowledge, the kind that can be applied to situations to bring about a desired result. Not all knowledge is useful in this sense; there is a kind of speculative or theoretical knowledge that can be very important for us without being practical and useful. There is some knowledge that is simply about the way things are and the way things have to be, about essentials and necessities; and our response to such knowledge may not be to put it to our use, but simply to recognize that things are that way and that there is nothing we can do about it. The patterns of time,

15. Ibid., p. 3.
17. Ibid., p. 3.
19. Ibid., p. 9.

16. Ibid., p. 16.
18. Ibid.

for example, are essential and necessary; the future becomes the past through the present. It is not strictly speaking useful for us to know this, not in the way it can be useful to know the intricacies of the tax laws or the symptoms and causes of arthritis, since we cannot do anything about or with the passage of time. Such knowledge is too basic to be useful; it expresses what we must simply take as it is, not what we can use in modifying the world.

But not all useful knowledge ought to be called professional knowledge. A good automobile mechanic may know a lot of useful things about cars, but we would not, I think, want to call him a professional. One reason for our reluctance has already been provided by Freidson. The mechanic's knowledge is not formal and systematic enough to become the basis of a profession; his knowledge is tied to the particularities of the automobile. If he knew not only a lot about cars, but also a lot of physics, mathematics, mechanics, metallurgy, chemistry, and electromagnetics, and if he could apply all this knowledge to the automobile, then he would be not just a mechanic but an engineer. He would not only know that certain things are true about cars, but would also know why they are true, and he would be able to trace the "why" through several layers of explanation. He might or might not be a better mechanic because of all this, since auto repair deals with this particular car and not with theory and explanation, but he would be able to do certain things that a mechanic could not do. He might, for example, be able to help in developing new synthetic materials for automobile engines.

When we say that the knowledge of the professional, though still practical, is more formal and abstract or general than that of the mechanic, we do not mean that the professional's knowledge departs from the world and expands into mere words or textbooks. To be more formal and abstract or general means to have a wider range, to work within a more comprehensive context and with more materials. The mechanic may know that the terminals of the battery must be kept clean and that batteries run down after three years or so, but the engineer can see the car battery as an instance of the same forces that are at work in radios, lamps, generators, and bolts of lightning. Because the engineer's knowledge is so wide-ranging, he can see other ways of doing what is done with a battery. Because, for example, a doctor's knowledge of medicine is so wide-ranging and because he knows why certain things happen, he can think of many different ways of treating the headache that I have been trying to treat with aspirin. One feature of the knowledge possessed by professionals, therefore, is its formal and wide or expanded character.

But if knowledge, even formal knowledge, is the only distinctive feature of the professional, it is still not clear how a profession can be distinguished from an art; *technē* was also defined classically as skill with understanding. The distinction can be sharpened by noting another important aspect of professional activity. If I go to an automobile mechanic, all I entrust to this person is my automobile, but when I approach a professional, I subject something more than a possession of mine to the professional's expertise: in a distinctive way, I subject myself and my future to his assessments and to his judgment. Using the word *prudence* in the classical sense, the sense given to it by Aristotle as a person's ability "to deliberate about what is good and expedient for himself" in a way conducive to the good life in general,[20] I submit my own prudence to that of the professional. In a limited way, I hand over the steering of my life to this person. I let him take over not just one of my things but my choices and activities themselves. I must do so, because I have wandered into an area of life in which my own knowledge does not equip me to steer by myself. Someone fell on my sidewalk and broke an arm and is suing me; I have developed severe headaches and blurred vision; I need to learn Russian because I will be stationed in Moscow. For a while I must do what someone else says I should, not what I simply decide to do myself. In engaging a professional, I do not abandon my own prudence; I do not delegate my prudence to someone else; but I do blend my prudence with that of the professional, or the professional's with mine.

It is true that the professional assumes responsibility for only a limited part of the client's life and that the client remains the ultimate agent in the relationship. As a client, I could always stop the transaction in question. But within that limited domain and with the importance that the domain may involve (my mental or physical health, my familial relationships, my legal standing), the professional deals not merely with my possessions but with me. If I go to a mechanic or to a dry cleaner, even one that provides "professional dry cleaning," I hand over my car or my jacket to someone else, but

20. Aristotle, *Nicomachean Ethics* VI, 5, 1140a26–29.

in dealing with a doctor or a lawyer or a teacher, I submit myself to be determined in my future condition by the one I consult; if I hire an architect to build a house for me, I am entrusting to that professional the design of part of my future life. This blending of my own prudence with that of the professional shows how knowledge can be common and shared even when it is practical knowledge, the kind that addresses and changes situations. It is not the case that only speculative thinking is common. I can share someone else's mind even in regard to what I should do, even in regard to my assessments and deliberations.

What we could call the phenomenon of nakedness, in its various forms, follows from the fact that a client or patient subordinates himself to the prudence of the professional. The client has to remove the cover used for both protection and privacy in his normal exchanges with others. The most vivid instance of such nakedness occurs in regard to medicine; patients must not only tell the physician about their experiences and activities, but may also have to remove their clothing, that most elementary of shelters. This is done so that the physician can carry out an assessment and an intervention on the patient's behalf. A client has to lay open to his lawyer everything that happened and everything that he did concerning the issue he has brought to the lawyer, and another client must tell his architect everything about how he wants to live in the building the professional will design for him. If in any such cases the client were to retain part of his cover or shelter in the relevant area, the appeal to the professional's prudence would be in vain; the very item that is kept concealed might be the key to the situation.

Some special obligations befall professionals because their prudence is being called upon to help steer clients' lives. The exercise of professional judgment and skill must, first of all, be for the client's good. This obligation does not stem from any personal benevolence or private virtue on the part of the professional, but from the very nature of the relationship between professional and client. The client addresses *this* individual not because of any personal characteristics as such, not as a friend to whom he has come for advice, but as the embodiment and agent of a certain kind of formal knowledge. It is only to activate this knowledge on his own behalf that the client has come to the professional. Second, clients need to shed their privacy only to the extent required by the exercise of the professional's judgment and skill. The physician does not need to be told about the patient's savings, and the real estate lawyer does not need to be told about the client's deafness. Third, the confidentiality required of the professional stems from the fact that things were told or shown to him only so that the expertise he embodies could be brought to bear on the life of the client. The professional's mind in this respect becomes like an expansion of the client's own mind and the information the professional acquires remains the client's own, unless and until the client wishes to disclose it to anyone else. Ultimately, the one thinking and acting, the one taking the initiative, is the client. The client has come to the professional, has initiated and established the relationship, and keeps it in being.

The obligation of professionals to put their knowledge and skill at the service of the client is vividly perceived in instances in which this obligation is broken. Suppose a client discovers that his lawyer is using information the client provides, and even perhaps soliciting information from him, for the lawyer's own financial benefit; or suppose a patient discovers that his physician is making decisions regarding his case in view of some institutional or personal purposes or gain that the doctor has. In such cases the prudence of the professional steers the client's life for the benefit of the professional, and yet the client has come to the professional to have his own good pursued.

It is instructive to distinguish the way we turn to a friend for help in deliberation and share in the friend's prudence from the way we turn to a professional. A friend is not specialized; my friend knows my whole way of being. I ask him for help in making a decision that affects me in my entirety; he helps me deliberate whether the course of action will be for my good as such, not just for my good health or for my legal standing. In contrast, I turn to a professional for help within a certain domain, the domain in which he is the expert. Furthermore, the "knowledge" I draw on when I turn to a friend is not a formal kind of knowledge. It is the friend's understanding of my general strengths, weaknesses, possibilities, and achievements, his understanding of my character, history, and expectations. It is a knowledge he has about me which is analogous to my own knowledge of myself. We, my friend and I, deliberate together about how the proposed action will affect the whole of my life, and although the final decision will have to be my own, the deliberation that leads up to it can be done in common. In contrast, the knowledge I appeal to in the professional is not primarily a knowledge about me in my entirety, but the knowledge of a domain in which I need expert assistance; it is a knowledge about general rules and principles, joined with the ability to apply them to particular cases. It would be out of place for me to ask the professional as such to deliberate with me in the way a friend would.

We have been describing the relationship between professional and client from the point of view of the client, whose life becomes directed, in part, by the prudence of the professional. We could reverse our perspective and describe the same relationship from the viewpoint of the professional. From this standpoint the professional is understood to be capable of exercising independent judgment; this ability is based on his knowledge, training, and experience. In listing some of the features of the professional, Philip Elliot, in *The Sociology of the Professions,* mentions "broad, theoretical knowledge used in non-routine situations to reach unprogrammed decisions. . . ."[21] The "unprogrammed decisions" of a professional are usually made in respect to other persons, in respect to clients. They are almost always decisions that steer the lives of others. The autonomy of the professional is not an isolated independence, nor is it one that deals with mere things.

Once a client has engaged a professional, the professional does not like to have his recommendations disregarded. As Everett C. Hughes writes, "The professional in some cases refuses to act unless the client—individual or corporate—agrees to follow the advice given."[22] By its nature, prudential deliberation is done in view of action, and if a professional is to share his deliberation with someone else, he wants to do so with the same certainty of action he would have if he were deliberating for himself alone. Most of us, surely, at one time or another, have had the embarrassing experience of admitting, say, to our physician, that we did not do what he told us to do: to lose weight, to take medicine, to get an X-ray. When this happens, the physician is not amused. He is not just worried about what will happen but offended by our neglect. He exercised his prudence, he deliberated on our behalf, and our failure to follow through was something like a personal affront. We did not just neglect advice, we slighted the physician's prudence.

The claim that a client subordinates his prudence to that of the professional may seem not to hold in the case of a profession such as engineering,

21. Philip Elliot, *The Sociology of the Professions* (New York: Herder and Herder, 1972), p. 96.
22. Everett C. Hughes, "Professions," *Daedalus* 92 (1963): 655.

in which the expert deals with materials and not with persons. However, it is quite clearly true of the paradigmatic professions, the four that originally were called "professions" in English: divinity, medicine, law, and "the gentlemanly occupation of the military."[23] It is true of many forms of social work, and it is true of the professions of architects, teachers, financial advisors, and the like. The feature of dealing rather directly with the decisions to be made by other people is an important element in the definition of the professional.

The relationship between professional and client is a fiduciary relationship. The client trusts the professional and entrusts himself—not just his possessions—to the professional. The professional is presented as trustworthy not primarily in the way a friend is found to be faithful, by having proved himself in many situations, but by having been certified as a professional. There is an elegant anonymity to professional trustworthiness. If I get sick away from home and must go to the emergency room of a hospital, I can in principle trust doctors and nurses I have never met before. I enter into a fiduciary relationship with them because they are presented as members of the medical *profession,* persons who are certified by the profession and who can, *prima facie,* be taken as willing to abide by its norms. I do not have exactly the same kind of trust if my car breaks down somewhere away from home; I am delivered over rather to the personal honesty, trustworthiness, and competence of the local mechanic. It is as though I had to find a temporary friend rather than being able to appeal to a professional.

The difference between a profession and an art, therefore, lies in the fiduciary relationship that is built into the profession but not into the art. The fiduciary relationship is based on the fact that in the paradigmatic professions, and in the paradigmatic practitioners of those professions, the client partially blends his prudence with that of the professional. Even members of a profession who do not treat clients directly can participate in this fiduciary relationship, because what they do—their medical research, their legal administration—receives its sense ultimately from its application to the lives of clients. Such persons do not merely promote an intellectual discipline; they develop a discipline that will bear on someone's prudence.

In this respect the profession of divinity, one of the four original "pro-

23. Freidson, *Professional Powers,* p. 22.

fessions," is an interesting case. We would be hard put to it to determine what the "art" of the clergy might be, and we would find it somewhat odd for clergy to form guilds. The profession of divinity seems to be the critical test for distinguishing between the arts and the professions. The clergy do have a certain specialized, theological knowledge, and do deal with a special domain of the "client's" life: with the client's relationship to God. But the relationship to God is "partial" in an unusual way, and it clearly engages the prudence of the client. The believer comes to the cleric for help in determining how to live in his relationship with God. In the clerical profession we seem to find the fiduciary relationship *par excellence,* and it may well be that the profession of divinity established a kind of field of force that emphasized analogous relationships in the other professions.

The natural and the conventional in professions

The professional relationship between practitioner and client can be morally interpreted in both a utilitarian and a deontological way. The profession is geared toward providing a service, and one can evaluate policies and performances in regard to how effectively and how extensively the service is furnished. But the one who benefits from the service is an autonomous human being, a person, and must be treated as such. This demand brings about deontological obligations for the professional, who must avoid paternalism in his involvement with the client. The professional's knowledge and judgment are offered to expand the prudence of the client, but they must not replace it. John Stuart Mill reminds professionals that they must aim at increasing the well-being of others, while Immanuel Kant reminds them that they must respect the client as a person. As Kultgen says, "Determination not to harm and if possible to help others to achieve such benefits as health, justice, desirable structures and artifacts, education, and solace is the utilitarian dimension of the professional's dedication to service. The deontological dimension is respect for autonomy."[24]

The utilitarian and the deontological perspectives bring out different moral aspects of the professional relationship, but even when taken together they do not exhaust the moral dimension. Indeed, they tend to make the relationship appear almost entirely conventional. They underemphasize the di-

---

24. Kultgen, *Ethics and Professionalism,* p. 352.

mensions of the relationship that are by nature. The professions as such tend to lay stress on convention and human art. As institutions, they have come about through the development of technology and bureaucratic social structures; even the knowledge associated with them has arisen in the context of technology and complex, capitalist social orders.[25] The knowledge of lawyers, accountants, and social workers, for example, is largely concerned with rules and regulations that cultures and individuals have devised, and it might seem that even medicine, with its dependence on technology, is primarily a matter of human contrivance, a matter of what we can make and what we can do. The professions then might appear to be purely human institutions sharply distinguished from the natural world, islands of human ingenuity dealing with human persons, exalting human techniques and human choice, regulated only by utility in service and respect for persons.

But the utilitarian and deontological emphases must be complemented by a recognition of those aspects of the professional relationship that are by nature. We can distinguish two ways in which "what is by nature" is at work in the professions: first, there are natural relationships and natural processes that precede the professions and provide a focus for them; and, second, because of this focus, the professions themselves can be seen to have a nature and a proper end.

As to the first point: Professional practice, although empowered by formal knowledge, is ultimately based on relationships that are established naturally, relationships that do not arise through human decisions but come to be as part of the natural human condition. The formal knowledge that empowers the professional is itself ultimately knowledge about such natural relationships, no matter how amply human convention and contrivance may have articulated the relationships. The profession of medicine, for example, ultimately depends on the fact that human beings become sick and become well again, but sometimes need the assistance of others who can adjust and improve the healing process. The whole of medical science and technology is about healing, and the process of healing has its own definition and nature. The natural process occurs before there is a profession of medicine. The physician and the patient are defined in relation to the healing process, to something established by nature. The teaching profession depends on the

25. Freidson, *Professional Powers,* pp. 3–4.

fact that we can and must learn things, and on the fact that such learning can be assisted by others, who have become identified as members of a profession; but all the conventions, technology, and knowledge that empower the teaching professionals would immediately turn to worthless dust if the natural process of learning were to disappear. The scale and complexity of formal knowledge and technology may give us the impression that the human world is made up entirely of our interventions and of ourselves as interveners, but the heady self-confidence to which our technological achievements may tempt us must bow before the natural order that comes first and remains always as the form and substance of our activity. Formal knowledge may empower the professional, but the professional is authorized by nature.

Indeed, the natural order in a professional relationship is what allows the relationship to be more than a merely contractual exchange, a purely conventional agreement in which the client comes asking for something and the professional is expected to deliver what is wanted. Both the client and the professional are subject to the nature of the relationship, and for this reason the professional has a certain authority over the client. A client *ought* to take proper care of his health; he is subject by nature to this obligation. Therefore the doctor can tell him what he *ought* to do according to the nature of things. The doctor is not limited to being able to say, "Well, you want to be healthy and you have come to me for help, so I recommend that you do this and that." Such a remark would be appropriate for, say, an automobile salesman or a clothier, someone who is merely assisting someone else in a purely contractual exchange (and in some cases even the clothier might be obliged by natural law to tell the client that he *really* should not go out in public wearing this thing). The governing principle in such cases is the desire or the will of the customer, not the nature of the client; but a professional is not a supplier, and a client is not a customer. Also, the formal knowledge of the professional is not mere information that can be useful to the client in satisfying his desires, but knowledge about the client in his own nature, in what he is. The knowledge of the professional can therefore help a client to understand himself better and thus be able to live more authentically according to what he truly is. A patient who lives temperately according to the medical knowledge of his physician is living more appropriately according to his nature as a human being, and so is a student who, through the knowledge and skill of his teachers, learns to think more precisely and more truthfully. The utilitarian and the deontological aspects of the professional relationship must be complemented by the goods and obligations in the relationship that are by nature.

The knowledge of the professional is concerned with the natural relationship between professional and client, and the skill of the professional is concerned with that natural dimension as well. The skill is exercised in imitation of nature: the physician promotes healing, the teacher promotes learning, the judge redresses wrongs, the social worker promotes familial cohesion and independence. The phrase "art imitates nature" does not mean that art makes a copy of the things that nature brings about; rather, it means that human skill makes things develop the way nature would make them develop, if it were not impeded in a particular case by sluggish circumstances or harmful deviations. When we exercise our skill, we let it be guided by the way things would occur according to their own nature. We imitate and assist the natural process, we do not subdue the natural process or replace it with a procedure of our own making. Professionals do not create what they achieve; they add their skill to a process that is already there, a process they try to bring to a more perfect completion. We imitate, we do not overpower nature; we do not wrestle nature to the ground.

The relationship between nature and human intervention (whether as art or as convention) is not as clear-cut as we might suppose. It is not the case that we have, on the one hand, nature pure and simple, say in some primitive people, and on the other hand, sheer human making and convention. Rather, in human affairs, nature and art, and nature and convention, always permeate each other. The natural manifests itself to us in and through the conventional and the skillfully transformed. The nature of a river is more fully disclosed when the river is bridged; the nature of wood is exhibited more vividly when wood is worked into a piece of furniture; the nature of familial relationships is more fully expressed when they are confirmed by good laws. Because nature and skill, and nature and convention, usually come to us as blended together and not as detached, it takes insight to ferret out the natural dimension in the human things that surround us; it takes insight to know what is at the base and the core of medicine, military affairs, legal transactions, and the like. It is easy to get so caught up in the arbitrary aspects of such things that we overlook the fact that something humanly substantial is going on in them. It is easy, for example, to claim that the law is simply what we lay down as being law, and to overlook the fact that whether we want it to be so or not, an issue of justice is always germinating in and through the law that we lay down. It takes insight to see what is the naturally just thing in a particular legal controversy.

Sometimes we have to bring the natural core to mind because the conventional has taken a course and a form that threatens its own natural basis: welfare programs may destroy families and human character, medicine may get caught up in procedures that impede health instead of promoting it, education may become so bureaucratized that young people are prevented from learning. When we criticize a way of doing something, and specifically when we criticize an established profession, we do so on the basis of a distinction we draw between the natural and the established. We claim to be able to see that the natural and the conventional, or the natural and the skilled, do not cohere. It is the generation of this distinction that presents both nature and convention or artifice to us; it is not the case that we first have nature fully given as a standard against which we measure our conventions and plan our arts. But it is not only in such negative cases, in which criticism is needed, that we see the distinction between nature and human intervention. In happier instances, in a more positive way, if we are insightful enough, we can rejoice at how well what we are doing seems to blend and fit with what naturally needs to be done in the activity we perform.

We turn now to the second way in which "the natural" functions in professions; the professions themselves have a definition and a *telos*. A profession is based upon a natural process that it tries to imitate and bring to as perfect a condition as it can. Through this focus, the profession itself, as an institution and as an activity, has its own nature and its own end: the formal knowledge and the skill involved in the profession are employed to bring this end about. The end of medicine is to restore and maintain health, the end of architecture is to construct buildings in which people can live and work, the end of teaching is the education of students. Such ends are built into the professions and they exist independently of the purposes the individual professionals may have in mind when they exercise their professions. A doctor may pursue his practice with the intention of becoming rich and famous, but medicine remains what it is whether or not his purposes cohere with its end.

The professional is obligated not only to his client but also to his profession. Professionals must act to preserve the profession. Their purposes, as

Francis Slade says, must be congruent with the ends of their professions.[26] In discussing medicine and the difference between healing and destroying life, Slade says,

Killing those upon whom they attend is forbidden to physicians by the Hippocratic Oath, not because it is morally wrong to murder people—the wrongness of murder is something that applies to all men and it is forbidden by whatever laws they acknowledge themselves to be subject to—but because to use the art of medicine to kill people destroys the art. The Oath, then, is for the sake of the art. The Hippocratic Oath does not forbid murder by medicine to physicians on account of the patients, but on account of the art of medicine.[27]

Thus, euthanasia is wrong not only because it injures another person, but also because it threatens the profession of medicine:

. . . If physicians acquired a reputation for killing rather than for curing, no one would wish to consult them. Since everyone would do everything possible to avoid them, there would soon be no physicians, for without patients the art cannot be practiced, and so could not be learned.[28]

Unprofessional conduct, therefore, such as violating confidentiality or financially exploiting the client, not only harms the client but damages the profession as well. Professions have ethical codes and they police themselves not only in order to protect vulnerable clients but to preserve themselves.

The religious dimension of professions

There is a religious overtone to the English word *profession*. Freidson, drawing on the history of the term provided in the *Oxford English Dictionary,* observes that the oldest meaning of the word was that of "a declaration, avowal, or expression of intention or purpose."[29] He says that this usage was "originally connected with taking consecrated vows" and that it stemmed "from the clerical foundation of the medieval university." The term implied "religious and moral motives to dedicate oneself to a good end."[30]

---

26. Francis Slade, "Ends and Purposes," in *Final Causality in Nature and Human Affairs,* edited by Richard Hassing (Washington, DC: The Catholic University of America Press, 1997), pp. 83–85.

27. Ibid., p. 84.   28. Ibid.

29. Freidson, *Professional Powers,* p. 21.   30. Ibid.

We might note that the word *profession* is derived from the Latin *profiteor,* the basic meaning of which is "to state openly, declare, avow."[31] The root is *fateor,* which means, in this context, "to admit, to assert, to state." This sense of a public declaration is an interesting correlative to the words *calling* and *vocation,* which are sometimes used to name one's decision to enter a profession. In response to being called, one goes on to declare publicly. To profess is also to confess.

Concerning the religious overtones of the word *profession,* Philip Elliot notes that before the Reformation the close affiliation of the universities with the church gave an ecclesiastical and hence religious tone to most professions.[32] But he also observes that modern professions arose with the development of secular branches of learning that were often "separate from the religious orthodoxy."[33] Such an origin would suggest less of a religious and theological dimension in the modern profession.

Is the etymological overtone the only religious sense left to the professions? Has the secular knowledge the professions are now based upon removed any religious and theological dimension from them? There are some aspects of the professions that can easily be given a religious meaning: dedication to the service of others can be seen as a form of charity, and respect for others, for one's clients, can be infused with respect for them as created in the image of God. Thus the utilitarian and deontological aspects of the professions seem easily able to accept a religious interpretation. However, the natural relationships that underlie professional relationships ought also to be given religious significance. They ought to be reverenced as parts of the world that are there before our intervention. To an Aristotelian, such things that are by nature would appear simply as part of the way the world is; but to one who believes in biblical revelation, they would appear as nature created by God. They would express a religious opportunity and obligation: it is a duty of the professional to preserve this natural foundation, to criticize its institutional distortions, and to promote its human cultivation.

One might think that the religious aspect of the professions consists in the motivation that religion can provide for the virtuous performance of professional activities. Religion would give a person greater reason to fur-

---

31. *Oxford Latin Dictionary* (Oxford: Clarendon Press, 1982).
32. Elliot, *Sociology of the Professions,* pp. 16–19.
33. Ibid., p. 20.

nish good service to others and to respect them. Motivation is certainly part of what religion contributes, but it is not everything. Religion provides not only motivation but also understanding; one could say that it provides motivation through understanding. Because we understand ourselves and others as created and redeemed by God, we are motivated to act with charity toward others, and because we see the world as created, we have a religious reverence for the nature of things. For example, the Christian religious understanding of the family, of human life, and of human sexuality will motivate a social worker or a health care professional to act in certain specific ways and to formulate certain policies in regard to families and young people.

In closing, I would like to mention a particular challenge to theology in the modern professions. In the past, Christian theology was able to find a religious sense in the knowledge that people acquired about the world and about themselves. Origen and St. Augustine gave a theological interpretation to the world of Plato, the Neoplatonists, and the Stoics, and St. Albert, St. Thomas Aquinas, and other Scholastics were able to do the same for Aristotle's world. The analogous challenge now is to provide a religious interpretation of the formal knowledge that distinguishes the professions. In what way can formal knowledge be seen as a reflection of the reason and wisdom of God? To clarify the religious dimension of professional knowledge is an important task, because the development of this knowledge will very likely continue apace in the future, and will continue to be one of the major cultural factors in human life. There is something metallic and mechanical about formal knowledge; like mathematics, it tends to eschew questions about the good (about what are now commonly but imprecisely called "values"). It is culturally important to determine whether such knowledge must indeed avoid questions of the good, why it must do so, and how questions about the good are to be formulated and how related to formal knowledge. To do all this is a philosophical and cultural challenge, but it is also a theological one. It is the task of showing how not only professionals as persons but also the formal knowledge that empowers them can be seen as reflections of God's wisdom.

RELIGION AND PSYCHOANALYSIS
Some Phenomenological Contributions

How is the relationship between psychoanalysis and religion to be examined? It might seem that the best approach would be to study what each of them has to say about the human condition. We might compare religion and psychoanalysis as two theories about the human estate, two competing claims to truth. But there would be something abstract about treating them in this way. Psychoanalysis is a special kind of science and art, and religion comprises a way of life as well as a set of beliefs of a special kind. In many ways the two are incommensurate. I propose therefore to join the issue of religion and psychoanalysis in a more concrete way by asking how the psychoanalyst can be related to the religious beliefs of his patient. The issue of psychoanalysis and religion arises in its sharpest form in the interaction between analyst and patient, and some dimensions of this interaction may be relevant to the issue itself. The interaction between therapist and patient is not a mere occasion that lets the question be raised, something that could be discarded when the two elements, religion and psychoanalysis, come to the center of our discussion. The situation in which this problem arises is part of the phenomenology of the problem and part of a possible resolution.

I will examine the relationship between religion and psychoanalysis by commenting on the work of Hans W. Loewald, who has provided both an authoritative interpretation of the writings of Freud and a favorable view of the place of religion in psychoanalytic theory.[1] My essay will discuss two topics: first, how the analyst can be related to the opinions of his patient, and how the patient can be related to the opinions of the analyst—in other words, how analyst and patient can quote one another—and, second, how the object of religious dispositions and beliefs, how "the divine," is to be understood. A third part will be devoted to bringing these two themes together. In developing these issues I will draw extensively on the principles of Edmund Husserl's phenomenology.

How the analyst and patient quote each other

Loewald mentions two features of psychoanalysis as a science. The first is that the essence of psychoanalysis is interpretation. Its task is to interpret whatever the patient makes known to the analyst and whatever can be deduced from what the patient makes known; its task is to interpret such things in terms of personal motivation.[2] A second feature of psychoanalysis is that the patient, the "object" of the science, is also able to enter into the investigative process: "there is no other field of scientific activity where the order of organizing potential is the same in the 'object' and the 'investigator.'" Loewald goes on to describe psychoanalysis as "calling forth . . . the investigator in the one investigated." (Could Oedipus himself be described by a better phrase?) The object of study in psychoanalysis is not just a target; the object is called upon to express a self-understanding and hence to interpret himself and his behavior, to enter into interactions with the analyst, into transference relationships, and eventually to reinterpret himself and his actions in the light of what the analyst has said and done. Loewald, in "On the Therapeutic Action of Psychoanalysis," says, "If an [analyst's] interpretation of unconscious meaning is timely, the words by which this meaning is expressed are recognizable to the patient as expressions of what he experiences."[3] The words spoken by the analyst "organize for him [the patient] what was previously less organized and thus give him the distance from himself that enables him to understand, to see, to put into words and to 'handle' what was previously not visible, understandable, speakable, tangible."[4] The patient

---

1. Hans W. Loewald, *Psychoanalysis and the History of the Individual* (New Haven: Yale University Press, 1978); *Papers on Psychoanalysis* (New Haven: Yale University Press, 1980).

2. Loewald, *Papers on Psychoanalysis,* p. 103.

3. Ibid., p. 238.   4. Ibid., pp. 238–39.

is able to assimilate "the organizing understanding which the analyst provides."[5] Patient and analyst must interpret each other. This dialogical process, which has been described as such by Stanley Leavy, is based upon the ability of the patient and the analyst to quote each other.[6] Even to begin the process, the analyst must be able to understand, and hence to quote, what the analysand says, and the patient, in order to bring the process to its end, must be able to share in the understanding of the analyst. The interpretative nature of psychoanalysis thus depends on the possibility of quotation.

A further refinement is necessary. "Possibility" can be taken in many senses. In one sense, we could investigate those conditions that render an individual psychologically capable of quoting someone else: we might ask whether this or that person has the detachment to cite someone else fairly, whether he has the acumen and linguistic resources to do so, whether this or that quotation is accurate, and the like. This kind of study presupposes a deeper level of investigation, one that examines how quotation as such is possible. It presupposes the ontology of quotation. Our discussion will move into this more philosophical issue. We will examine how quotation as such occurs, how it differentiates itself from other modes of thought, awareness, and being, and how it occurs in the special context of the psychoanalytic relationship. The study of psychoanalytic quotation will shed light on the special form of intentionality at work in psychoanalysis.

One of the characteristics of higher-level mentation is that it permits many persons to possess the same meaning. No matter how private our own appropriation of a meaning may be, the core of the meaning, the sense, can be achieved by many. That is what permits agreement, but it also permits disagreement and confusion; people may think they are each formulating the same sense when in fact they are not. The publicness of meaning was recognized in antiquity and was forcefully restated in our time by Edmund Husserl in the critique of psychologism that he made, in 1900, in his *Logical Investigations*.[7] Sameness of sense is made thematic in quotation, when we restate the same "thing" that someone else says or thinks, and restate it precisely as having been stated or thought by that other person.

5. Ibid., p. 239.

6. Stanley A. Leavy, *The Psychoanalytic Dialogue* (New Haven: Yale University Press, 1980).

7. Edmund Husserl, *Logical Investigations,* translated by John N. Findlay (New York: Humanities Press, 1970), pp. 90–224.

Although the core of meaning between quoted and quoter can be the same, there can be several perspectives, each formally different from the other, from which we can possess the one meaning. There can be several formally different voices that each state one and the same sense. Let us consider the patient, the analysand, as the fundamental voice, as $voice_0$. Then, an ordinary interlocutor with that person would count as $voice_1$, which speaks from $perspective_1$. An ordinary observer of the conversation between the person and his interlocutor, a third party who simply watches and listens, would count as $voice_2$. The analyst is $voice_3$, spoken from $perspective_3$. Finally we can distinguish $voice_4$ and $perspective_4$. This is what we could call the voice and perspective of the philosopher. His stance is to reflect on the voices and perspectives of all the others, and also to think of the world and the things in it as they show up in the perspectives of all the others, as they are spoken about and disclosed by all the other voices. Of special importance for our concerns is the fact that the philosopher also reflects upon the interaction between patient and analyst, and he examines this interaction formally as a process of manifestation; he does not serve as a superior analyst who might give the original analyst tips on improving his technique. The philosophical perspective is to analyze the process of disclosure as such, and to consider the participants formally as agents and datives of manifestation. The present essay is done from $perspective_4$ and is written and read in $voice_4$.

There is nothing to prevent one and the same person from working in more than one of these perspectives; the analyst may become a simple interlocutor for a moment ("Will you be able to take the subway home?"), or he can reflect philosophically on what he is doing as an analyst. But although the same person may speak in different voices, he should be careful not to blend and confuse what he says in one voice with what he says in another. A distorting fusion of horizons would result and perplexing ambiguities would follow; such overlaps provide the soil for category mistakes.

Before we determine more fully the nature of the psychoanalytical voice, let us amplify somewhat $voice_0$, the voice of the analysand. This voice is by definition a fragmented one. Some of what it says is spoken by the person who has come for analysis, but some of what it says is spoken by voices that have become entangled with the voice of that person: the voice of his father or mother, for example, or his own childhood voice as responding to his father or mother. The mixing of voices yields incoherences of speech and action. Things are taken and stated by this person in ways that are not in keeping either with what they are or with what he is. The analysand comes to the analyst to gain the ability to untangle these voices: to become able to speak in his own voice and merely to quote the voices that ought not to be his own, to become free either to appropriate them as his own or to dissociate himself from them. In his present state he is so entangled with them that he cannot quote, appropriate, or deny them. He has no distance from them, no distance to the someone talking in him who really isn't he himself. The patient has not sufficiently grown out of the early stages in which there is not enough "I" to make a difference between what I say and what you or they say. The analyst helps $voice_0$ distinguish between his own appropriating voice, $voice_0{}^x$, and the voice he wishes either to confirm or negate, $voice_0{}^y$.

The task of the analyst is to help the analysand make these distinctions. The analyst can help him do so because he, the analyst, can hear levels of voices that the ordinary interlocutors and observers cannot hear; the analyst can hear these voices in the patient because he has heard them in himself through his own analysis, and because, through his training, he has acquired categories with which to name the many and various voices working through one speaker. He has disentangled $voice^x$ and $voice^y$ in himself and is free to hear similar voices in the patient and thus to help the patient to acquire his own voice. He can regress with the patient to lower levels of mentation, but can at the same time keep the higher levels intact and so, as Loewald often says, remain ahead of the patient much as the parent remains ahead of the child and helps the child to come to terms with the world.[8]

Let us contrast the voice of the analyst, $voice_3$, with other voices we have distinguished. The voices of the ordinary interlocutor and of the observer, $voice_1$ and $voice_2$, both have their own point of view on the world. Things seem to them to be in a certain way. Both these voices will agree with $voice_0$ in some respects and disagree in others; when they disagree, they will take the propositions of $voice_0$ as mere opinions and as false ones. They will say that the person is simply wrong in what he says. The $voice_3$ of the analyst is different in that the analyst does not, as analyst and formally speaking, have an alternative view of the world. He works into and stays within the per-

8. Loewald, *Papers on Psychoanalysis,* pp. 93, 229–30.

spective$_0$ of voice$_0$; he takes seriously everything that is stated by the patient's voice and does not reject anything as merely a false opinion.

On the other hand, the analyst does not simply absorb the world of the patient; he sustains a special kind of detachment and exercises a special kind of quotation: not the kind exercised by voice$_1$ and voice$_2$, the kind that merely tests the opinion to see whether it is true or not, but a new kind, one that listens to what is said in order to find out who is speaking and to bring the presence and power and source of that voice to the attention of the patient. The analyst hears more than is said. What is said is treated as a clue to who is saying it. The analyst is to discover the truth in the falsity of what the patient says, he is to discover the past event that is being repeated even as the patient thinks he is involved only with what is going on now. And when the termination of analysis occurs, the patient should have come to distinguish his own voice from the others that had been speaking in him, but the analyst also changes from living within the perspective of the patient to being an ordinary interlocutor or observer, to speaking in voice$_1$ and in voice$_2$ in regard to the patient. Indeed, it is interesting to raise the question of when it is that the analyst shifts from voice$_3$ to voice$_1$; even during the time of analysis, the analyst cannot stop being someone who has his own view of how things are, someone who can say that what the analysand claims is not the case, someone who gradually "leads" the patient to himself and to the way things are.

In discussing the voices engaged in psychoanalysis, I have understated the affective dimension in this distinctive human relationship. Although psychoanalysis involves conversation and dialogue, its core lies in the transference that occurs between patient and analyst. This transference is substantially preverbal. The verbal dimension is essential to transference, but it lies on the surface. Transference is the reworking of affective attitudes and interactions that have been internalized by the patient; in analysis the patient is to reexternalize these interactions and attitudes, to direct them toward the analyst, who will respond in such a way as to help the patient to untangle appropriate and inappropriate feelings.[9] If in his early years the patient was, say, held in contempt by significant persons, and if he internalized this interaction and now holds himself in contempt, the transference allows him to

9. Ibid., pp. 259–60, 309–11, 335.

reestablish the original interactions externally, to rework them and to make the crucial emotional distinctions, those that will allow him to react with appropriate feelings to new situations instead of blindly and persistently repeating the interactions of the past. The preverbal affective attitudes and interactions have to be reeducated; the analyst, the new object for the feelings, does not react in the way "the other person" used to act and react. The untangling that is done in regard to voice$_0$ is primarily an affective untangling; the voice$_0$ in question is a voice pervaded with affectivity. As Loewald puts it, "narrative is drawn into the context of transference dramatization, into the force-field of re-enactment."[10]

There is something like quotation, something analogous to verbal citation, in the transference relationship and in the analyst's reaction to it. The analyst has to "catch" and reflect a feeling in the way he feels, much as a listener must capture and return someone else's opinion in the words that he, the listener, uses. The patient, as time goes on, may become able to pick up the feeling at a distance himself, to feel the feeling as though quoted, then feel it as to be either appropriated or denied. Thus there is a preverbal, affective dialogue in psychoanalysis, and the verbal exchanges and quotations draw their substance from it. The affective exchanges set the stage for the "timely" verbal intervention; they establish when the moment to determine something by words has arrived, when the time for the appropriate intervention and distinction has come. The words are there for the affectivity.

I should make a refinement concerning the ontology of quotation, whether verbal or emotional. Because of certain philosophical presuppositions, but also because of natural inclination, we are very much tempted to think that when we quote someone else, we take over into our own awareness some sort of "mental representation" that exists in that person's psychic world. Loewald himself is aware of this misunderstanding regarding "mental contents" and he criticizes it. He writes, "I also question the . . . common equation of self and self-representation, or of object and object representation," which, he says, arises because of "confused thinking in regard to the term 'mental representation.'"[11] When we say we think this or that, what we really mean is that we believe the world shows up in a certain way; when we

10. Ibid., p. 366.
11. Ibid., p. 351.

quote someone else, we state that the world appears to him in such and such a way, and we may either agree or disagree with that proposal. Even when we emotionally "quote" others, when we feel what they feel, as felt by them, we do not merely perceive one of their feelings or sympathize with their mental states; rather, we let certain things appear to us as charged emotionally, but as being so charged for the other persons. What people are trying to get at when they speak of mental contents or mental representations is not some sort of mental thing, but the way things and persons in the world seem to be. Thus when the analyst quotes the patient, he is not trying to discover what mental contents the patient has but trying to discover how the world appears to the patient, how the patient believes the world to be. Thinking is always articulation of some part of the world, thinking is always "outside"; even feeling is always a presentation of something worldly; and quotation is articulation of part of the world as it is proposed or articulated or felt by someone else. Quotation is an articulation to the second degree; it is not a peek inside, not a peek at someone's mental screen.[12]

If the analyst's ordinary voice$_1$ is always in the background when he engages his professional voice$_3$ in analysis, the opposite is also true: when the analyst becomes involved in ordinary transactions, his professional voice$_3$ and perspective$_3$ cannot be expected to disappear altogether. Hans-Georg Gadamer has commented about this in his debate with Habermas. He criticizes the attempt to introduce a new sort of art and science similar to psychoanalysis, an "emancipating reflection" that would try to remove impediments to public communication and free society from ideological constraints.[13] He claims that ordinary public discourse has its own hermeneutic integrity and that claims made in it should be answered on their own terms. Suppose there is a political disagreement and one of the speakers heatedly, even angrily, presents an argument for a particular course of action; this person has a right to be answered with political arguments, not with a psychological analysis of the causes of his anger.[14] To blindside the speaker, to turn

12. See Robert Sokolowski, "Making Distinctions," in *Pictures, Quotations, and Distinctions: Fourteen Essays in Phenomenology* (Notre Dame: University of Notre Dame Press, 1992), pp. 27–51.

13. Hans-Georg Gadamer, "Replik zu Hermeneutik und Ideologiekritik," in *Gesammelte Werke* (Tubingen: J. C. B. Mohr, 1986), volume 2, p. 257.

14. Ibid., p. 260.

from the terms of the argument to an analysis of his voice$_1$ (in effect, to turn his voice$_1$ into a voice$_0$), is to destroy the integrity of public discussion; the intrusion of psychoanalytical expertise is "an upsetting factor," a *Störungsfaktor* in normal social exchanges.[15] Gadamer admits that the technical ability of the analyst is bound to assert itself; even in ordinary conversations, the analyst will notice certain things. Speaking in voice$_1$ to an analyst is like writing a letter to a graphologist; you are "delivered over to him" even if you do not intend to address his analytical ability.[16] But both the analyst and the graphologist must respect the content of the normal message and respond to it on its own terms. When they notice what is hidden to everyone else, they themselves must not become blind to what everyone else sees, the manifest content of what is being stated.

This brings us to the case of religion and the way quotations can take place in regard to religious language. What voice does the analyst use when quoting and discussing religious belief? And what is the content of religious expression?

How the religious dimension is to be understood

The third chapter of Loewald's book, *Psychoanalysis and the History of the Individual,* is entitled "Comments on Religious Experience." Loewald begins this chapter by reminding us of Freud's negative view of religion. Freud thought that religion was "an illusion to be given up as we are able to overcome our childish needs for all-powerful parents."[17] Freud's interpretation of religion was challenged by his friend Romain Rolland, who claimed that the experiential root of religion was an underlying feeling of being at one with the entire world. Freud said that he himself did not experience this sensation, which Rolland called an "oceanic feeling" or a "sensation of eternity," but he claimed that if it was experienced by some people, it might well be explained psychoanalytically as derived from the primary narcissistic stage in which the child has not yet developed ego boundaries between himself and his mother and between himself and the world.[18] But Freud, says Loewald, "did not pursue his basic hunches, and under the weight of

---

15. Ibid., p. 259.
16. Ibid.
17. Loewald, *Psychoanalysis and the History of the Individual,* p. 57.
18. Ibid., pp. 59–60, 68.

his authority religion in psychoanalysis has been largely considered a sign of man's mental immaturity."[19]

Loewald's own view, rather tentatively developed, is that religion may express not an immature regression, but a wholesome recognition of archaic mentation. He asserts that secondary processes should always be kept in touch with the primary processes that underlie them, at the risk of falling into "the madness of unbridled rationality,"[20] and religion may be the expression of the archaic levels of psychic life that remain continuously present in us, no matter how easily we may overlook them. The point is not to allow primary processes to drown the secondary, but to keep access to the wellsprings of the primary process open even during the mature activation of secondary processes; the creative language found, among other places, in authentic religious expression may serve to express the moment at which "the density of the primary process gives way to the discursiveness and articulation of secondary process."[21] Secondary processes, says Loewald, are not static states into which we enter, but activities that must be kept continuously alive, activities that must constantly draw nourishment from the primary process: "the range and richness of human life is directly proportional to the mutual responsiveness between these various mental phases and levels."[22] Freud tended to think of religion as dependent upon a need for an all-powerful, "enormously exalted" father who would protect the believer, but on his own admission he could not account for the belief in maternal divinities that seems to have preceded belief in paternal gods.[23]

After observing that Freud spoke particularly of the boundaries between ego and the outer world, Loewald introduces the "equal if not more basic differentiation" in the development of mental life, "that of temporal modes."[24] The differentiation of past, present, and future is as basic as—perhaps even more basic than—the distinction between internal and external, and certainly both distinctions arise in function of each other. The importance of the temporal modes is emphasized in many passages in Loewald's

19. Ibid., p. 57.
20. Ibid., p. 56.
21. Loewald, *Papers on Psychoanalysis*, p. 203.
22. Loewald, *Psychoanalysis and the History of the Individual*, p. 61.
23. Ibid., p. 57; *Papers on Psychoanalysis*, pp. 8–9.
24. *Psychoanalysis and the History of the Individual*, p. 61.

work.[25] His own treatment of religion, in the chapter we are examining, is developed largely in terms of temporality and eternity.

Loewald says that the idea of eternity should not be confused with that of everlasting duration, which is time projected indefinitely; rather, "in the experience of eternity, time is abolished."[26] Temporality accompanies secondary forms of mentation, but a glimpse of primary forms would involve the de-articulation of present, past, and future, in an extreme condensation. "The primary process in pure form is, I believe, extant in the experience of eternity."[27] Loewald describes instances in which we might catch such glimpses, moments in which time seems to be surpassed or undercut; in such cases "the secondary, rational form of mentation loses its weight. It is overshadowed or pervaded by the timelessness of the unconscious or primary process."[28] We try to express, in secondary-process categories, these experiences in which we touch the timelessness of the id, and then we speak, for example, of everlasting life after death. Loewald insists that such experiences are not simply illusions but "bring us in touch with levels of our being."[29] He observes that psychoanalysis can help formulate a positive sense for the experience of eternity and for the religious expressions to which it leads. This would be of great benefit because, he claims, religious experiences are "aspects of unconscious mentation . . . that in much of modern civilization are more deeply repressed than 'sexuality' is today."[30] He calls for a "genuine appropriation" of the forces at work behind the expressions found in religious traditions.

In response to Loewald's interpretation of religious experience, one might be inclined at first to object that he postulates religion as directed only inwardly, only toward the psychic primary process, whereas religious belief is concerned not only with the psychic but with the worldly as well. But such an objection would not be effective, because Loewald claims that primary process is not "internal" as opposed to "external." On this most basic level, inner and outer have not yet been differentiated. In the primary process there is neither an ego nor objects, no inside as opposed to outside;

---

25. *Papers on Psychoanalysis*, pp. 43–52, 138–47, 149–73.
26. *Psychoanalysis and the History of the Individual*, p. 63.
27. Ibid., p. 65.   28. Ibid., p. 67.
29. Ibid., p. 69.   30. Ibid., p. 74.

there is only the matrix within which boundaries are to be drawn.[31] There is nothing in Loewald's interpretation that would deny the possibility of cosmological divinities.

The primitive unconscious does possess features that are attributed to the gods in pagan religions. It is all-encompassing, and it contains powers that we will forever be unable to master. These powers, furthermore, are not just a spectacle before us; they are causes of our human condition. Somehow or other we come to be because of them, and we remain permanently under their influence. It is not inappropriate for us to respect these causes of our being in a way analogous to the manner in which those who believed in the Homeric gods might have respected the forces that were thought to have brought the human estate, and the world of that human estate, into being. Loewald makes a successful attempt to remythologize the chthonian gods.

It seems to me, however, that in his difference with Freud, in his criticism of Freud's tendency to take religion as the wish for and the fear of an all-powerful father, Loewald neglects the role of the forces that were personified and reverenced as the Olympian gods. It would be difficult to consider Apollo, the god of music, law, prophecy, order, and pattern, as an expression of the id. Apollo is supposed to tame the dark gods of the underworld. That which arises as other to the primary unconscious is also one of the causes of our being, and it is equally unmasterable by our own deliberate efforts. It is true that the establishment of boundaries, and subsequently the establishment of orders and patterns, are achievements that we ourselves must carry out; but the very *possibility* that such things can be at all is not our achievement. As possibilities they transcend our own powers, and they are as "divine" to us as are the dark and chaotic forces. We can appropriate only what is already given as capable of being appropriated.

Loewald's interpretation of the meaning of religion, together with the modification I have introduced, allows an analyst to translate the religious beliefs of a patient into the expression of certain basic and irreducible levels of being. Loewald's interpretation allows the analyst to consider religious beliefs not as delusions but as the expression of something both real and important. It becomes possible for the analyst to "quote" the patient and to quote him with assent, but only after the belief of the patient has been trans-

31. *Papers on Psychoanalysis,* pp. 127–29, 167, 185.

lated into categories that are familiar and acceptable to the analyst, categories that express something positive in psychoanalytic theory. The quotation has to be mediated through a translation, and it is possible that the patient will not recognize the translation as valid. He might think that the translation says something other than the belief he wishes to express.

Such a concern about the accuracy of translation would be less likely to occur if the patient's idea of the divine were that of a god who is part of the world, as the divine was, say, for the Greek and Roman poets and philosophers. For these thinkers, the gods are and must be part of what is. The gods are the best, most powerful, the most important and most independent, the encompassing parts, the parts that somehow order all the rest, but they could not be except as part of the whole. Loewald's interpretation of the divine might give another name to such divinities, and it might locate the gods in another kind of part of the whole, but it would not really transform the divine into another kind of being. The translation would not be very different from calling Thor by the name of Jupiter.

Biblical faith and understanding

The problem of the accuracy of religious translations becomes more urgent, however, in the case of a patient who believes in the God revealed in biblical religion, the God who created the world and is not merely a part within it. In this sense of the divine, the world is understood as existing not under the sway of ineluctable forces, not just there and fated to be as it is, but as existing through the freedom of the Creator. The believer—in this case the patient—also understands himself to have been created, to have been chosen to be. His relationship to God is not taken to be like his relationship to his primary unconscious, nor like his relationship to the ordered patterns that transform the unconscious into secondary forms of mentation.

The Bible, and the religious traditions stemming from the Bible, present not only a recommendation about what our attitudes and behavior should be; they also present something to be understood about the nature of things, about the world, about being. Distinctions are made, and the primary distinction concerns how the divine or the ultimate is to be understood. In biblical religion, the divine or the ultimate is not simply a principle of order or an originating force that is part of the world; it is understood to be distinct from the world, to be Creator of the world. The word *Creator* has a very exact sense in these traditions; it does not mean merely a "maker" or merely one who brings order into chaos or light into darkness. The Creator is understood as being so distinct from everything other to himself that he would have been (or would be) even if the world had not been. Such an understanding is required for the full freedom and generosity of Creation; only someone who does not need to give and who does not gain from giving can be so completely generous as the Creator is understood to be. And as a correlative to this independence and generosity, the world itself is understood not as simply being there but as having been given being by the Creator; and the believer is understood not only as the outcome of natural forces, evolution, and parental generation but also as having been freely given being by God. In this biblical understanding, there is something like freedom and generosity at work in the very being of the created whole.

The biblical understanding of God as Creator does not arise for the patient as a gradual transformation of his own personal experience. It is presented to him by a religious tradition as a possibility of belief. That tradition itself is understood to be more than just a human achievement, whether individual or social; it is understood to have involved revelation as its specifying element, no matter how much the revelation may have been embedded in the structures of human psychic development. The "translation" of the patient's beliefs, therefore, must not lose this understanding of God as other not only to the patient and his unconscious but other to the whole created world as well, and as capable of being, in undiminished goodness and greatness, even if there were no world.

In his essay entitled "Internalization and the Superego," Loewald briefly mentions Christianity as "initiating the greatest intensification of internalization in Western civilization."[32] He says that the death of Christ represents for the believer the radical loss of "the ultimate love object, which the believer loses as an external object and regains by identification with Him as an ego ideal." This occurs, Loewald says, in accord with the psychic processes of loss, mourning, and internalization. He calls this event "the death of God as incarnated in Christ." His remarks are provocative and point the way toward further reflection on psychoanalysis and Christian belief, but some refinement needs to be made. The term "the death of God" is misleading, because

---

32. Ibid., p. 260.

in Christian belief the Godhead did not die when Christ died. Christ the man died, and this person who died was God, but his divinity did not die. God, as the ultimate object of love, did not die, is not lost, and is not to be mourned. Loewald's remarks show the contemporary relevance of the definitions of the Council of Chalcedon, which in A.D. 451 declared that the two natures of Christ, the divine and the human, retain their integrity in the Incarnation, and that the attributes of each nature as such do not become attributes of the other as such; the Godhead as such does not become mortal and does not die, no more than the humanity of Christ becomes eternal or omnipotent.

I think that the set of relationships and transformations Loewald is getting at in his remark about the death of Christ are better determined in terms of Creation than in terms of Redemption. The believer, in his understanding of Creation, holds that the entire world, himself included, might not have been, and God would still be in undiminished goodness and perfection. Both the believer and the world are held to exist through God's unnecessitated choice. The "loss" that is envisioned in this belief is the possible nonbeing of everything except God, not the loss of God. God is understood as that which could not die or be lost in this way. This belief is an understanding of how the world and the things in it can be; it is an intellectual comprehension. It is not presented as one of the affective object-relations the patient has developed during his life. The patient in question may, of course, cathect these objects in ways that are not in keeping with what they are understood to be, just as a particular patient may cathect, say, food in ways that are not in keeping with what food is as nourishment (as in the case of persons suffering from anorexia). A distortion brought about in a patient's appreciation of an object may be important in the treatment of the patient, but it does not destroy the sense that the object has as it is understood apart from that appropriation. In the case of the biblical understanding of God, the sense is determined by its expression in the Bible itself and in the ecclesial, theological, and spiritual tradition that stems from what is narrated in the Scriptures.

The biblical understanding of God, like all understandings of objects to which we can be related, indicates a pattern of behavior. It implies as a response biblical morality and virtues, such as faith, hope, and charity in the Christian biblical tradition. It also implies a biblical self-understanding on the part of the believer. If a person thinks he has been created by God, that he is known by God, and, in the Christian tradition, that he has been redeemed by the incarnate God, he will see his life and his relations to others in a distinctive light and will feel obliged to act in an appropriate way.

The biblical understanding of God goes beyond the senses of the divine expressed in both the chthonian and the Olympian gods, since the biblical God is not part of the world; nevertheless the biblical understanding does bear some resemblance to these two senses and it could therefore be misinterpreted as one of them. Like the chthonian gods, the biblical God is understood to be an ultimate origin for everything that is subsequently determined, and like the Olympians, he is understood to be a final end or completion of the things that are. Because of these resemblances, and because similarity is often taken for sameness, a writer like Loewald could misinterpret the biblical God in terms more appropriate to a worldly divinity. But the way the Creator is an origin and an end is radically different from the way the pagan deities are understood to be sources and causes.[33]

Loewald criticizes psychoanalytic theory for its tendency "to understand the very organization of the psychic apparatus in terms of defense"[34] and for its tendency to see "the relationship between organism and environment, between individual and reality . . . as basically antagonistic."[35] He says that psychoanalytic theory has been influenced by modern social estrangements and complexities, and that it has "taken for granted the neurotically distorted experience of reality"[36] that he finds so widespread in contemporary life. Loewald thinks that Freud's misinterpretation of religion as an obsessional neurosis might stem from this modern social context and this overemphasis on defensive reactions. He suggests that ego development should not be interpreted primarily in terms of warding off intrusive stimuli and trying to restore a stable state; it should be seen more positively as growth into higher levels of integration achieved through ever greater synthetic functions of the ego. "The ego is an agency which organizes," and new achievements can mean "a gain in its organization and functioning."[37] He says, "With further

---

33. See Robert Sokolowski, *The God of Faith and Reason: Foundations of Christian Theology* (Washington, D.C.: The Catholic University of America Press, 1995).

34. *Papers on Psychoanalysis,* p. 27.

35. Ibid., p. 28.   36. Ibid., p. 30.

37. Ibid., pp. 44, 74.

and higher ego organization, far from getting closer to a state of rest, there is more life."[38]

The biblical understanding of God, together with the self-understanding it proposes for the believer and the form of activity it implies for him, can be interpreted as an opportunity for greater expansion and integration. It can be taken to open a new possibility for development of the ego, even for certain kinds of renunciation, mourning, and internalization. Whether or not it can truly be interpreted in such a positive way depends on two things: on its own intrinsic intelligibility, and on the effect it has on human lives. Thus there are two questions that can be put to the biblical understanding. One is philosophico-theological: Is this an intelligible understanding and not an incoherence? The other is psychological: Has this understanding been lived by persons who are not neurotic, and has it motivated distinctive patterns of behavior, or is it somehow essentially a neurotic or defensive projection?

A falsifying voice and quotation

By way of conclusion, I will make only one point concerning the way psychoanalysis might approach these two questions. As we have seen in the citation from Gadamer, both the handwriting expert and the psychoanalyst, when they enter into public discourse, must resist the temptation to overlook the face value of a message and to see primarily what the message reveals about the speaker. This temptation has been especially hard to resist because of the kind of natural science that was introduced by Francis Bacon, Galileo, Descartes, and Newton, and because of the kind of voice that was associated with this science. The modern scientific tradition considers the rigorous mathematical method of science as the only way of truly describing the world; everything else we are aware of becomes taken as a subjective projection, a mere appearance, a secondary quality. A distinction is then introduced between a physical "outside" and a psychic "inside," between an "outer world" and an "inner world." The only voice with the authority to speak truthfully about the outer world is the voice$_s$ of the one who can master the scientific method. This voice$_s$ tells the hard truth about the way things are; the other, nonscientific voices just tell us how things seem.

In this scientific tradition, it becomes plausible for the expert in psycho-

38. Ibid., p. 74; see also pp. 176–77, 234.

analytic method to assume that he has the truth about the psyche and that he can hope to unlock the secret of all its projections, that he might be able to explain why things seem to us as they do, while leaving to the physicist the task of telling the truth about the external world. The Cartesian physicist, moreover, quotes the ordinary opinions of other speakers only with suspicion, taking them as *mere* opinions,[39] and the analyst may be inclined to do the same. This is the wrong kind of distance to take toward the statements of others; it is a misleading objectivity, one that emerges from the context set by the unfortunate dichotomy between inner world and outer world, a dichotomy related to what Loewald referred to as "confused thinking in regard to the term, 'mental representation.'"

To adjust this context and to dissolve this dichotomy, one would need to show how the voice$_s$ behind scientific method is established and how it is related to the other voices I have talked about in this paper. I will not pursue this discussion now; I will only remark that natural science itself no longer speaks only of things like force and energy but has begun to employ such concepts as "signal," "representation," "information," "computation," "code," and "program," concepts that are now seen to straddle the natural and the intellectual,[40] and that natural science has become acutely aware of the role of the observer even in physics; the strong dichotomy between nature and psyche seems to be giving way to a more flexible relationship between the two. As these developments continue, and as they have more and more impact on our general self-understanding, they will provide a less constricting context for determining the place of the psychoanalytical voice$_3$, which, as Loewald has so often stated, is a voice of conversational exchange, not simply of detached observation.

---

39. See René Descartes: ". . . I am finally compelled to admit that there is not one of my former beliefs about which a doubt may not properly be raised; and this is not a flippant or ill-considered conclusion, but is based on powerful and well thought-out reasons. So in future I must withhold my assent from these former belief just as carefully as I would from obvious falsehoods, if I want to discover any certainty." *Meditations on First Philosophy,* First Meditation, translated by John Cottingham, in *The Philosophical Writings of Descartes* (New York: Cambridge University Press, 1984), volume 2, pp. 14–15.

40. See Elmar Holenstein, "Maschinelles Wissen und menschliches Bewusstsein," *Studia Philosophica* 46 (1987): 145–63.

CHURCH TRADITION AND THE
CATHOLIC UNIVERSITY

There are a number of things that are obviously required for a Catholic university to remain and to flourish as a Catholic institution. It must have a sufficient number of faculty and students who share the Catholic faith and an even greater number who are dedicated to the university's religious mission; it must implement its mission in its curriculum and public activities; it must be attentive to the spiritual welfare of its students, faculty, and staff; and its administrators must be devoted to its Catholic identity. These requirements, which are mentioned in *Ex Corde Ecclesiae,* are well recognized. I wish to make two other points concerning the identity of Catholic universities, one dealing with the internal workings of the university and one dealing with the Church. I think that both these issues are important for the current controversy about how Catholic universities can maintain their heritage and avoid becoming simply secular institutions, as many of the Protestant universities and colleges in our country have become.

Theology, the Magisterium, and academic freedom
My first point, touching on the internal structure of the university, is somewhat practical and empirical. It deals with the politics and the sociology of the faculty, with the way faculty members work out issues of university governance and policy, and also with the influence that some faculty members have on others.

My thesis is that those faculty members who teach theology and the disciplines that are closely related to theology have a particularly strategic role to play in working out a successful harmony between the university and the Church and between reason and faith. In particular, they have an important and specific role to play in maintaining the Catholic character of a university. Their role consists in showing to the rest of the faculty how the belief and the authoritative teachings of the Church can have a place within the academic world. These faculty members are in a position to show other scholars that the Church and its authoritative teaching can be a source of truth, one that can be recognized and reflected upon in a scholarly way. To show this in theory and in practice is to get at the core of the identity of a Catholic university.

For a Catholic university to be successful as Catholic, the faculty at large must be enthusiastic about the contribution their work can make to the intellectual cultivation of Christian religious belief. They have to see this contribution as a good, something to be pursued and developed, something to which they can dedicate their energies. They also have to see the cultivation of the Catholic intellectual heritage as compatible with their scholarly disciplines and scholarly activities; that is, they must be able to see how their specifically intellectual work can contribute to the Christian heritage, and also how their academic work can be inspired by Christian faith and nourished by it. As professionals, they have to see that the two ventures of being academics and being involved in a Catholic enterprise are not only compatible but mutually reinforcing. The opinion that faith and reason can help one another must be a widespread conviction among the faculty if a university is to remain Catholic.

But there is a problem in making such an opinion widely accepted in a contemporary university. The secular sciences and academic fields as they are now constituted claim to be independent of any authority external to their disciplines. They claim that their ways of thinking begin within each discipline itself, with principles, methods, and sources of that discipline, independent of any authority outside it. This claim rests on a conviction concerning the nature of human reason: reason is seen as self-authorizing and autonomous, as generating its own principles and not accepting anything on authority, as setting itself up as the beginning and the judge of thinking. In this perspective, accepting things on faith has a tinge of gullibility and un-critical submission, of what Kant called heteronomy, which he saw as the deepest betrayal of reason.

Very many people in academic life, very many faculty and students, spontaneously accept this Enlightenment understanding of reason and the university. This understanding is behind the concept of academic freedom demanded in the university and it is embodied in most of the slogans of academic life. Such an understanding of reason, academic freedom, and au-thority is implied in the commonplaces, the *topoi,* the premises that can be taken for granted in public speeches and public discussions about academic matters. For most academics, reason and its freedom seem to be at odds with authority and with the acceptance of authority. The teaching authority of the Church, therefore, is looked on with a mixture of suspicion and anxiety when it claims to be a factor internal to the academic discipline of theol-ogy.

In Catholic institutions the theologians stand at a crucial point in this apparent conflict between reason and faith. In this regard, what the theo-logians do is of great importance politically and socially within the univer-sity. If they say that their own academic discipline has as its object the living belief and tradition of Christianity as interpreted by the teaching Church, they can play an especially important role in showing that reason and faith are compatible; they can play an important role in helping the other faculty members to see this compatibility. They can not only argue for but also illus-trate a more adequate understanding of the relationship between scholarly reason and the authority that preserves the truth for us.

No one else can do this in the way that the theologians can. If people in some other discipline, such as history or politics or philosophy, try to argue for the compatibility between Church teaching and reason, it will seem that they are trying to impose a constraint on someone else, on the theologians. The actual influence of these other scholars will be weaker no matter how good their arguments may be; their influence will be weaker rhetorically and dialectically because of who they are, because they are not the ones most affected by the point they are making. However, when the theologians make this point, their word has greater weight, because they are regarded as the experts in this matter and because the issue of authority affects them most of all. If, on the other hand, the theologians try to maintain the more rationalistic or Enlightenment notion of academic freedom, the faculty at large will tend to believe and support them and will tend to see conflicts between academic reason and ecclesiastical authority. This is in fact how the dynamics of faculty politics works.

Looking at the matter rather formally, teachers of theology and their related disciplines can follow two different paths in respect to Church authority and academic inquiry. First, they can recognize the teaching Church as an authoritative source within the discipline of theology. If they do so, they will greatly help the rest of the faculty see the possibility of integrating their scholarly, intellectual efforts with the faith of the Church. But, second, they can accept the rationalist understanding of science and academic freedom and try to apply it to their own discipline of theology. They may see the authority of the Church as external to their discipline, and in times of controversy they may call upon the faculty to help them protect their theology from such "outside" influences. Given the widespread acceptance of the Enlightenment understanding of academic freedom, very many if not most of the faculty will tend to support them. To put it concretely, if the teachers of theology call out, "We are under assault; come and help us in our academic distress," the faculty will generally respond, "We must help the beleaguered theologians."

The theological faculty can move even farther in this direction. They may warn the rest of the faculty that the teaching Church will interfere not only in theology but in other disciplines as well. This is a common rhetorical device, often used in the heat of controversies dealing with academic freedom. The teachers of theology and its related fields will try to marshal faculty support by frightening the rest of the faculty into supporting them. Here, the claim will be "If this Church intervention comes to pass, you too will be vulnerable," and the faculty will tend to reply, "We must help them, for we are in danger ourselves."

Obviously, if the second of these two paths is followed, the university will come to a standstill in its development of the Catholic intellectual life. Over time, its identity as a Catholic institution will be diluted. The school's identity will be weakened at its academic core. The first path, on the other hand, the one that acknowledges the respective authorities of both the scholars and the Magisterium, will be productive and illuminating. It will promote theological development and will serve the Church. It will, furthermore, also make an important contribution to academic life generally, even outside the domain of theology and its affiliated disciplines. It will do so by locating academic intelligence and research within a wider human context. It will show that truth is achievable outside the academy and its specialized scientific disciplines, and it will show by example how academic thinking can respect the intelligence of cultural and moral traditions, even while making their own contribution to them. The example of theological thinking can thus help bring about a better integration of the specialized disciplines, even the natural sciences, into the wider realm of human life.

Thus, the proper integration of academic and religious truth can play a strategic role in contemporary culture, and the teachers of theology are at a pivotal position in this issue. They can help overcome the Enlightenment prejudice, which is itself now under severe attack by the irrationality of deconstruction. A proper understanding of faith and reason will not only help preserve the Catholic identity of colleges and universities, but also provide a better resolution for the crisis in which the humanities and sciences now find themselves.

The university and the liturgical life of the Church

I now come to my second major point, which deals not with academic matters directly but with the Church and its teaching and practice. I submit that in current controversies about the university and the Magisterium, the Church has put itself and its own authority at a disadvantage because of the comprehensive revision of the liturgy that was carried out after the Second Vatican Council. The impression was made, even though it may not have been intended, that the Church was distancing itself from its inherited liturgy, and this impression has had an important impact on the relationship between the academic scholar and the teaching Church.

In making the following remarks I will be speaking about the psychological and social impressions that have been made in the past thirty-five years. I am not saying that the Church had no right to change the liturgy, nor that the new order of the liturgy is illegitimate in any way, nor even that the Church should not have changed its liturgy. I am saying that the way the academic world looks at Church authority has been influenced by changes in the Church's liturgy.

Let us recall that the liturgy is truly the one thing needful in the life of the Church. The liturgy is not a mere accessory to the Church's work; it is the point of contact between the believer and God, the place where the Church lives its life to the highest degree. It is the moment when the Church is most itself. The liturgy is not just an instrument in the life of the Church; it is the life of the Church fully and sacramentally expressed.

In the 1960s, the Church restructured its liturgy in a way that it had never done before. The manner in which the liturgical changes were made was unprecedented. It reflected a specifically modern impulse to make things new. We must recognize how distinctive this action was. The restructuring is now a matter of fact and history, a choice that was made in the life of the Church. No one can cancel what has been done, but the urgent question does arise, Where do we go from here? What trajectory do we follow? As we move on, do we recede still farther from the old rite of the liturgy, or do we attempt to emphasize, visibly and palpably, the continuity between the old rite and the new? We stand at an important intersection in the life of the Church, and our next steps will be of critical significance. Furthermore, as we take these next steps, whose authority will guide us? To develop this issue, and to show its relevance to the Catholic university, I wish to examine the nature of Church authority.

The authority of a bishop is that of a shepherd. His pastoral rule is based not primarily on laws or the will of the people but on the tradition that has been inherited. It is not just that the tradition provides the Church with the episcopal office; rather, the inherited tradition of liturgy and doctrine is what the bishop is supposed to preserve. The shepherd is given custody of something that he must protect and hand on. The pastor rules the flock, but he does so as the custodian of the liturgical and doctrinal life of the Church, which provides the measure for his rule. This liturgical and doctrinal life has developed in an organic way, and the authority of the bishop is there to preserve the living whole that he has inherited.

There are two passages in St. Paul's first letter to the Corinthians that bring out this dependence of pastoral authority on tradition. In chapter 15 St. Paul teaches the Corinthians about the Resurrection of Christ, and he introduces this exercise of his teaching office by saying, "I handed on to you as of first importance what I also received" (I Corinthians 15:3). In chapter 11 he makes authoritative decisions about the eucharistic liturgy and he introduces these remarks by saying, "I received from the Lord what I also handed on to you" (I Corinthians 11:23). St. Paul's pastoral authority is based on the need to preserve and transmit what was handed on to him.

Likewise, the strength of episcopal and papal authority rests on the duty to preserve and transmit the tradition the Church has received. The tradition is what the bishops and pope appeal to when they exercise their authority; they can decide certain things and can say and do certain things because they are handing on what they have received. Their authority is both measured and justified by the inherited tradition. This dependence of their authority on what they are to preserve is true not only theologically but also psychologically, sociologically, and rhetorically. People more easily recognize the authority of the pastor when he appeals to the tradition he has to maintain. The inherited tradition is the staff on which pastoral authority rests.

The changes introduced into the liturgy after the Second Vatican Council were an attempt to protect, preserve, nourish, and apply the liturgical life of the Church for the good of souls. But the changes were very comprehensive and they were done very suddenly. They were not incremental. They were beneficial in many ways, but they also caused some serious difficulties, which ought to be faced.

One difficulty was that some people got the impression that the hierarchy claimed the authority to redesign the liturgy, not just to hand on what they received. Instead of being seen as preserving and cultivating what was received, the Church was perceived by some to be reconstructing it. The shepherding authority of the hierarchy seemed to be changed into another kind of authority, that of the executive. Indeed, subsequent demands that Church officials change the inherited discipline of clerical celibacy and the restriction of ordination to men show that many people think that the pope and the bishops can make changes "at the stroke of a pen." If the Church could change the liturgy as much as it did, why can it not change many other things as well? The liturgy seemed to become something that is *established* primarily by law and decree, rather than being a living tradition of the whole Church that is *protected* by laws and decrees.

At first glance, one might suppose that such a shift in the meaning of authority, from shepherd to executive, would serve to make the hierarchy more powerful. The bishops and pope seem charged not only to shepherd what they receive, but also to reconfigure it according to what they deem necessary and appropriate. The liturgy and the life of the Church seem to be even more under their control. But in fact, this apparent shift in the meaning of authority has weakened the authority of the bishops, and for two different reasons.

First, the authority of the hierarchy became subordinate to that of the historians and experts of the liturgy. When the bishops are seen as shepherds, when the point of episcopal authority is to preserve what has been inherited, the measure of what is to be done is ready to hand and visible to everyone: it is the liturgy that had evolved organically over time as a result of countless decisions and adaptations made by countless individuals, under the guidance of the Holy Spirit. You do not need to be an expert to know what it is: it is there in front of everybody in the way the Church lives its life. The Church must still distinguish between essentials and accidentals, and must apply the tradition to current situations, but what is to be preserved is there for everyone to see.

However, if a major redesign of the liturgy is to take place, what can serve as the measure for the change? You cannot use what you have in front of you as a guide; by definition, the thing you have in front of you needs to be reconfigured. You have to get to something more essential. Given the historicist temper of our day, the logical place to look for a norm and measure became the liturgy as it was supposed to be at the beginning, in the early Church. This earliest form will be the measure for what we ought to have now. And who knows what this earliest form was like? Not the hierarchy, certainly, but the experts, the scholars who know the languages and the sources relevant to this matter and who form hypotheses about it. Because of the project of liturgical revision, the hierarchy seems forced to yield some of its authority to those who are expert in the liturgy and its history. The pastoral authority to preserve what has been received is given over in part to those who know the hidden original form of what has been received.

In fact, in the Church controversies of the past two decades, the popular image of the biblical scholar or the liturgical historian has become the image of the person who gets at the truth of the liturgy, in contrast with the "prejudices" of those who adhere to the received tradition. To illustrate this, I would like to appeal to an offhand remark made by Martin Stannard in his biography of Evelyn Waugh.[1] Waugh, as everyone knows, was devoted to the

---

1. Martin Stannard, *Evelyn Waugh: The Later Years 1939–1966* (New York: W. W. Norton, 1992).

old liturgy and tried to prevent major changes in it. His biographer does not sympathize with his stand, at one point even calling it "logically absurd."[2] During his exposition and critique of Waugh's ideas on the liturgy, Stannard makes the following remark: "Scholars had already scraped away the encrustations of ceremony which had grown slowly since the second century."[3]

This brief remark contains a whole philosophy. Since the second century, for nineteen hundred years, we have had encrustations of ceremony, not a living liturgy, not an organic tradition. Since the second century alien elements had intruded on and distorted the life of the Church. Furthermore, it is the scholars who can "scrape away the encrustations" and get at the pristine form, the original, the "true" liturgy that should be restored. This casual remark is an excellent example of the challenge to the authority of the shepherd of tradition. It implies that what we have inherited, rather than being what we must hand on, first needs to be redrafted in view of what existed before the accretions began to grow. This, then, is one way in which the authority of the teaching Church has been weakened because of the changes that have been introduced in the liturgy.

The second way in which it has been weakened comes from another direction. If the historical and scholarly challenge to the Church comes from those who are experts about the past, another kind of challenge comes from those who claim to be experts about the present. These are the pressure groups in the Church, those who claim to know what the present age demands, who say they know what changes are appropriate for modern man. Right now the most conspicuous claims are those being made on behalf of feminist groups, but other voices have been raised on behalf of the young, the intellectuals, various social classes or ethnic groups, people who have different moral opinions, or modern forms of political life. Once again, the hierarchy becomes vulnerable to such claims once it decides to restructure the liturgy, because groups such as these claim to know how the liturgy ought to be adapted to the modern world.

Thus, the authority of the shepherd is dealt a two-pronged attack when its custodial character is diluted and it is less directly measured by what it has received. Experts about the past claim special knowledge of what is inher-

2. Ibid., p. 463.
3. Ibid., p. 462.

ited, while the experts about the present claim special knowledge of what is needed here and now. Such challenges arise because of the thoroughgoing revision of the Church's liturgical life.

To bring this problem into sharper focus, I suggest that we consider an analogous situation and look at the liturgy of the Orthodox Church in Russia. That Church is now free, after having suffered seventy years of severe oppression. The K.G.B. did horrible things to the Russian Church, but the Church never changed the liturgy. The liturgy that was preserved under persecution and that is now openly practiced is simply the inherited liturgy. It has not been updated and its "encrustations" have not been scraped away. Would this Orthodox liturgy speak more effectively to modern man, in Russia or anywhere else, if it had been updated? What impact would it now have if it had been redesigned during the past thirty-five years? Should we in the West encourage the Russian Church, now that it is free, to modernize its liturgy as quickly as it can?

Again, I am not saying that the Roman liturgy should not have been modified, nor do I wish to deny the benefits of the new rite, but I am asking where we should go from here. I am also saying that whatever is done next will have an extremely important effect on the authority of the Church. The next steps will be crucial, because if the Church revises its liturgy even more to suit the temper of the times, it will reinforce the risky aspects of the choice it made some forty years ago. It is of great importance for the Church to heal the apparent breach between the old liturgy and the new, and do everything possible to make it clear to everyone that its *novus ordo* is not something radically different from what it has received. In this regard, it does seem to have been unwise for the Church to have prohibited the old rite of the liturgy for about fifteen years after the new rite was introduced.

What do these remarks about the liturgy have to do with academic freedom and the nature of the Catholic university? I think they help explain why many academic scholars think that their work is parallel with rather than subordinated to the pastoral and teaching authority of the Church. Scholarly work and expertise seem to have been given an authority to determine the new shape of the liturgy and, by implication, the teaching of the Church. Scholars are the experts in the original forms of liturgy and doctrine, and if revisions are going to take place, it is the scholars who seem to be in the best position to determine what the changes should be. Church

authority is displaced and the Church inevitably becomes more vulnerable to pressure groups and their demands. Even the papacy is presented as
though it were something of an intruder on the domain of liturgy and theology, and the pope is described not as an authoritative figure but as a man
who is trying to impose his personal conservative viewpoint.

Our present situation would be very different if the authority of the
Church were seen to be primarily the authority to preserve and hand on
the visible tradition that has been inherited. If the bishops seem to be under
siege in regard to liturgical practice and Church teaching, it is because the
basis and measure for their authority to rule, the inherited tradition that they
are to hand on, seems to have been yielded by them and taken by others. The
tangible and evident authority based on tradition gives way to an authority
based on reason and academic expertise, and the culture of the Enlightenment makes great inroads into the life of the Church.

Two distinctions concerning academic freedom

I have finished the two major points I wanted to make in my talk, one
dealing with the faculty of a Catholic university and the other dealing with
the authority of the teaching Church. In closing, I wish to make two distinctions.

The first is taken from a book by Yves Simon entitled *A General Theory
of Authority*.[4] In that work Simon makes a distinction that is of great help in
discussions about academic freedom.[5] Some people claim that we ought to
submit Church doctrine and practice to the give and take of academic debate, to controversy and refutation, to the marketplace of ideas. Such free inquiry works well in the sciences. If Church doctrines are true, will they not
be vindicated in such debates? Won't the truth be able to take care of itself?
In response to such a claim, Simon would say that the marketplace of ideas
may serve very well to determine the truth of what he calls "positive" statements, claims that are empirical and easy to communicate, the kind that En-
rico Fermi called "sharp statements." But there are other kinds of assertions,
which Simon calls "transcendent" statements, and these cannot be expected
to survive in such give-and-take. Such statements are not easy to communi-

4. Yves R. Simon, *A General Theory of Authority* (Notre Dame: University of Notre Dame
Press, 1962).

5. Ibid., pp. 104–27.

cate and to decide. They cannot take care of themselves in the marketplace of ideas; they need an authoritative institution to protect them. I think that Simon's distinction between positive and transcendent statements show why the Church cannot be a debating society or an academy but must be the place where the deepest truths about God, the world, and the human condition are authoritatively preserved.

Furthermore, that fact that Church teachings and other transcendent truths are not decidable in the marketplace of ideas does not make them into a second-best sort of truth; they are not less rigorous and less verifiable than the truths reached by academic scholarship and experiment; rather, they are deeper truths and require a different kind of communication and verification. They involve the engagement of an entire life and the protection of an authoritative teacher, not just a scholarly method.

A second distinction I wish to bring to mind is that between academic freedom and freedom of speech. These two things are very often confused, even by judges in law courts, let alone commentators in the media. Academic freedom is not simply one form of the right we have to express our opinions in public. Academic freedom is not protected by the first amendment. It is not the right of free speech, but the right of a scholar to be guided by the methods, principles, and sources of his discipline, and to be free of pressures that might force him to say things in his professional work that are not warranted by his discipline. Academic freedom is supposed to protect a scholarly discipline, not the right of a citizen to speak freely. In regard to Church teaching, academic freedom is not the right of a scholar to say what he thinks the Church ought to be teaching; rather, it is the right to reflect, in a scholarly way, on what the Church teaches, on the inherited deposit of faith.

The cost of secularization

What does the future hold for Catholic institutions of higher education? Will they remain Catholic, or will they become secular? There is ample evidence for the danger of secularization, and I would like to comment on what is at stake here.

If this secularizing comes to pass, our current generation will see an enormous alienation of Church resources, the loss to the Church of its institutions of higher education, both small and large, both colleges and universities. This loss would be momentous and would call to mind the losses suffered by the Church during the Reformation in England and the great secularizations in Europe. It would greatly weaken the Church's ability to educate her people and influence contemporary culture. The educational inheritance of the Church in America, the institutions that were built up over the past two centuries by the sacrifices of the laity, religious, and clergy, may well be handed over to the secular culture to be used for its own educational purposes, in the service of its own values. No persecution will have brought this about; if it does occur, it will have been done freely. It will have happened quickly, within one or two generations, but great historical changes can happen in a short span of time, and such changes once done cannot be undone. What had been built up over many generations can be given away in one.

Moreover, this alienation, if it occurs, will have taken place right at the moment when the culture to which our institutions were given was entering into spiritual disarray. We will have been misled by voices that told us that what we as Catholics had achieved was not good enough. We were encouraged to make our colleges and universities into a gift to the nation, right at the moment when what the nation really needed was not our institutions but the education that our institutions were providing. To draw an analogy from the Old Testament, if this donation of our institutions to the secular world should come to pass, it will be like an inverted exodus, an exodus run in reverse. Whereas the Israelites despoiled the Egyptians, escaped from slavery, and entered into freedom, we will have trudged back into Egypt, handed over our institutions, and asked others what we should do with ourselves. None of us knows how God will judge those who allow this to happen, but history certainly will not be kind to them.

PHILOSOPHY IN THE SEMINARY CURRICULUM

I wish to discuss the purpose of a seminary program in philosophy as well as the structure and content of such a program, but I will begin by making a few institutional and pragmatic remarks.

Three practical points

The determination of a seminary curriculum is not primarily the work of the faculty, but of the institution that sponsors the seminary. To use modern secular categories, a seminary provides a professional formation; in this respect, it is much like a law school or an engineering or architecture program. We are all familiar with the stringent requirement that professional associations impose on professional schools. Such schools have to prepare their students for a certain role in society and they get evaluated from time to time. The faculty of such a professional school cannot do anything they like with the curriculum; they have to comply with the overall guidelines of the professions if they are to be accredited. A seminary is like this also. The Church sponsors the Catholic seminary and has the authority and the right to determine the curriculum prevailing in it, because the students in that program are being trained and educated to serve in a certain capacity, and the Church ought to be able to specify what she wants them to know and what they must be able to do.

It is not the case that the seminary is like an experimental center for the faculty, who can do whatever they want with it. The same is true, incidentally, for colleges and universities; they too do not belong to the faculty. It is not the case that the faculty that temporarily occupies an educational institution at a given moment has the power to set the course of that institution from that time onward. The course and structure of an educational institution is set first of all by the nature of that institution, by its *telos,* and the faculty alone are not authorized to define that nature and that end. To return to the specific case at hand, the Church, which establishes and sponsors seminarians, determines the courses that should be made available to seminarians in them.

What about academic freedom? Are the faculty not supposed to be able to exercise their minds freely, and to present things as they see fit? The strategic distinction in reply to this question is this: academic freedom is not the same thing as free speech. The two are very often confused, even by law courts and sophisticated elites. It is as citizens that we have the right to free speech; as citizens we can speak our minds in regard to public issues. Academic freedom, however, is not a kind of superior version of free speech, one that empowers faculty members as even more authoritative citizens, as super speakers, people whose opinions are much more valuable than those of others because they are expert in a certain field of study. Academic freedom is the right to teach and publish in accord with the methods, principles, and sources of a given scholarly discipline, and it does not extend beyond that. It is a freedom that is constrained by an objective body of knowledge and by the nature of its subject matter; it is not a freedom to express an opinion, say, about ecclesiastical or governmental policy. People who work in a seminary may have such freedom of speech as citizens and as members of the Church, but not formally in their role as seminary teachers.

I have made two points; first, that a seminary program is to be determined by the institution that sponsors the seminary, and, second, that academic freedom is not the same as freedom of speech. A third practical point I wish to make is something that Francis Slade once observed, that the seminaries that were established by the Church after the Council of Trent were the first modern attempt at a kind of universal or general education, an education that was geared not specifically to form other scholars, but to provide for large numbers of students, with different intellectual talents and interests. This too has to be taken into account in preparing a seminary curriculum and in determining the role of philosophy in it.

The 'telos' of a philosophy curriculum in the seminary

It is obvious that in their spiritual and professional formation seminarians need courses in theology, liturgy, canon law, and the like, but why do they need philosophy? Why has the Church traditionally made philosophy a part of the seminary curriculum? This requirement has been strongly restated by Pope John Paul II in his encyclical *Fides et Ratio,*[1] where he says that philosophy is "fundamental and indispensable to the structure of theological studies and to the formation of candidates for the priesthood" (§62). After complaining about a lack of philosophy in such programs, he says, "I cannot fail to note with surprise and displeasure that this lack of interest in the study of philosophy is shared by not a few theologians"[2] (§61).

One of the major reasons why philosophy is important in conveying the Christian faith can be found in the doctrine of the Incarnation. The Church teaches that in Christ the two natures, human and divine, were complete and intact; neither was diminished or destroyed by virtue of the hypostatic union. In particular this means that in contrast with the various Christological heresies (the Arian, Apollinarian, Nestorian, monophysite, and monothelite), the Church teaches that human reason, which specifies our human being, remained intact in Christ. It is not the case that the Divine Word somehow replaced human reason and the freedom that followed from it. If the integrity of reason is preserved in Christ, it is also preserved in the Christian and in the Church. The Word of God does not only bring a new revelation of the life of God and his covenant with man; it also confirms and heals our reason, that which specifically makes us human and makes us persons. Philosophy is the most intense exercise of human reason; it is the activity in which reason comes to the fullest possession of itself. Part of the mission of the Church, as *Fides et Ratio* tells us, is to restore faith in reason.

One of the major challenges in restoring faith in reason is the fact that in our modern world reason has been taken to be primarily scientific ra-

---

1. *Encyclical Letter Fides et Ratio of the Supreme Pontiff John Paul II to the Bishops of the Catholic Church, On the Relationship between Faith and Reason* (Boston: Pauline Books and Media, 1998).

2. See also *Fides et Ratio,* §60: "I have myself emphasized several times the importance of this philosophical formation for those who one day, in their pastoral life, will have to address the aspirations of the contemporary world and understand the causes of certain behavior in order to respond in appropriate ways."

tionality, and so the Church must show that scientific rationality is not the most fundamental kind, even though it is a legitimate and noble exercise of intelligence. In fact, to take scientific reason—in the natural, social, and psychological sciences—as the most basic kind of reason ultimately leads to irrationality. As such scientific thinking tries to handle the specifically human things, like human freedom and knowledge, political life, moral action, and so on, it becomes obvious that it cannot do so, and since people would have assumed that the only true form of reason is found in the rationality of science, they then conclude that they must abandon reason in approaching such things, and they turn to irrational ways of thinking such as extreme existentialism and deconstruction, which arose as rebounds from scientism.

Now, of course, a parish priest should not be expected to deal with problems raised by the technical aspects of science, such as questions in quantum physics or the various theories of evolution or linguistics, but he has to be able to deal with the popular impact of such things. The faith in scientific reason, with a corresponding loss of faith in any other kind of reason, has had a major influence on how people understand themselves, and these misunderstandings do surface in the local parish, not only in universities. Think how often psychological explanations are taken to be the definitive and final answer to human problems. A book like C. S. Lewis's *The Abolition of Man* is an excellent example of how such issues can be treated in a popular but profound way. Even the catechesis of the Church herself needs a philosophical element if it is to avoid being reduced to sentimentality, which is a popular version of deconstruction. I would like to quote the French philosopher Alain Besançon on this topic. In a book entitled *Trois tentations dans l'Église,* he discusses the Church in France and says: "For a generation the catechesis of children has been troubled and uncertain. It no longer aims at putting into their heads stable dogmatic formulas, learned by heart, but tries to breathe into them a state of soul that is vague, affectionate, and kindly towards everyone."[3] The intellectual element of catechesis is lost when this occurs, and people's faith becomes thoughtless. This lack of a thoughtful faith makes Christians vulnerable to indifference and a loss of what they think the faith to be, and liable to conversion to other beliefs.[4]

3. Alain Besançon, *Trois tentations dans l'Église* (Paris: Calmann-Levy, 1996), p. 216.
4. Besançon speaks especially about conversions of Christians to Islam. See *Trois tentations,* p. 11: "The new situation is that Islam, now entirely freed of the various European dominations,

Clearly, the aim of a seminary philosophy program is not to make seminarians into *philosophers,* academic experts, in the full sense, but it is to try to make them *philosophical,* to have a sense of how questions can be pursued, to have a number of strategic distinctions and definitions clearly in mind, to be able to respond with philosophical understanding to questions people raise. Many of the issues that people bring to priests are simply human problems and not exclusively theological or religious ones, and in most cases even if they are more specifically theological they also have a human or philosophical component. The aim of a seminary philosophy program is to equip the seminarian and then the priest with a certain vocabulary and certain intellectual habits. He should become better able to use such words as *responsibility, meaning, the human person, human nature, moral obligation, virtue* and *vice,* and to use them thoughtfully. He should be able to bring out with some clarity important natural things, things that are accessible to reason.

Philosophy helps us articulate the way things are and the way they appear to us. It can be of great value even for homiletics. A very good way of presenting the Christian things is to contrast them with natural things: to develop some human good, some human truth that people know from their own experience, and then to show how the Christian truth both confirms this good and goes beyond it. The Christian sense of God, for example, is best conveyed to people by developing for them the human sense of an ultimate meaning in the world, and then showing how Christian revelation transcends it, and fulfills that meaning even while speaking about a God who is not part of the world. The theological virtues of faith, hope, and charity are best presented not just by themselves but in contrast with the natural virtues, which we understand spontaneously from our natural experience; the theological virtues are best brought out by showing how they go beyond natural human agency. The theological virtue of charity, for ex-

---

is installing itself in Europe by massive immigration; and that this establishment coincides with a moment of social and doctrinal weakness of the Church. History reminds us that these are exactly the circumstances that in the past surrounded the massive Christian defections to this other religion." See also Bat Ye'or, *The Decline of Eastern Christianity under Islam: From Jihad to Dhimmitude,* trans. Miriam Kochan and David Littman (Madison, NJ: Fairleigh Dickinson University Press, 1996), p. 66. Both authors show how the doctrinal divisions in regard to Christology weakened the Christian societies in the Near East and Northern Africa. Such historical precedents should make us even more concerned about the doctrinal and liturgical trivializations that have taken place in parts of the Church in the past few decades. The effects can be not only religious but social and cultural as well.

ample, can be effectively brought out by showing how it differs from—but is also related to—human friendship. What we seek in friendship, as our highest moral good, is ultimately found and fulfilled in charity in a way that we never could have imagined without revelation. Furthermore, if charity needs friendship as its base, as that from which it should be distinguished, charity also perfects human friendship and lets it be more fully what it is by its own nature. Christian faith thus elevates, heals, and perfects reason, but it also appeals to reason, because faith presents a message and a truth that is to be understood, not just a law that is to be obeyed.

Thomism and phenomenology

We can better understand the purpose of a philosophy curriculum if we spell out a bit further the kinds of things that we would expect a seminarian or priest to know, and the kind of intellectual habits that he should acquire in regard to philosophy. Before doing so, however, I wish to give a name to the kind of philosophy that I think should be taught in the seminary. I would like to call it "streamlined Thomism." I think that seminarians should learn the essentials of Thomism, but they should not be expected to become medieval philosophers. Some may wish to do so, but for most of them, in their general education, it would be better to convey the fruits of Thomism, not the whole tree. In learning such a streamlined Thomism, seminarians would be introduced to the great tradition in philosophy, because in Thomas's writings we find not only his own thought but many of the essentials of the thought of Aristotle and the Platonic tradition. Thomas gives the student access to the great classical tradition of philosophy. A seminary program should distill for the students the central teachings of Aquinas, formulated in a classical vocabulary but also adapted and supplemented in view of our contemporary needs and understandings. I think there should be a new revival of Thomism in the educational effort of the Church. Certainly, the important historical research into Aquinas and medieval thought that has occurred in the past 150 years should continue, but for a more general education, especially in the seminary but in college programs as well, a kind of distilled, modern Thomism should be formulated. In the past three or four decades Thomism has been replaced in Church institutions by an eclectic and historical study of philosophy, but such an approach never comes to a conclusion and does not form the mind in the way a Christian philosophy should. A return to a Thomistic approach would be very desirable.

I would also like to suggest that this streamlined Thomism could profit very much from insights that have been achieved by phenomenology. This use of phenomenology could help Thomism come to terms with modern thinking, with modernity. It would help Thomism address contemporary problems in a classical way and it would, I think, make Thomism more interesting and keep it from appearing historically "dated." The encyclical *Fides et Ratio* seems to take phenomenology to be rather like phenomenalism; this may be the meaning of the passage that reads, "We face a great challenge at the end of this millennium to move from *phenomenon* to *foundation*. . . . We cannot stop short at experience . . ." (§83). I do not think that phenomenology has to be interpreted in this phenomenalist manner, even though many writers and scholars who work in that tradition may take it that way. But we need not be limited by the ideas of Sartre or Merleau-Ponty, for example; why can we not interpret phenomenology in our own way, and take advantage of the manner in which it allows us to treat the modern problem of appearance?

One way of interpreting the phenomenological method is the following: it consists in making strategic, elementary distinctions. When we make such distinctions, we work with phenomena, with the way things appear, but we certainly do not just rest with superficial phenomena. If we distinguish between, say, anger and hatred, and work out the essential character of that distinction, or if we work out the difference between pictures and words, or that between essentials and accidentals, we are not working with "just" the phenomena. We *are* getting to the foundation of things, we are getting to an elementary understanding and are not remaining just with experience. We are elevating experience into philosophical understanding. If we work things out this way, the whole absurd modern problem of idealism versus realism just drops away as a serious issue. We do not and indeed we cannot "prove" that there is an external world or that there is such a thing as truth; to get tangled up in problems like this is to get lost in a whole host of ridiculous, artificial puzzles from which we will never free ourselves. Instead, we should simply make a lot of clarifications and distinctions in regard to basic issues, and the truth of such insights will evidence itself. I think phenomenology can help us do so in a simple, direct, and understandable way, and I also think that analytic philosophy is not nearly as helpful. The philosophical work of Gilbert Ryle and J. L. Austin held much promise, but I think that most other analytic philosophers have never gotten out of the Cartesian box and are of less assistance in the project of a streamlined Thomism.[5] Phenomenology, if it can avoid jargon, can formulate philosophical problems in the way that people spontaneously experience them, but in my opinion analytical philosophy is far less able to do so.

Examples of what a philosophy curriculum should help students to know

What sort of things, then, should seminary students get to know? They should, for example, get a sense of causality and its various kinds: efficient, material, formal, and final, as well as instrumental. They should be taught the difference between the essential and the accidental in things, and be shown that whenever we name an object, whenever we speak about something, some of the essentials of that thing are being put into play, that if we speak at all we cannot avoid what is often disparaged as "essentialism." It would be especially important to convey to students the concept of the nature of things, to show that things do have natures, that they are not merely shapeless, meaningless entities that we can make use of as we see fit for our own purposes. Along with the concept of nature, it would be very important to convey a sense of the ends that things have, their internal final causes, their teleologies, and to distinguish such *ends* from the *purposes* we have when we make use of things. A clear grasp of nature, ends, and purposes is obviously crucial, for example, in the discussion about the family and human sexuality; how could the Church's moral teaching about such matters ever make sense to a seminarian or priest if the ideas of nature, ends, and purposes were not clear to him?[6]

5. On the Cartesian nature of the philosophy of Frege (and hence of the form of thinking inspired by him), see Richard Cobb-Stevens, *Husserl and Analytic Philosophy,* Phaenomenologica 116 (Dordrecht: Kluwer Academic Publishers, 1990). On the value of the work of Ryle and Austin, see the excellent book by David Braine, *The Human Person: Animal and Spirit* (Notre Dame: University of Notre Dame Press, 1992), pp. xx–xxi.

6. The most effective presentation I have encountered of the concept of end or internal final cause or *telos* can be found in two essays by Francis X. Slade: "On the Ontological Priority of Ends and Its Relevance to the Narrative Arts," in *Beauty, Art, and the Polis,* edited by Alice Ramos

In the realm of human action and the human person, the student should learn the meaning of human responsibility and choice, and the way they are differentiated from nonresponsible conduct, the role of compulsion and ignorance as exculpatory, the differences between virtue and self-control, between vice and weakness, between intellectual and moral virtues, the way the theoretic life is lived in regard to knowledge and art, the meanings of justice and friendship, the sense of personal identity over time, the role of memory and anticipation, the way actions shape a character and shape the person himself, the meaning of the principle of double effect. It would be especially important to cover the philosophical definition of the various human appetites, inclinations, and emotions, such as love and hate, pleasure and pain, anger, indignation, cruelty, kindness, gratitude, resentment, envy, admiration, contempt, and the like. It would be extremely important and extremely interesting for the student to understand these things, to bring a rational appreciation to our human emotive life. One might even ask, with some exasperation, "Why on earth would anyone *not* want to teach such things?" not only in the seminary but in college programs as well.

I think that this examination of the human things should discuss not only ethics and the human person, but also some political philosophy, which was sorely underemphasized in neoscholastic thought: it should show what political society is as opposed to the family and other prepolitical associations, the nature of citizenship, the various kind of political communities, and the shifts and changes that occur in political life. This kind of study would not try to make priests into ersatz politicians but would try to make them capable of evaluating public policies and helping people to be good citizens and to preserve their freedom. The clergy must be helped to avoid credulity and oversimplification in regard to public life.[7]

In regard to human cognition, the program should help the student appreciate what words are, how words are used to make judgments, how judgments are blended into arguments. It should discuss the most common fallacies, and distinguish rhetoric from dialectics. It should show the difference

---

(Washington, DC: The Catholic University of America Press, 2000), pp. 58–69; and "Ends and Purposes," in *Final Causality in Nature and Human Affairs,* edited by Richard Hassing (Washington, DC: The Catholic University of America Press, 1997), pp. 83–85.

7. On the role of political philosophy in Christian thought, see my essay "The Human Person and Political Life," chapter 12 above.

between perception and understanding, and also bring out how we take responsibility for the things that we speak, how the human person, the agent of truth, expresses the nature of things when he communicates with others. The role of other people in helping us to know the truth, the role of tradition, the way an ancient text can still speak to us now, with undiminished force and clarity, should also be discussed: the hermeneutic problem of a text, the question of how there can be an identity of meaning in a text over a long period of time and in very different contexts, is obviously of great importance for the study of Holy Scripture, and it is one among many of the questions that deal with human cognition. It would also be good to show the difference between science and common sense, and science and philosophy. The program should show what science *can* tell us as well as what it *cannot* speak about, and why. It should also show that while science gives us truth, it is not the only way of reaching the truth about ourselves and about the world. Furthermore, it is not the task of philosophy to somehow *prove* that there is such a thing as truth; rather, it is its task to bring out the various ways of achieving truth, and precisely in making these distinctions philosophy will have established the possibility of truth. The discussion of truth, of course, also involves a discussion of the various forms of error, ignorance, and concealment.

The ideas I have sketched out are highly interesting things. It is good to know them; they are valuable in themselves; perhaps I am naive, but I find it hard to imagine that someone who has been introduced to them would not be happy and grateful to have this knowledge. Such knowledge, which is part of our cultural heritage, addresses so many things that are extremely perplexing to people in our current world, and indeed in any world. Furthermore, such ideas provide an excellent context in which to study theology. Finally, priests who know such things would be in a better position to help the laity understand many of the problems that they have to face in our present culture.

I have one final point to make about the value of a program in philosophy. There is one very significant distinction that very much needs to be made in our present situation, both in the Church and in society, and I think that a program in philosophy can help us make it. It is the distinction between thinking and speaking *rhetorically* and thinking and speaking *philosophically*. Far too much discourse is simply rhetorical, even when the speakers pretend to be giving an analysis. Far too often people think they are presenting the truth of things, or they pretend to be presenting the truth of things, when they really are arguing, and arguing rather emotionally, for their own point of view. The very grasp of this distinction, the very insight that surreptitiously or deliberately we may be speaking *only* rhetorically, is a tremendously important thing. It makes us aware that we must try to do something other than speak rhetorically, that we must speak analytically, thoughtfully, and philosophically. The very appreciation that such a thing is possible is of overriding importance. It is also salvific, in its own way: it gives us hope that there is something like the truth of things that can rescue us in a complicated and confusing situation. It encourages us to look for true friends and advisors, and not just allies in a struggle. It makes us more willing to look for guidance from the Church and from tradition. A well-ordered program in philosophy can help the Catholic clergy to be beacons of light in a foggy world, agents of reason and not of sentimentality. To bring about this philosophical spirit would be of prime importance not only for the Church but for society as well.

Curriculum, textbooks, and resources

I think that there is little mystery about the external form that a seminary curriculum in philosophy should adopt. It should look very much like a traditional major in philosophy. Let me present what I would consider the ideal. It should consist of at least ten courses, each with three credits, for a total of 30 credit hours. The courses I think are essential are the following: History of Philosophy (9 credits), Metaphysics and The Philosophy of God (6 credits), Philosophy of Nature and Science (3 credits), The Human Person (3 credits), Ethics and Political Philosophy (6 credits), Logic and The Theory of Knowledge (3 credits).

I think that the remarks I made earlier are sufficient to justify the categories in this list. I should say something, however, about the first category, the history of philosophy. This course is essential because it provides what I would like to call the "spine" of Western thinking. It would lay out the standard sequence of historical periods: ancient, patristic, medieval, modern, and contemporary. To know this sequence is very important for the study of theology, and it is better to treat it in philosophy than in theology, because so much of it is purely philosophical. This historical sequence would help the student locate various authors and it would also help him locate himself and his own culture. Furthermore, if the student were to be taught things like the various forms of causation or the various forms of human conduct, it would be important for him to know when these concepts were expressed and how they were reinterpreted over time. This course would involve some reading of classical texts. It might also be desirable to have still another course, beyond those I have listed above, one that would be devoted to classical texts in Christian philosophy, in which the student might read in a deeper way some of the major works of Christian writers.

I would also like to suggest that it would be a good idea to develop textbooks for the courses listed above. The tendency now is for teachers to develop their own courses on the basis of primary texts and selected readings, but I think it would be advisable to have books that summarized the most important concepts in each of the courses I have mentioned. A textbook of this nature need not be coextensive with the entire course, but it could provide the core content of the course, the basic material that definitely ought to be covered. More material could be added at the discretion of the teacher, but the basics should be made available in a systematic way. I think that students benefit from a good textbook. It provides order in the course, and it makes sure that the essentials have been presented. Such texts could also be a great help to teachers.[8]

The question of a seminary curriculum in philosophy brings us to the question of Christian philosophy as such; it is a special version of that more general problem. Our discussion about the seminary can help deepen our appreciation of the way in which revelation confirms and enhances the power of human understanding. It brings us back to the relationship between faith and reason.

8. I would like to recommend two particular authors for their profound, modern, and yet traditional treatment of the topics that should be covered in a seminary curriculum: Yves R. Simon and Robert Spaemann.

INDEX

Christian Faith & Human Understanding was designed and produced in Bembo by Kachergis Book Design of Pittsboro, North Carolina. It was printed on 60-pound Natural Offset and bound by McNaughton & Gunn Lithographers of Saline, Michigan